Becoming a Talent Magnet

THE SIOP PROFESSIONAL PRACTICE SERIES

Series Editor
Douglas H. Reynolds

TITLES IN THE SERIES

Performance Management Transformation: Lessons Learned and Next Steps
Edited by Elaine D. Pulakos and Mariangela Battista

Employee Surveys and Sensing: Challenges and Opportunities
Edited by William H. Macey and Alexis A. Fink

*Mastering Industrial-Organizational Psychology: Training Issues
For Master's-Level IO Psychologists*
Edited by Elizabeth L. Shoenfelt

*Mastering the Job Market: Career Issues for Master's-Level
Industrial-Organizational Psychologists*
Edited by Elizabeth L. Shoenfelt

Overcoming Bad Leadership in Organizations
Edited by Derek Lusk and Ted Hayes

*Talent Assessment: Embracing Innovation and Mitigating Risk
in the Digital Age*
Edited by Tracy M. Kantrowitz, Douglas H. Reynolds, and John C. Scott

*Becoming a Talent Magnet: Lessons from the Field on Attracting and
Recruiting Great People*
Edited by Mark A. Morris

Becoming a Talent Magnet

Lessons from the Field on Attracting and Recruiting Great People

Edited By

MARK A. MORRIS

OXFORD
UNIVERSITY PRESS

OXFORD

UNIVERSITY PRESS

Oxford University Press is a department of the University of Oxford. It furthers
the University's objective of excellence in research, scholarship, and education
by publishing worldwide. Oxford is a registered trade mark of Oxford University
Press in the UK and certain other countries.

Published in the United States of America by Oxford University Press
198 Madison Avenue, New York, NY 10016, United States of America.

© Oxford University Press 2024

CIP data is on file at the Library of Congress
ISBN 978–0–19–093851–2

DOI: 10.1093/oso/9780190938512.001.0001

Printed by Integrated Books International, United States of America

This book is dedicated to my daughter Caroline, a brilliant author whose creative talent is matched only by her courage and heart.

Contents

Contributors   ix
Introduction   xiii
   Mark A. Morris

1. Workforce Planning   1
   Robert E. Ployhart and Mark A. Morris

2. The Employment Value Proposition: Differentiating Yourself
   Among a Sea of Employers   32
   William J. Shepherd

3. Sourcing   62
   David Dorsey and Matt Allen

4. Job Postings, Ads, and the Age of the Aggregator   95
   Valerie N. Streets

5. Recruiting Technology   114
   Mark A. Morris

6. Talent Metrics and Analytics in a Sea of Data   139
   Alexis A. Fink, Tanya Delany, and Jay Steffensmeier

7. Onboarding During Transformational Times: Responding
   to Business Trends with Technology and Best Practices   162
   Deborah K. Ford and Talya N. Bauer

Conclusion   189
   Mark A. Morris

Index   193

Contributors

This book owes its value to the valiant efforts of the chapter authors who volunteered to share their considerable talents and experiences during a worldwide pandemic, author changes, and many other challenges. The brief biographies below reflect roles held during the chapter writing and are only a glimpse of their impressive accomplishments. I gratefully salute them all.

Robert E. Ployhart is the Bank of America Professor of Business Administration in the Department of Management at the Darla Moore School of Business at the University of South Carolina. His research focuses on human capital resources, staffing, and applied statistical models. Rob has published over 130 scholarly articles and chapters, and three staffing-related books. He has served as an Associate Editor for four journals and is a Fellow of SIOP, AOM, APA, and APS. Rob received his PhD from Michigan State University, MA from Bowling Green State University, and BS from North Dakota State University (all in psychology).

William J. Shepherd, PhD, is an industrial/organizational psychologist who has worked in HR consulting and at both Wendy's and Huntington Bank in senior HR leadership roles. Will's work has spanned a wide variety of talent management areas including employee engagement, employee assessment, succession planning, and leadership development. His work has been recognized by SIOP with the "Wiley Award for Excellence in Survey Research" three times, the "M. Scott Myers Award," and twice jointly by SIOP and SHRM with the "Human Resources Management Impact Award." Will obtained his doctorate in I/O psychology at Bowling Green State University. He has taught as an adjunct professor at multiple institutions including over 10 years at Ohio State. He has been an active Division 14 volunteer, including as a former Chair of the SIOP Professional Practice Committee. He is a licensed psychologist and Fellow of SIOP and APA. His research has been published in leading journals including the *Academy of Management Journal*, *Journal of Applied Psychology*, and *Personnel Psychology*.

David Dorsey has over 25 years of experience as a human capital consultant, researcher, and senior leader. David currently serves as a Vice President and the Director of the Business Development Division at the Human Resources Research Organization (HumRRO) and was previously a Senior Executive in the U.S. government, serving in defense and intelligence. Prior to working in government, David was a Vice President at Personnel Decisions Research Institutes (PDRI) and has conducted innovative research and development in the areas of understanding adaptive performance, building assessments for mission critical skills (e.g., cyber, language, data science), innovating performance management, using modeling and simulation technologies for learning, understanding career paths, and building corporate-level data science platforms and communities. David has produced over 70 book chapters, articles, and presentations. He is the recipient of two major research awards and an award for being a top leader in government and was elected as a SIOP Fellow.

Matt Allen is an Assistant Professor of Management in the College of Business Administration and on the executive team at the National Counterterrorism, Innovation, Technology, and Education Center (NCITE) at the University of Nebraska Omaha (UNO). Matt received his PhD from the University of Oklahoma in I/O Psychology and holds a BS in Psychology from the University of California, Riverside. He has over 15 years of experience as a consultant, professor, and manager specializing in applied research and implementation of evidence-based solutions for, among others, the military, intelligence community, and federal law enforcement. Prior to his current role, Matt served as the manager of HumRRO's Talent Assessment and Analytics Program and as the manager of a strategic HR function in the Department of Defense. Matt's publications and presentations range from insider threat, cybersecurity, leadership, individual difference assessment, to organizational research methods.

Valerie N. Streets is an Organizational Development Strategist in Global Operations at Dell Technologies. She has previously held Behavioral Scientist and Consulting roles at Infor, Gartner, and the Society for Human Resource Management. Valerie earned her PhD in I/O Psychology from Old Dominion University and completed a Postdoctoral Fellowship at The University of Tulsa, where her research focused on areas such as diversity and inclusion, coaching, decision-making, and recruitment.

Alexis A. Fink is VP of People Analytics and Workforce Strategy at Meta (formerly Facebook) and has led People Analytics teams at several major tech companies such as Intel and Microsoft. Alexis has also done extensive work in organizational transformation, organizational culture, leadership assessment, and the application of advanced analytic methods to human capital problems. She has published two books and numerous articles and book chapters. Alexis is the new incoming President-Elect of SIOP as well as a SIOP Fellow and recipient of SIOP's Distinguished Service Award in 2019. She was Chair of the IT Survey Group, an industry consortium dedicated to employee surveys. Alexis earned her PhD in Industrial/Organizational Psychology at Old Dominion University.

Tanya Delany is head of Lifecycle Assessments in the Talent Management team at Phillip Morris. She spent more than 11 years at IBM in selection and analytics roles, rising to Director of Selection, Onboarding and Metrics. Tanya has contributed to the SIOP Principles (2018) revision and is a SIOP Fellow.

Jay Steffensmeier is head of Global Hiring Science at Amazon, where he has spent the last 12 years building out the talent assessment function and state-of-the-art instruments to support Amazon's high growth rate and candidate volume. Prior to Amazon Jay worked at Microsoft and Sprint in selection roles. Jay received his PhD in I/O Psychology from Clemson University and his BS in Psychology from Drake University. Jay won the SHRM/SIOP HR Impact Award in 2018 for his work on simulations for hiring at scale and has served on numerous SIOP panels and committees.

Mark A. Morris has led global Talent, Learning, People Analytics, and Organizational Effectiveness functions for Amazon, Sodexo, Lockheed Martin, and JCPenney. Mark has chaired sessions and authored articles in *Personnel Psychology*, *Human Performance*, and other journals and taught business classes at the University of Washington and the University of Texas at Arlington. Mark was a co-founder of the Dallas Area I/O Psychologists and served as Chair of SIOP's Professional Practice Learning Resources Committee. Mark earned his BA in Psychology from the University of Texas at Austin and his PhD in I/O Psychology from the University of Houston. His awards include the MacNaughton Award for Employment Interviewing, two Chairman's Awards from JCPenney for linking human capital to business results, and two diversity research awards from the Academy of Management.

Deborah K. Ford is dedicated to driving a connected employee experience that reinforces diversity, equity, and inclusion. She has led teams in start-up organizations just beginning their journey and mature organizations with diverse stakeholders, global impact, and ambitious goals. She most recently acted as the VP of People for the "Flying Taxi" company, Kittyhawk, led by Google founder, Larry Page, and self-driving car pioneer, Sebastian Thrun. Deborah has a strong ethos dedicated to redefining the ways we work for the future in support of faster iterative processes, speed to value, collaborative decision-making, and growth mindset. She received her MS from George Mason University and her PhD from Portland State University in Industrial/Organizational Psychology.

Talya N. Bauer (PhD, Purdue University) is the Cameron Endowed Professor of Management. She is an award-winning teacher and researcher. She conducts research about relationships at work including recruitment, applicant reactions to selection, onboarding, and leadership. Her work has been supported by NSF, NIH, the SHRM, and SIOP Foundations and has been published in research outlets such as the *Academy of Management Journal, Journal of Applied Psychology, Journal of Management*, and *Personnel Psychology*. She has worked with dozens of government, Fortune 1000, and start-up organizations and has been a Visiting Scholar in France, Spain, and at Google Headquarters. She currently serves as Associate Editor for the *Journal of Applied Psychology* (and is the former Editor of *Journal of Management*). Her work has been discussed in the *New York Times, BusinessWeek, Wall Street Journal, Harvard Business Review, USA Today*, and NPR's *All Things Considered*. She is a fellow of SIOP, APA, and APS.

Introduction

Mark A. Morris

Amazon

The need for this book was driven by the importance of the talent acquisition (TA) function combined with the dearth of scientific research supporting important decisions in that same space. I reached out to 42 experienced recruiting directors in my LinkedIn network prior to starting this book in 2018 to ask them what TA book they relied on for solid research, and 16 responded. The most common answer was "there isn't one," or some version of "I rely on *Harvard Business Review* articles or surveys from search firms." This book should help fill the gap as it is not sponsored by any vendor and is written by a blend of experienced practitioners and scientists (academics). The intended audience includes both talent management professionals (industrial/organizational psychologists, organizational effectiveness leaders, etc.) who design in this space and the senior human resources business partners (HRBPs) and TA directors who execute and depend on these programs and systems to deliver results.

Few would argue that the hiring process is not a key value add for any HR function, and research-based books exist in plenty for elements of the hiring process, such as onboarding or selection testing. However, most research in the recruiting space has focused on selection testing (a small piece of the puzzle but the easiest to measure) or interviewing. The book is intended to add a new dimension to the currently available work, which is often heavily or directly derived from vendors.

Overall, my impression is that we as a field have an opportunity to do much more original research in the TA space, but it is understandable that highly competitive pressures reduce the incentives to make findings public. To draw an analogy to selection testing, each company's TA situation is similar to that of building a test for a specific job. First you do a job analysis, then develop items or buy existing tests off the shelf that can reliably measure important parts of the job. The difference is validity generalization. In the

Mark A. Morris, *Introduction* In: *Becoming a Talent Magnet*. Edited by: Mark A. Morris, Oxford University Press.
© Oxford University Press 2024. DOI: 10.1093/oso/9780190938512.001.0001

selection world, we have certain types of tests whose validity generalizes to a wide variety of jobs and settings. In TA, this is tougher because you have more moderators. Even referrals, which are widely seen as "something everyone should do more of," are not as universally useful. The reader may well wonder: What ARE some good "universal" guidelines? While compiling this volume some key fundamentals have emerged that are not dependent on the size of a company. Some of the suggestions below will take much longer in large, complex, global businesses:

- **Do workforce planning at least once every year.** Involve your finance team to determine headcount and, at the least, do a spreadsheet forecasting demand for important jobs so you can think about how to supply the talent.
- **Automate repeatable processes.** An easier application process, the presence of a tough job market, and the creation of a more positive candidate experience will result in more applications. How to process these fairly and ensure compliance reporting? You need technology to automate and manage this, or you'll miss out on government incentives and possibly have liability exposure. Plus, you'll create a negative experience for candidates, which can hurt your employment brand and reduce the average talent level of your applicants.
- **Track hiring metrics.** How many people did you interview, and hire? What percentage were diverse? Where did you source them? Which sources were best? What was the cost per hire? How long did it take from posting a requisition to acceptance? What do your dispositions look like? What is the new-hire 90-day retention rate? Based on your organization's situation some of these will be more relevant than others, but you should have some metrics that meet your business rhythm and hold yourself and your team accountable. These metrics enable you to set service-level agreements with candidates, such as Amazon's "2 & 5 Promise" (applicant will hear from Amazon with a decision two days after the phone screen and five days after an onsite/virtual interview loop).
- **Map out your hiring process.** It is always useful to see a process mapped out, as it can show where slowdowns and bottlenecks occur and usefully align hiring managers, HRBPs, and TA teams on the workflow. An optimal hiring process is key to have before obtaining, upgrading, or configuring TA technology because it will help to define required

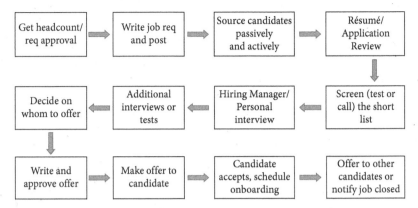

Figure I.1 Sample hiring process

capabilities. For example, if you are hiring massive amounts of hourly employees in a retail environment, your hiring system needs to be able to do a screening assessment with decision rules. A common hiring process is shown in Figure I.1.

From the candidate's perspective there is a parallel process, and I recommend mapping it out too and comparing the two to understand the entire ecosystem. If you make a change in the interview scheduling due to the applicant tracking system, how will it impact the employee side of this equation? Do they now have to wait longer? Share their calendars? Any changes you contemplate should consider both views.

Each chapter of the book describes a particular element of the hiring process from the perspective of research-informed practice. It is my sincere hope that the content of this book provides you with some ideas, tools, or inspiration to take your TA function to the next level.

Figure 1.1 Sample hiring process

1

Workforce Planning

Robert E. Ployhart
University of South Carolina
Mark A. Morris
Amazon

Why do companies carry the cost of an human resources (HR) department? In practice, HR exists to support workforce planning (WFP), as nearly all the actions taken by a Fortune 500 corporate HR team are aligned to the mission of getting the right talent in the right place at the right time. Business units can plan staffing needs, but only HR can bring the talent to the table through hiring, compliance, sourcing, and onboarding, thereby leveraging the networks of business leaders. In many industries, talent wars are the differentiator between success and failure, either to pursue a scarce resource or to take the best player from the other team and add them to your team. For firms competing to find qualified people for hard-to-fill jobs, being a talent magnet is a significant competitive advantage. While being a talent magnet requires the full commitment of many stakeholders in a business, this book will focus on what the HR, talent management (TM), and talent acquisition (TA) teams can own and drive.

As we emerged from the pandemic in 2022, a survey of 1,657 hiring leaders (HireVue, 2022) lists "lack of quality candidates" as the number-one talent issue for the second straight year (cited by 40% of respondents): 55% reported that they were experiencing higher attrition and there was a 43% increase in talent teams who feel under-resourced. Even during times of high unemployment where there is a larger available labor pool, high-performing employees are a key competitive differentiator, with an average of 400% higher-than-expected productivity for top 5% performers (O'Boyle & Aguinis, 2012). In one author's experience, some jobs lend themselves to an even higher multiple of return on salary. For example, elite software engineers allow qualitatively different types of products and services, and greater speed to market for both customer-facing and internal products creates first-mover

Robert E. Ployhart and Mark A. Morris, *Workforce Planning* In: *Becoming a Talent Magnet*. Edited by: Mark A. Morris, Oxford University Press. © Oxford University Press 2024. DOI: 10.1093/oso/9780190938512.003.0001 strategic advantage and becomes a force multiplier of efficiency. If talent is the most important resource in the modern economy, then TM is the most strategically impactful of all HR activities. TM is defined in practice to include recruiting, selecting, developing, rewarding, retaining, and succession planning (Collings & Mellahi, 2009). Numerous authors have defined solid, research-based practice guidelines for most of these components, but little practical guidance exists in terms of how to truly differentiate a firm from its competitors in terms of attracting talent. TA is defined as a systematic process by which firms *strategically* target skill sets, roles to fill, talent sources, and candidates, and then develop attraction strategies to obtain employees with the competencies needed to achieve their strategic goals (Ployhart, Weekley, & Dalzell, 2018). It is often under-utilized, with HR leaders staffing recruiting functions with entry-level talent, and requires sales-type skill sets that can be under-valued within HR, especially by industrial/organizational (I/O) psychologists. Fresh graduates who are fortunate enough to excel in filling roles are often recruited away themselves to do agency work (executive search), with commissions that can run to five times their annual salary as an early-career internal recruiter.

Like all components of TM, TA forms an essential piece of WFP. Nearly every act of a corporate HR department or its vendors can be considered part of a WFP strategy; in fact, surveys of and interviews with chief HR officers often identify this as the biggest challenge and core responsibility of that job. A more effective TA function increases the return on investment of every downstream HR activity because the incoming employees are more capable (leading to reduced training time and higher performance), more likely to fit the culture, and more likely to remain. With costs of turnover estimated at $5,000 per employee even for low-level hourly jobs, and up to 33% of annual salary for typical management jobs, even a small reduction can offer significant financial benefits, in addition to creating less internal disruption to teams and providing more consistent relationships with customers.

In 2020, after the tragic deaths of George Floyd, Breonna Taylor and others, many leading companies made a greater commitment to diversity and inclusion, particularly to improve representation in senior roles. While part of this typically involves building and developing internal talent pipelines, TA is the only way to actually change a firm's demographic and cultural diversity. It is important to note that many diversity metrics are captured only in the United States and are not available in most other countries due to privacy laws like General Data Protection Regulation (GDPR) that restrict the collection of personal data. Creating a diversity-friendly climate where tough, uncomfortable conversations can be safely held has been shown to be related to positive business results (e.g., McKay, Avery, Liao, & Morris, 2011). Therefore, a good workforce plan should include elements of needed representation by level and job family and a hiring process designed to source and select diversity-friendly leaders. Bersin (2021) as well as our experience at Amazon suggests that internal talent marketplaces, especially at large, complex firms, become as much a player in talent movement as external attrition in a workforce plan and must be accounted for when planning an organization's staffing needs and allocating and deploying talent. Retailers moving to more of an online delivery model during the pandemic needed to staff up in web delivery and logistics while redeploying top talent in frontline roles. Healthcare firms redeployed to infectious diseases and testing from other specialties, even calling in retired medical professionals to meet staffing and training challenges.

Finally, firms compete in different ways, which create different talent needs; a firm's competitiveness is based in part on acquiring the bundle of talent unique to the firm's strategy and culture, and in the appropriate amount, time, and place (Cappelli, 2008).

Attracting the desired talent with the necessary qualities and quantities is extremely difficult. Firms that do TA well have created a strategic resource that is rare, valuable, difficult to imitate, and costly to duplicate (Barney & Wright, 1998). These characteristics ensure that talent contributes to a firm's ability to create value and sustain competitive advantage. Being able to effectively attract and select the best talent makes recruitment and selection (staffing) a strategic organizational capability. In this sense, the engine that fuels a firm's strategy, financial and operational excellence, brand, and culture is TA. TA obviously must fit within the constellation of other HR activities and the firm more broadly, but our point is that TA is the starting point for HR strategic impact.

However, global changes in technology, demography, culture, and the nature of work have disrupted the practice of TA. Long-held metrics, prized since Jac Fitz-Enz started Saratoga, are shifting to better reflect the performance of today's recruiters. For example, some companies are moving from "time to fill" to "time to accept" as a more accurate measure given a high proportion of passive candidates for some open requisitions. Passive candidates often have to give more notice, which can inflate the time to their start date, but are often the best candidates from a quality-of-hire standpoint so are worth the wait, especially in hard-to-fill or higher-level roles. Quality of hire continues to emerge as an important metric, with more data available through competitive intelligence using LinkedIn promotion velocity and salary increase rates, as well as for internal research on which sources of talent get the best performance ratings. Across the United States, SkillSurvey (2021a) reports that 80% of respondents rated quality of hire as "extremely important."

Unfortunately, the rapid development of TA practices has far outpaced science and research (Ployhart, Schmitt, & Tippins, 2017). The result is a shortage of guidance on how to attract and accumulate the very resource that most influences competitive advantage. Without guidance or accepted best practices, each organization deals with TA according to its culture and job level, experimenting within some common constraints like regulations requiring minimum job posting times or background checks (usually 72-hour service-level agreements). Some give it focus and attempt to develop practices based on trial and error. Others outsource talent acquisition completely to vendors or recruitment process outsourcing (RPO) firms, believing the cost reductions and efficiencies enable them to be more competitive. Almost everything is up for grabs, from sourcing, to technology, to application and hiring processes, to onboarding. These firm-specific approaches make it difficult to do meta-analyses to determine their effectiveness and establish a broader scientific accumulation of evidence-based impact.

In this chapter we offer our perspective on what it takes to become a talent magnet. Our perspective is informed by broad scientific principles, the research literature (whenever possible), and direct experience working in and with global organizations. We seek to accomplish two goals. First, we start with science and explain why considering talent as a strategic resource is fundamental to understanding the importance of TA. Second, we consider the practical challenges involved in TA and provide recommendations, when possible, about how to move past the challenges to become a talent magnet. We then conclude with practical implications and recommendations for future research.

The Science of Talent

In our experience, the amount of attention given to TA practices (e.g., different types of technology, recruitment methods) is much greater than the attention given to understanding the talent resource itself. We consider talent to be the constellation of knowledge, skills, abilities, and other characteristics (KSAOs) needed to perform the job and achieve the organization's strategic goals (Ployhart et al., 2018). However, we also recognize that talent is embedded within a broader group and organizational context. Focusing purely on KSAOs needed to perform one's job is necessary but insufficient. For example, capable employees leave organizations because they don't fit the culture or they clash with their manager and coworkers. Therefore, we believe that talent is also about having the appropriate values, interests, and preferences so that one may effectively perform the job in a way that also fits within the firm. Our view of talent thus blends and integrates approaches in prior research (Sackett, Lievens, Van Iddekinge, & Kuncel, 2017; Schmitt, 2014).

The fact that talent is the KSAOs and values that fit a job and the organization's culture and strategy suggests that talent is a resource that can be deployed for competitive advantage. The fact that it cannot be owned by a firm but can instead only be accessed by employees voluntarily applying their skills means that talent is a strategically valuable resource (Coff, 1997). In contrast to other organizational resources (like financial capital, land, etc.), there are several unique features about talent resources.

First, talent resources are unevenly distributed in different regions of the world. The more specialized the nature of the talent, the less likely it is equally distributed. Due to mobility and market forces, different regions have become hubs for different types of talent. These hubs are sometimes referred to as "talent hot spots." For example, Silicon Valley is widely recognized to be a hub for technological talent, Boston for biomedical talent, and New York and London for financial talent. Specialized talents, like natural resources, are not equally distributed around the globe.

Second, unlike natural resources, talent resources have (to a large extent) free will and choice. This means talent is mobile and fungible, and employees with high-demand skills can often move between employers and regions with some ease. For example, cybersecurity experts and computer scientists are currently in high demand. However, entry-level employees working jobs in retail or food service are likewise highly mobile. In general, the market for the last several decades has been one that supports and encourages employee mobility (Cappelli & Keller, 2014). Firms have been less likely to invest in their personnel, contributing to less employee loyalty, and thus driving employees to mobility to enhance their careers and salaries. Thus, employees today have less loyalty to their employer and are relatively impatient if opportunities do not come quickly.

Third, at the same time, the preferences of employees and the needed kinds of talent are always changing. The value (and thus demand) of talent is highly affected by the needs of business. As firms seek to compete and gain advantage, the types of talent they need likewise change (Kryscynski & Ulrich, 2015). What is in demand today will likely morph and change into different demands tomorrow. This is particularly the case given that the pace of change seems faster today than it was even 10 years ago, and thus organizations must strive to be agile while simultaneously being focused. The lifespan of organizational strategy and the tenure of chief executive officers (CEOs) has become compressed, so what it means to fit a job and culture is increasingly volatile.

Fourth, because talent is in demand, but also because the market for talent changes rapidly, employees are often impatient during the recruitment process. It is increasingly recognized that the candidate experience is an important part of the employee lifecycle, and that early experiences with the firm as a potential employer become strong influences on the employee's subsequent onboarding experience (McCarthy et al., 2018). In the modern era, reputation and brand have become more important because candidates can share information about employers easily and widely (e.g., Glassdoor). This has created a major push to ensure the recruitment process is short, positive, and engaging. A recent survey (SkillSurvey, 2021a) reports that only 56% of organizations gather candidate experience data after a hire.

Thus, talent resources are geographically heterogeneous, mobile, opinionated, and, to a certain extent, self-centered. Employees expect a positive recruitment experience and want to be engaged. They are less likely to endure an employer who doesn't provide opportunity and a competitive salary. Thus, a perfect storm exists whereby those with in-demand talent are courted with "high-touch" recruitment practices from competitors, which only adds to the existing impatience and reluctance to tolerate an employer that does not provide sufficient opportunity. Add to this the projections about talent shortages and skill gaps, and it becomes obvious that talent is a strategic resource that is valuable, rare, difficult or costly to acquire, and difficult to substitute—that is, talent is a strategic resource that contributes to competitive advantage.

Practical Challenges (and Some Solutions) for Becoming a Talent Magnet

We will list some common challenges to effective TA, and then discuss each along with some recommendations for addressing them. Some of the most significant practical challenges in TA involve:

1. WFP and TA's role
2. HR ownership versus the hiring manager
3. Accurately forecasting talent demands by job, location, and workforce
4. Optimizing recruiter requisition loads
5. Attracting high-quality candidates
6. Assessing and selecting to balance candidate experience and valid/efficient selection
7. Improving velocity of the hiring process while balancing candidate experience
8. Headcount/requisition approvals
9. Interviewing process (usually the single longest piece of time in the hiring process due to calendar challenges)

WFP and TA's Role

Amit Mohindra, former head of workforce analytics at McKesson, offers the following definition of WFP (2015):

> [A] *business* process that applies the *rigor* of financial planning and analysis to optimize the workforce on three fronts—*capacity* (headcount size and cost); *mix* (worker type and location); and *capability* (skills and experience)—to execute the organization's business *strategy*.

Many organizations (including Sodexo North America and Lockheed Martin) use HR business partners (HRBPs) in conjunction with leaders from sales, operations, and TA to plan staffing needs based on expected wins and losses of new business, as well as historical patterns of turnover, seasonality, and retirement eligibility of incumbent populations.

Strategic WFP can be more complex. As Levenson and Fink (2017) suggest, it can be driven by organizational redesigns. TA should be involved as soon as the organizational design is finalized, so that as communications are happening to affected employees, TA understands any new roles that are defined. This will help ensure that accurate candidate needs are captured and that job postings and hiring criteria are on point.

TA is typically most involved in the "buy" strategy, whereas the learning and leadership development team owns the "build" strategy. When buying talent, it is often necessary to identify specific targeted roles at specific competitors and even specific employees who are seen as top talent. For example, if you lose enough contracts to Jennifer's killer presentations you may seek to recruit her for your team, simultaneously upgrading your talent and downgrading that of your competitor. This is an aggressive approach but can be highly effective.

HR Ownership Versus the Hiring Manager

There is often tension between HR and the hiring manager. Two scenarios are common.

The first occurs when the hiring manager is in a power function like operations or sales, because it is likely that they have more power than a support function like HR. If they have a candidate already in mind, they may wish to skip the process and put their person in the role regardless of job posting compliance rules or whether the candidate is truly competitive either internally or externally. A lack of diversity in a candidate can present additional complications.

In the second scenario, some hiring managers may wish to over-delegate the task of finding a new player for their team. If the line manager already has a candidate in mind, either internal or external, HR may find it challenging to enforce a good, consistent selection process that protects the company, ensures fairness, and results in the best candidate getting an offer.

Therefore, the key is for HR to demonstrate *how* it adds value to the process—by enlarging the slate of diverse qualified talent; making the process faster, yet more consistent and rigorous; and enhancing quality of hire.

Accurately Forecasting Talent Demands by Job, Location, and Workforce

Staffing forecasts depend on several variables. Companies with clean, standardized data and job architecture will be at a substantial advantage because they will require minimal manual cleaning of data and can run and update forecasts frequently as conditions and seasons change. In addition to the current state of the data and systems, forecasts depend on the availability of talent in key roles and the sophistication of predictive analytics in that organization. An advanced flight risk algorithm incorporates pension plan and retirement eligibility, uptake rates, total turnover by role controlling for age and performance/potential levels, union status, etc. These are just some of the variables used to forecast needs, along with marketing timing, historical staffing levels, growth rates, external labor supply trends, new market entries/new contracts, etc. TA refers to the labor pool of active job seekers, the base rate of qualified candidates, and internal company strategy of pursuit priority.

Scenario planning is a valuable approach to WFP. For example, let's say you are hiring drivers for a delivery truck business. This is hard-to-fill job in the United States with more openings than candidates, and thus a terrible selection ratio. As a result, the WFP strategy is likely to be "build your own" by investing heavily in new-hire skills training to take previously inexperienced citizens and give them the minimum skills needed to drive the trucks safely. If you have a business model that pays below-market rates, you are basically trapped in a talent strategy of constant churn where you are hiring large amounts of inexperienced people with high failure rates and betting everything on your onboarding and new-hire training to save the day in terms of customer satisfaction, safety, and contractual compliance. For each major job family they hire, most companies have to make the decision of whether this is staffing or selection. If the job is simply a commodity, where performance makes little difference and the base rate is low (i.e., the job is easily learnable for most applicants), then it is staffing. Consider, as an example, large retailers during holiday season. If the job is one where small skill differences create huge outcome advantages (e.g., professional sports, software development, sales), then selection needs to be much more rigorous. Another variable is geography, which affects labor supply shortages, market pay rates, and ability to relocate for both internal and external candidates. If part of your employee value proposition (EVP) is being able to work from home, then relocation and geographic pay rates are less powerful, but for jobs that require a physical presence these are key considerations. Most hiring is local, but talent availability is also affected by macroeconomic factors, so many recruiters follow unemployment data (3.7% as of the start of 2020), which can indicate a tight labor market and different expectations for time-to-fill and time-to-accept metrics for recruiters. SkillSurvey (2021a) reported an average time to fill for all jobs of 43 days, while a 2023 Society for Human Resource Management (SHRM) survey reported a time to fill of 48 business days(Maurer, 2024).

TA is often the driver of HR in growth companies because the company's growth frequently depends on the ability to provide workers. In growth scenarios like Amazon (which had 31,000-plus full-time job openings as of November 2019), WFP and hiring plans for TA are almost synonymous. There is little opportunity to do organizational design–based planning as Levenson & Fink (2017) recommend; rather, a workforce plan is often focused on budget-approved headcount by level and job family, location, and current attrition rates. "Post and pray" strategies cannot work at this scale, so sourcing analytics and a site strategy must inform company decisions about where to locate new facilities—a plentiful labor supply is critical. Even the typical reliance on work-from-home tactics to expand the applicant pool or on the usual one-third of hires coming from referrals is not sufficient when hiring hard-to-fill roles in high-volume/high-growth environments. Automation is a requirement, from scraping and surfacing, to tech tools like Connectifier and hireEZ for your Chrome extensions, to an applicant tracking system (ATS) and candidate relationship management (CRM) software that allow you to track, contact, and follow up with analytical support and automated emails to keep dozens of candidates warm simultaneously.

A recent study by Gartner TalentNeuron's big-data engine showed that throughout 2018, about half of all jobs posted by S&P 100 companies were for the same 39 roles (Gartner, 2019). There were 662 jobs in the study across the United States and the United Kingdom. Focused roles were in information technology, research and development, sales, marketing, and customer service. Specific job titles in the United States included software developer, marketing manager, and systems engineers, while in the UK titles were financial manager and customer service representative. Recent articles in *Forbes* and rankings by SHRM (2018) also add nurses, skilled trades, drivers, home health aides, medical manager, information security, and mechanics to the list of hard-to-fill jobs. Below is a reasonable composite for the United States for 2019 based on these rankings, my own experiences filling many of these roles, and Bureau of Labor Statistics occupational outlook data for the "Hard Eight"—the toughest jobs to fill:

1. Software developer
2. Sales (representative, manager, inside sales, etc.)
3. Engineers

4. Drivers
5. Mechanics and skilled trades
6. Nurses
7. Accountants/financial managers
8. Medical managers

If your organization is tasked to fill these jobs despite below-average pay and a weak employment brand, you might want to consider growing candidates internally because recruiting passive candidates will be very challenging. A list of the "Top 12" skills in demand, based on LinkedIn's research on all job postings on their site, combined with my own experience and benchmarking, is as follows (it includes competencies and technical skills):

1. Agile learning
2. Mobile app development
3. Cybersecurity
4. Sales leadership/solution selling
5. Data analysis/artificial intelligence/machine learning
6. User experience/user interface (UX/UI) design
7. Creative problem-solving
8. Video production/augmented reality/virtual reality (AR/VR)
9. Influencing
10. Digital marketing/social media marketing
11. Collaboration
12. Cloud computing

In addition, with the trend toward skills-based talent practices, a new Gartner survey (Reul, 2022) breaks down needed skills for leaders (eight-plus years of experience) into these categories: growing, core, declining, and emerging. Project management, communications, and collaboration are considered "core," program management and transparency are "growing," and courage and inclusion are "emerging."

Optimizing Recruiter Requisition Loads

Managing a team of recruiters means managing a workload of requisitions. While many recruiters can carry 20 to 30 full-time equivalent requisitions at any one time, this can vary quite a bit. Factors affecting workload include scarcity of talent for the role, employment brand, competitiveness of compensation, geography, and level of the role. A hard-to-fill role requires more sourcing, more legwork, and more networking to get qualified leads. A weak employment brand means a worse conversion ratio of leads to candidates because it is less appealing to potential employees. Compensation that is not competitive, or a geography that is unappealing, is likewise a factor that adds difficulty to filling a requisition. Even for a good company with good pay, a highly educated and in-demand software developer may not want to relocate to Nebraska (sorry, Cornhuskers!). While remote work can result in challenges around cultural assimilation, retention, learning curves, and onboarding, it can certainly open up new avenues to source and attract scarce talent.

A talent magnet company will focus on improving these factors so that recruiters can be more efficient and will selectively use vendor support (at lower dollar cost per candidate) to do initial screening, name generation, and sourcing and then hand a high-quality shortlist to the recruiter for more in-depth review and interviewing. It is further recommended to keep recruiters in role at least two years to learn the commonly filled jobs in that space, which speeds up intake and improves credibility with both candidates and their hiring managers. In commodity-based staffing (e.g., drivers, cafeteria workers, seasonal cashiers), where selection options are few due to limited applicant flow, manager disinterest, or high-base-rate jobs, a recruiter can successfully manage as many as 50 requisitions. Executive recruiting is a different space entirely, as these candidates often expect more time and attention and can have complicated total rewards packages that recruiters need to understand in detail (e.g., option strike prices, bonus matching policies, restricted stock units, vesting schedules). An appropriate workload here (or when hiring senior software developer roles) can be as few as five open requisitions at any one time. Good recruiting metrics, as cited in Chapter 6 in this book, are recommended to the discerning TA or HR leader as a leading indicator that a requisition load is too heavy or too light for a given team or individual.

Attracting High-Quality Candidates

One of the strongest attractions TA teams can bring to bear is a clear, focused, and appealing EVP (see Chapter 2 in this volume for more). In general, an EVP approach uses a marketing segmentation model to target specific types of people (e.g., teachers on summer break, retirees, students) and crafts a sales pitch for how a given role at this company will meet their needs. A more aggressive approach is to identify specific roles at competitors and to target their incumbents with a sales pitch geared to valued advantages of the company. For example, if you worked at Macy's and knew that your general managers (store managers) had a better bonus plan than at Target, you might get a list of those incumbents at Target and reach out to them on LinkedIn with a carefully scripted message hitting on the bonus plan. Of course, once you get a few former Target employees in your organization, you can use their personal networks and referrals to gain more, all the time collecting names of high performers by asking things like, "Who were the sales leaders in your district?" until you've poached the top 20%. Be aware that this is not recommended, as some companies (including Target!) have responded to this type of recruiting by increasing their pay well above market rates to poach back ruthlessly to deter this type of activity. A strong external network that feeds you intelligence can also be quite useful here as you can find out about layoffs, contract losses, store closures, etc. where people will be at least uncertain and possibly open to a new opportunity. A 2022 survey of 4,049 employees in the third quarter of 2022 from Mercer (2022) found that compensation and flexibility were the top attractors sought by the 33% of employees seeking a new role.

Assessing and Selecting to Balance Candidate Experience and Valid/Efficient Selection

Previous research on personnel selection has spent considerable time describing good processes for assessment, from structured interviewing (e.g., Campion, Palmer, & Campion, 1997) to validating assessment scores (e.g., Murphy, 2012; Schmitt, 2014). Much of this research has focused on technical issues relating to improving reliability and validity. The technical issues are obviously critical, but there are several additional considerations that merit additional discussion.

Even the most proven and legally defensible selection approaches with good return on investment (ROI) are not immune to a loss of political support. We've seen this firsthand in retail and hospitality environments, where a lack of applicant flow for frontline positions (which are often treated like a commodity-based staffing) meant a lack of support for ANY test that screened out even a small percentage of the remaining paltry number of candidates. In one case, a small location averaged less than one candidate per opening. Selection ratios like this are not a good environment for testing, yet we are legally and professionally bound to be consistent across enterprises, even when some sites/locations are much larger and benefit from vast differences in applicant flow. Although an easy-to-understand ROI case is always recommended, it is important to have an exception process signed off by legal and operations, as well as your HRBP and TA team for situations with very low applicant flow. We've also found it helpful in those cases to provide local recruiting resources to hiring managers at those low-flow sites, including links to the employee referral program; signs, videos, and other collateral; lists of best practices from similar sites (e.g., where to source candidates), and a spreadsheet to help them calculate appropriate referral bonuses based on cost of turnover. Typically for frontline workers you want to pay out $500 after 90 days to the referring employee, but you can go as high as $1,000 if you stagger it over six months. Since employees are twice as likely to stay in hourly jobs in many companies after that period of time, and the cost of turnover is usually four times that amount, you are likely to return 100% on your investment across large numbers of new hires. It is also worth looking at Chapter 7 in this book on onboarding if you are in a situation where your business model is not competitive on compensation and you are heavily dependent on your onboarding program.

Improving Velocity in the Hiring Process While Balancing Candidate Experience

Candidates are looking for an easy experience where they are treated professionally, and they may judge a company by its hiring process. When an ATS allows applicants to use their LinkedIn profile to autofill applications, which they then only need to review and edit, this saves time, making the experience more positive. Therefore, increasing velocity helps the company AND improves the impression that candidates receive.

One of us has mapped out the hiring process at multiple companies, and we've found that some usual suspects typically emerge that account for large chunks of the time to fill a role: intake, sourcing, interview scheduling, background checks, and offer-letter generation. While background checks often get a bad rap for delaying a hire, they are in fact the shortest time on average of these "big rocks" of the hiring process. TA teams can track background checks separately, often with a service-level agreement (SLA) with a vendor like Goodhire, Accurate, or HireRight. Per SHRM, about 70% of companies conduct these checks on all job candidates, usually as a condition of employment after the offer but before the start date. These checks usually involve 48- to 72-hour turnarounds, depending on what is done. The most common model is employment and education verification, a social security number check, and, if job-related, a credit check and criminal history check. More research is done for sensitive positions, and a drug test can add $50 or so to a typical $30 background check, plus another week of time. If not properly integrated into the ATS, then manual steps will be needed, adding time to the hiring process.

Some forward-thinking companies do pre-boarding (e.g., reading and acknowledging company policies/handbooks, voluntary self-identification of veteran status) before the employee has actually started so as to accelerate their time to productivity and allow the company to collect government money (e.g., the work opportunity tax credit).

Offer letters are a key element of the candidate experience. They must reflect promises made by the recruiter and hiring manager and must also stay within company policies. They are often approved by HRBPs, the compensation team, or both. Offer letters are legally binding documents and can be used as proof of employment to obtain loans and for other legal purposes, so they are typically prepared with care. Between these requirements for preparation, incorporation of expectations (often necessitating a conversation) and approvals, this step can take significant time, sometimes two weeks or more for a complex case involving exceptions. Other steps in this process will be discussed later in the book.

Applicant reactions are generally more positive (Ryan & Ployhart, 2000) to unstructured selection where they feel they have more room to maneuver and influence the process. Long multiple-choice tests are not as popular. In situations where talent is scarce or hard to fill, the power these highly-sought-after candidates yield is so great that they can demand very high wages and even a different "express lane" of hiring practices outside a company's normal approach. For example, they may get higher-touch recruiting attention, and from higher levels. They may be able to bypass standardized tests (although they are likely to have a technical interview by a job expert to get a true sense of their actual capabilities) and may be eligible for special benefits and sign-on bonuses usually reserved for executives.

Applicants report a more favorable experience when the hiring technology matches their expectations; when sourcers and recruiters are highly responsive to questions; when they are treated respectfully and inclusively; when interviewers are on time and prepared and know their stuff; and when they get good feedback and closure. High marks are also given for consistency around pay and other promises. Heartless communications from an ATS lack the personal touch that make candidates feel valued but are often necessary for efficiency reasons with large applicant populations for many jobs. A poor candidate experience (e.g., with a person, a job site/careers page, the application or interview process, ATS) can not only lose you that individual candidate but can also result in a poor review on Glassdoor, Indeed, or Niche that can affect your employment brand and reduce applicant flow and the quality of applicants, especially for passive candidates. According to Careerarc (2016) survey of 826 job seekers, 72% of candidates with a negative experience will share it with others or online, so it is important to track.

Headcount/Requisition Approvals

Another one of the time taxes paid by an organization in the hiring process involves the layers of approvals. This can take the form of getting headcount approved as part of an annual financial plan or budget or approval from a senior leader to re-allocate existing headcount. It is typically required as a step to open a requisition. High-velocity companies in retail and tech may push down these decisions to lower-level managers to speed up hiring, especially in a competitive market, and or empower them to hire as long as they stay within their contract or budget numbers (this is common with site general managers). Headcount typically represents a permanent fixed cost for the organization, so companies employ processes to create "friction" to ensure that it is truly needed before adding it to the expense line, even in fast-growth situations. Since approvals can significantly impact the hiring process in terms of waiting to post the requisition, they should be clearly defined (e.g., a level 4 leader can hire up to level 3 budgeted headcount without additional approvals). Coordination with the finance department on headcount planning is a key element here.

Approvals can also affect the hiring process once the requisition has been posted. Some hiring managers must get approvals to make a hiring decision for a particular candidate. It is also common in less hierarchical organization for hiring managers to allow peers or other interviewers to "veto" a candidate, especially if they are key stakeholders for that role (and if they aren't, why are they in the interview process?). Some forward-looking firms have specially trained hiring "ninjas" who interview outside of their area in order to ensure that culture fit or high standards are being applied consistently.

Interviewing Process

If you are looking to reduce your cycle time for hiring, the interviewing process is often a good place to start. The first step is to identify exactly how many people are truly stakeholders who need to be comfortable with this hire; typically a hiring manager, a peer, and at least one internal customer as well as an HR representative are included. A recruiter will often do a screening call. Interviews can often be done faster and cheaper via Skype, Chime, FaceTime, or other online video tools. This book will not go into the structured interview process, as it has been thoroughly described by many excellent books and articles (e.g., Campion et al., 1997) and is widely used. Interestingly, some companies will use the Situation, Behavior, Impact structure around work example questions, others around demonstration of cultural principles, and still others around competencies.

Due to calendars, the interview piece of the hiring process is usually the single longest chunk of time, so when pressure comes to reduce time to fill, it can be a target. In 2009, Fernandez-Araoz, Groysberg, and Nohria reported in the *Harvard Business Review* on the results of their interviews about hiring practices with HR managers at 50 global companies and a group of executive-search firms. They found that common practices were actually much less common and more variable than expected, even within the same companies. In 12% of companies, candidates for senior positions went through 21 or more interviews before a hiring decision was made!

It appears that there is a need for some guidance, especially around the question of how many interviewers is enough for a given position. Some considerations when designing a process or building the interview slate are as follows:

- *How senior is the role?* Executive jobs that impact many areas will necessarily have more stakeholders who will want to sign off, and the scope of the role can justify more care and time to be taken in the hiring process. In addition, a broad role may involve multiple skill sets and experiences that need to be assessed by different people (not everyone is qualified to evaluate a candidate on ALL of their job-related competencies). Some companies include a "culture fit" person in the interviewing slate whose only responsibility is to ensure that the person will not clash with the highly valued company norms.
- *How fast must the hire happen?* In some cases, there may be a high cost for every day of delay (e.g., fines from a customer, risk of contractual breach, expensive contractor fees, risk of further turnover from strained internal resources covering the work).
- *What is the cultural context?* Some companies are comfortable with a lower level of formality in selection and often move casually. Fernandez-Araoz and colleagues reported finding that 50% of hires are done on the gut instinct of the hiring manager. Other companies are culturally systematic or have very high quality standards, and this influences the rigor of the hiring process.
- *What is the level of capability of the organization with regard to human capital?* Companies with highly trained managers and advanced analytic tools for hiring (and a track record of using these successfully) are much more likely to use structured interviewing and other selection processes that take more time. You also need fewer of them to "check" on the others if they are skilled and objective talent evaluators. If they have never used an ATS, you will need to approach the entire process differently (see Chapter 5 in this book). Recruiter productivity should be factored into any planning tools or forecasts.

Purpose

Most companies use multiple interviewers for several purposes (e.g., to spread ownership, to reduce uncertainty, to spread risk, to collect more information). There may be a risk aversion or lack of confidence in hiring, so they "round up" so that everyone has some ownership of a potentially bad decision. From a practical basis you may need several different people so that you can accurately assess all the vital skill sets required for success on the job. However, you don't necessarily need multiple people to assess each competency. Fific and Gigerenzer (2014) showed that expertise overlap affected the needed number of interviewers.

Candidate Reactions

Interviewing is as much a recruiting event as an evaluation, so you want at least one person on the slate who will give a fair but appealing impression of your company to the candidate. After all, they may be a future customer at some point, and any top-talent person you can attract is one less working for the competition. Top-talent candidates often have choices, and they know it—you can count on the fact that other organizations are recruiting them aggressively, so don't forget this piece if you expect to compete for in-demand talent or hard-to-fill openings (see Wilhelmy, Kleinmann, Konig, Melchers, & Truxillo [2016] for more on signals interviewers use to create a good impression). From the candidate standpoint, they benefit from exposure to more than one or two leaders if they are to gauge their fit with the organization, but you don't want them saying, "What do they still need to know about me?" Use feedback from Glassdoor or Comparably ratings and reviews as well as acceptance rates to track how you are doing on this front.

Good Design

It is assumed that you follow structured behavioral interview processes based on trained interviewers, solid scoring criteria, and job-related behavioral questions to which you are diligently recording interviewee responses and your own observations (Campion et al., 1997). There practices are well established and commonly understood, yet applying them can sometimes be difficult. Based on the considerations above, you will want to vary your number of interviewers around some basic guidelines (but always keep it to the minimum necessary number):

- For hourly positions, two interviews are enough. These jobs usually have higher turnover, so you just want a second set of eyes to reduce potential bias from the first interviewer and confirm/validate. The interviewers should include the hiring manager and a future peer to the candidate or peer to the hiring manager if available.
- For most exempt/management jobs, I recommend four interviewers on the slate. They should include the hiring manager, the matrix manager

(depending on the organizational structure), senior peers, and internal customers. Increase this number if you have multiple stakeholders who will be affected by the role, or if it is highly visible/controversial. Decrease this number to three if the people involved are geographically dispersed or rarely available and it would unacceptably increase time to fill.

- For executive jobs (C-suite and their direct reports), target an average of seven interviewers per hire. In addition to the hiring manager and multiple peers of the candidate you should have corporate-level leaders from key relationship functions interview as well (internal customers), the CEO, and possibly board members if the new hire will interact with them. Always include a senior operations or line manager with Profil and Loss responsibilityso they can "own" the hire if it is a functional or staff area. If you are doing an assessment center or in-depth testing, it is prudent to stretch this out a bit so you don't have fatigue affecting the results or annoying the candidate. Carefully select your interview slate to fit the level and complexity of the role, sequencing it so that the most senior interviewer is last, to protect their time.

- It is best to have a standard process with some flexibility so that it doesn't break when faced with the inevitable exceptions. Make sure each interviewer on the slate knows the role, the candidate, the schedule, and what they are looking to assess, so they can accurately assess it. If you can pull this off while ensuring that minimal time and stress are put on both the organization and the candidate, then you are well on your way.

Research Needed to Understand How to Become a Talent Magnet

As we have seen, the practice of TA faces many difficult challenges, and there is often little systematic, evidence-based guidance on what practices work best within the typical practical constraints. Clearly, research should be conducted to address each of the challenges identified in the prior section. These challenges do not fit neatly into academic silos, but therein lies the opportunity to disrupt the recruitment and selection literature and conduct research that is new and innovative. However, the greatest difficulty in conducting this type of research is the speed by which TA practices change, relative to the speed with which academic research is conducted and published. Simply put, research that is started today will likely be out of date by the time it is published.

In this section we take a different approach and seek to identify research topics for challenges that are just emerging. In this way, we hope research conducted today will be able to inform practice just as the key practical issues emerge at scale. We try, as Wayne Gretzky famously said, "to skate to where the puck is going, not where it is."

Recruiting for Jobs That Don't Exist .

As the nature of work continues to evolve quickly and radically, the lifespan of many jobs is getting shorter and new jobs are being created at greater rates. It is often claimed that technology eliminates jobs, but the introduction of many types of technology often results in the creation of entirely new types of jobs. For example, consider the current nature of cybersecurity jobs, which were scarcely even present just a few years ago. Similarly, organizational strategies change and evolve quickly, so firms must develop capabilities for creating the talent resources needed to pursue new initiatives. This means firms may be recruiting for jobs that they currently do not have and in some cases may not even exist. New executive roles, such as chief transformation officer or chief innovation officer, may be created to provide leadership for new initiatives. In all of these examples, research needs to explore how TA can occur in a way that is effective and timely.

First, research is needed that examines how firm strategy, talent strategy, and WFP can be bundled in a way that is synergistic and seamless. It makes little sense for a firm to pursue a bold new strategy if it does not have the people or capabilities to deliver on that strategy. Hence, in volatile and uncertain environments, firms must learn how to develop a talent strategy that delivers the talent where it is needed, when it is needed, and with sufficient quality.

Second, research must examine how to effectively translate talent strategy into action. For example, how do firms create capabilities for forecasting future talent needs and creating the talent resources with speed and agility? What are the best practices that underlie such capabilities?

Third, research needs to determine how recruitment practices and messages will need to change to identify and then attract the desired talent. For example, how will existing recruiting practices and approaches need to change to message jobs that don't currently exist? Most workers come to identify with their occupation and job, so how does one message an entirely new type of career, and how does a firm help potential candidates broaden their professional identities? The TA practices of old were created in a world of fairly static jobs; the future looks to be volatile and uncertain, and thus research must identify practices that enable firms to stay ahead of the curve.

Recruiting for Jobs That Are Going Away

The flipside to recruiting for jobs that don't yet exist is recruiting for jobs that are disappearing (or have a terminal lifespan). There are many such jobs that are in decline, most notably in manufacturing and basic service roles (e.g., cashiers). There are many projections suggesting that AI and related technologies will make jobs that involve routine operations obsolete (e.g., bookkeepers, telephone operators, basic data-entry personnel). One might also see the transportation sector (e.g., trucking and delivery) being radically disrupted if self-driving vehicles become widespread. Of course, just because a technology can replace humans does not mean that it will. The questions become how a firm can identify which jobs are disappearing, forecast future demands, and then recruit new candidates into the role in a responsible manner.

First, research is needed to identify which jobs are disappearing. Broad industry trends can be observed using O*NET and related economic and government databases, as well as industry-specific forecasts, organizational consortium groups, and a firm's own business and workforce strategies. Second, research is needed to identify how a firm can forecast the talent needs in jobs that are in decline or being phased out. Research suggests that turnover can be a contagious process (Felps et al., 2009), so employees working in a job that is disappearing may preemptively decide to leave the job or firm. Such turnover can make it difficult to forecast talent needs because if the turnover process is contagious, the turnover rates may be clustered together and trends can spike quickly, making it hard to spot before it is a serious problem. Third, the most difficult challenge is how to identify and attract individuals into roles that are not going to last long into the future. It seems inappropriate and potentially unethical to recruit without acknowledging to candidates that a position is being phased out; how one can message such an outcome while still attracting candidates will require new ways of thinking.

For example, the firm may already be developing a succession plan for the phased-out roles, such that when the jobs are ultimately gone, the firm will have new roles the employees can transition into. Regardless of the specific issues, recruiting talent into disappearing jobs is likely to be entirely different from prior TA research. This will require new theories and research to make sense of a challenge that is likely to become more common.

Identifying the Right Balance of AI to Human Judgment

Although AI is not quite "ready for prime time," we have every reason to believe it will eventually make its way into TA—the only question is, to what extent? At present we do not believe AI is ready to be the sole mechanism for identifying and sourcing talent. Thus, research needs to determine the appropriate balance between AI and human judgment.

Fortunately, this is a topic where I/O psychologists have some experience and history. In the early days of biodata, the field suffered from "dustbowl empiricism" in the sense that any biodata items correlating with performance criteria were retained and used as a basis for hiring (Stokes, Mumford, & Owens, 1996). It did not matter whether the items were appropriate, sensible, theoretically justified, or discriminatory; they only needed to relate to performance. This approach obviously gave way to more theory- and construct-based biodata methods; this was especially important given the passage of the 1964 Civil Rights Act. Note that with the construct-based approach, empirics and analytics were still used, but rational human judgment (theory) was also highly relevant. As another example, use of regression-based approaches is the statistically optimal way to combine multiple predictors (Kuncel, Klieger, Connelly, & Ones, 2013). The best a human can combine predictor information is what regression does every time. However, regression models can only combine what is included in the model, and predictor intercorrelations (multicollinearity) can create difficult-to-interpret solutions. It is therefore recommended that regression models and human judgment (theory) be used jointly to develop the predictor equation.

Similar approaches should be used with AI and big-data models. Human judgment and theory should be used to inform the model and identify the relevant sources of information. Then, the analytic methods can be applied to build the empirical model. This model should then be evaluated in terms of theory and substantive criteria to ensure it is appropriate, sensible, ethical, and legal. All of this seems fairly straightforward, but there are many research needs to understand *how* these AI–human collaborations should occur. For example, people are generally poor users of statistical information and suffer from a variety of biases and heuristics. Research needs to determine whether AI can be used to reduce these biases and, alternatively, how these biases may contradict the estimates provided by AI.

Ensuring AI Doesn't Have Bias Built into the Algorithm

Following from the point above, it can be difficult to determine if an AI algorithm is biased or discriminatory. Regression models are reasonably transparent in the sense that they rely on relatively few predictors and the weights are easy to observe. In contrast, AI models rely on multiple sources of input data, nonlinear relationships, and contingent relationships. AI models are like stepwise regression on steroids. Further, AI models can learn and adapt with time. In fact, we heard a chief HR officer from one Fortune 100 firm saying that they introduced an AI architecture with a predetermined algorithm, and it adapted to the point where they no longer knew the algorithm and were trying to figure it out!

And this sense of "intelligence" is what contributes to the concerns around bias and AI. If one cannot articulate the nature of the AI architecture and algorithm, then one cannot evaluate the possibility of bias in the system until the bias is found in terms of differences in hiring rates (i.e., adverse impact, disparate impact). A case in point is HireVue, which has begun to provide facial-recognition algorithms to its suite of virtual interview platforms. As of this writing, serious questions are being raised (as well as a federal complaint) about the appropriateness of the facial-recognition software, not the least of which concern whether the information is job-related and discriminatory against underrepresented groups. The facts that many organizations use this software, including Unilever and Hilton and that venture capitalists are pouring massive amounts of money into AI talent systems suggest many will be watching how HireVue's case unfolds in the legal and legislative arenas.

Here is another context where I/O psychologists are uniquely prepared to make important technical, professional, and ethical contributions. I/O psychologists know assessments and they know the law relating to staffing.

Research is needed to determine the validity, reliability, and subgroup differences for AI models. Research is also needed to determine whether AI models offer benefits beyond traditional methods with known validity and subgroup differences. Research needs to understand how AI models learn and how to build learning algorithms that will avoid the use of illegal or inappropriate data. All of these questions are poorly understood, and I/O psychologists will be well served by researching them immediately. For more on AI tech see Chapter 5 in this book.

Diversity, Equity, and Inclusion

Diversity, equity, and inclusion are routinely in the top 10 most important issues raised by chief HR officers, talent leads, and Society for Industrial and Organizational Psychology (SIOP) members. Since the deaths of George Floyd and Breonna Taylor in 2020, the world has moved well past affirmative action and the compliance focus that characterized the aftermath of the Civil Rights Act of 1964. Modern organizations realize that diversity is now a strategic priority, as the world is diverse, customers are diverse, and innovation often stems from diversity of people and thought (Roberson, 2019). Yet building a diverse workforce that can work together requires an emphasis on inclusion, which is the valuing of differences (Roberson, 2006). Hence, both diversity and inclusion are needed to make an effective workplace where differences are valued, appreciated, and leveraged for performance and competitive advantage.

Unfortunately, too much research is still locked in a "compliance" and affirmative action framework. Research is sorely needed to identify how to attract a diverse and inclusive organization. For example, research needs to identify the key practices that are most effective in recruiting diverse candidates and building inclusion. Research needs to explore how diversity and recruitment are similar and different. Research also must examine how inclusion can be messaged to attract talent. In some of our own research within organizations, we have found that perceptions of diversity and inclusion efforts differ across races, ethnicities, gender, and age. Hence, a major challenge is understanding how to attract talent using customized approaches targeting specific subgroups, and then blend these subgroups into a cohesive unit through inclusion practices.

Blending the Ownership of Recruitment Between HR and the Line

A characteristic of successful HR operations is that they strive to develop shared ownership and accountability with the line (Ready, Hill, & Thomas, 2014). When HR and the line share ownership, HR interventions are more likely to be aligned with strategy, to achieve business results, to be supported by the line, and to be implemented by the line. Yet too many HR people fail if they don't think like business leaders. They don't understand how the business makes money and they don't understand accounting and finance (which is the language of business). They also tend to view business problems from a purely HR perspective. For example, in executive education courses, one of the authors often asks HR managers to list their top three challenges. The challenges are usually HR-centric: reducing turnover, lowering cost-per-hire, and so on. Rarely do they focus on business challenges: increasing profitability, increasing market share, differentiating against competitors. This is one of the reasons HR is often perceived negatively in organizations.

Research is needed to better understand how to blend ownership between HR and the line. For example, research is beginning to examine how middle managers are critical to implementing HR policies and practices (Sikora, Ferris, & Van Iddekinge, 2015). More of this research is needed to understand how HR practices can be implemented more effectively, as well as identifying potential barriers and areas of resistance. Likewise, research is needed to better understand how HR efforts are perceived and messaged at the executive level. How can chief HR officers better convey the value of talent and HR efforts to CEOs, executive team members, and boards? In our research at the University of South Carolina's Center for Executive Succession, we have found that understanding top management team/board dynamics is critical to the effectiveness of the chief HR officer. Research needs to examine how the chief HR officer builds relationships with these executives to create shared accountability between HR and the line.

Developing Models of Effective Recruiting

Becoming a talent magnet means the organization must develop the capability to forecast, identify, and attract talent, so that the required talent is available in the right quality, quantity, place, and time. Past research on recruitment is helpful and informative but is perhaps out of tune with respect to the technologies, speed, and nature of modern TA. Research is sorely needed to understand how recruitment strategies and practices may differ across industries and organizations. Much more strategic recruitment research is needed to understand how recruitment aligns with business strategy. Likewise, understanding the appropriate blend of external and internal recruitment is critical, as prior research has tended to treat these as either/or choices. Note that conducting this research will require a shift away from studying only individuals and individual-level outcomes (e.g., job acceptance). Rather, between-firm research will be required to understand how firms develop the strategy and capability to become a talent magnet.

Evaluating Tools

WFP models include Supplier, Input, Process, Output, Customer (SIPOC), which outlines key stakeholders (HR, finance, recruiting, sales/business development, etc.); uses inputs like revenue growth rates, recruiter capacity, sourcing effectiveness ratios, attrition rates, and internal talent supply; and automates processes like communicating status, postings, offer letters, and scheduling to eliminate bottlenecks like interviewer calendars. SIPOC outputs include dashboards incorporating predictive analytics for forecasting demand. These dashboards offer integration with site strategy, show external trends from the labor market, internal migration patterns, conversion ratios, and hiring plans tracking headcount by location, and level, This enablesa TA leader to manage resource planning and staffing and redeploy as needed. Customers would include hiring leaders, finance and HR leaders, and other appropriate stakeholders. Vendors like Visier can model and predict attrition rates and enable visualization of business intelligence. Companies with core competencies in data management, technology, or analytics will likely build their own custom solution to more easily integrate with legacy systems. In addition to mass hiring plans, succession planning can be a part of WFP to identify critical roles and single points of failure that could disproportionately hurt the business—this should inform bench-building priorities, which will influence recruiting requirements for feeder jobs into these roles. Keep in mind while modeling that a low-tenure workforce is likely to see higher attrition, as 40% of employees who leave voluntarily do so in the first six months (SkillSurvey, 2021b). A sample WFP tool is shown in Figure 1.1.

Exempt UK staff		Total HC Forecast	
1200	Total 2019 Headcount	1344	Total 2020 Headcount
360	Planned New hires	144	New HC due to Growth Expected of 12%
306	Exits last 12 mos	486	All projected exits (inc new hires)
18	Annual Hires per Recruiter	630	Total Hires needed in 2020
20	Recruiter Headcount	-270	HC above/below forecast given current resources/productivity

	2020 Bench by Critical Role	2020 Forecast Needs by Critical Role	External Needs (considers role of internal bench)
GM	0	2	2
Assistant GMs	1	4	3
Supervisors	4	8	4

FTE Headcount be Pay Grade	Forecast Exits + New Roles	Internal Bench by Grade	Replacement Hiring Needs by Grade/Level
Grade 1	680	192	0	192
Grade 2	310	85	33	52
Grade 3	150	34	15	19
Grade 4	50	8	4	4
Grade 5	12	2	2	0
Grade 6	6	0	1	0
TOTAL		321	55	267

			43%	Bench Metric/Pct Ready Now
				Does not include entry level hires

Figure 1.1 Sample workforce plan

Conclusion

"The purpose of most organizations is to create value for their stakeholders. Value is created through increasing revenues and/or decreasing costs" (Ployhart et al., 2018, p. 3). As businesses must constantly adapt their strategies in response to rapid change and disruptive competition, talent is the only resource that can effectively navigate such uncertainty and complexity. In this sense, talent is the lifeblood of the modern organization, and becoming a talent magnet is the only viable option for ensuring a firm's survival. Yet much needs to be learned about how to become a talent magnet. The academic literature is flooded with rigorous studies that offer valuable insights, but too many critical questions remain unanswered or are not even considered relevant academic topics. In this chapter we hope to have offered some guidance for how to become a talent magnet. We hope to have also offered directions for how academic research can be refocused to answer questions that are timely and critical for organizations.

References

Barney, J. B., & Wright, P. M. (1998). On becoming a strategic partner: The role of human resources in gaining competitive advantage. *Human Resource Management, 37*, 31–46.

Bersin, J. (2021). The mad scramble to lead the internal talent marketplace. https://joshbersin.com/2021/12/the-mad-scramble-to-lead-the-talent-marketplace-market/

Campion M. A., Palmer D. K., & Campion J. E. (1997). A review of structure in the selection interview. *Personnel Psychology, 50*, 655–702.

Cappelli, P. (2008). *Talent on demand: Managing talent in an age of uncertainty.* Boston: Harvard Business Review Press.

Cappelli, P., & Keller, J. R. (2014). Talent management: Conceptual approaches and practical challenges. *Annual Review of Organizational Psychology and Organizational Behavior, 1*, 305–331.

CareerArc (2016). The state of the candidate experience. https://www.careerarc.com/lp/candidate-experience-study/

Coff, R. W. (1997). Human assets and management dilemmas: Coping with hazards on the road to resource-based theory. *Academy of Management Review, 22*, 374–402.

Collings, D. G., & Mellahi, K. (2009). Strategic talent management: A review and research agenda. *Human Resource Management Review, 19*, 304–313.

Felps, W., Mitchell, T. R., Hekman, D. R., Lee, T. W., Holtom, B. C., & Harkman, W. S. (2009). Turnover contagion: How coworkers' job embeddedness and job search behaviors influence quitting. *Academy of Management Journal, 52*, 545–561.

Fernandez-Araoz, C., Groysberg, B., & Nohria, N. (2009). The definitive guide to recruiting in good times and bad. *Harvard Business Review, 87*, 74–84.

Fific, M., & Gigerenzer, G. (2014). Are two interviewers better than one? *Journal of Business Research, 67*, 1771–1779.

Gartner (2019). Gartner TalentNeuron data. https://www.gartner.com/en/newsroom/press-releases/2019-05-02-gartner-talentneuron-data-shows-49--of-all-job-postin

HireVue. (2022, February). Global trends report: The state of talent experience 2022. https://www.hirevue.com/resources/report/report-hirevue-2022-global-trends-report.

Kryscynski, D., & Ulrich, D. (2015). Making strategic human capital relevant: A time-sensitive opportunity. *Academy of Management Perspectives, 29*, 357–369.

Kuncel, N. R., Klieger, D. M., Connelly, B. S., & Ones, D. S. (2013). Mechanical versus clinical data combination in selection and admissions decisions: A meta-analysis. *Journal of Applied Psychology, 98*(6), 1060–1072.

Levenson, A., & Fink, A. (2017). Human capital analytics: Too much data and analysis, not enough models and business insights. *Journal of Organizational Effectiveness: People and Performance, 4*, 145–156.

Maurer, R. (2024). Recruiters say their job job a little easier in 2023. https://www.shrm.org/topics-tools/news/talent-acquisition/recruiter-nation-report-2023-2024

McCarthy, J. M., Bauer, T. N., Truxillo. D. M., Campion, M. C., Van Iddekinge, C. H., & Campion, M. A. (2018). Improving the candidate experience: Tips for developing "wise" organizational interventions. *Organizational Dynamics, 47*, 147–154.

McKay, P. F., Avery, D., Liao, H., & Morris, M. (2011). Does diversity climate lead to customer satisfaction? It depends on the service climate and business unit demography. *Organization Science, 22*(3), 788–803.

Mercer. (2022). US 2022 Inside Employees' Minds report. https://www.mercer.us/content/dam/mercer/attachments/private/us-2022-inside-employees-minds-report.pdf.

Mohindra, A. (2015). The three "laws" of workforce analytics. https://www.linkedin.com/pulse/three-laws-workforce-analytics-amit-mohindra/

Murphy, K. R. (2012). Individual differences. In N. Schmitt (Ed.), *The Oxford handbook of personnel assessment and selection* (pp. 31–47). Oxford: Oxford University Press.

O'Boyle, E., & Aguinis, H. (2012). The best and the rest: Revisiting the norm of normality of individual performance. *Personnel Psychology, 65*, 79–119.

Ployhart, R. E., Schmitt, N., & Tippins, N. T. (2017). Solving the supreme problem: 100 years of recruitment and selection research at the *Journal of Applied Psychology*. *Journal of Applied Psychology, 102*, 291–304.

Ployhart, R. E., Weekley, J. A., & Dalzell, J. (2018). *Talent without borders: Global talent acquisition for competitive advantage.* Oxford: Oxford University Press.

Ready, D. A., Hill, L. A., & Thomas, R. J. (2014). Building a game-changing talent strategy. *Harvard Business Review, 92*(1–2), 3–8.

Reul, L. (2022). The skills of tomorrow: How critical roles are evolving. https://reportds.s3.us-east-2.amazonaws.com/The+Skills+of+Tomorrow%3A+How+Critical+Roles+Are+Evolving+gartner_business_quarterly_3q22.?utm_campaign=TALENT%20EDGE%20WEEKLY&utm_medium=email&utm_source=Revue%20newsletter.

Roberson, Q. M. (2006). Disentangling the meanings of diversity and inclusion inorganizations. *Group & Organization Management, 31*(2), 212–236.

Roberson, Q. M. (2019). Diversity in the workplace: A review, synthesis, and future research agenda. *Annual Review of Organizational Psychology and Organizational Behavior, 6*, 69–88.

Ryan, A. M., & Ployhart, R. E. (2000). Applicants' perceptions of selection procedures and decisions: A critical review and agenda for the future. *Journal of Management, 26*(3), 565–606.

Sackett, P. R., Lievens, F., Van Iddekinge, C. H., & Kuncel, N. R. (2017). Individual differences and their measurement: A review of 100 years of research. *Journal of Applied Psychology, 102,* 254–273.

Schmitt, N. (2014). Personality and cognitive ability as predictors of effective performance at work. *Annual Review of Organizational Psychology and Organizational Behavior, 1,* 45–65.

Sikora, D. M., Ferris, G. R., & Van Iddekinge, C. H. (2015). Line manager implementation perceptions as a mediator of relations between high performance work practices and employee outcomes. *Journal of Applied Psychology, 100,* 1908–1918.

Skillsurvey (2021a). Recruiting report: Building future talent pipelines and ensuring post-hire success. https://www.hrmorning.com/wp-content/uploads/2021/06/EBK_048___Recruiting_Trends___Talent_Acquisition.pdf

Skillsurvey (2021b). Lead the retention revolution. https://www.icims.com/wp-content/uploads/2022/08/iCIMS_SkillSurvey_Retention-Revolution-ebook.pdf

Society for Human Resource Management. (2018). These are the hardest jobs to fill right now. https://www.shrm.org/resourcesandtools/hr-topics/talent-acquisition/pages/hardest-jobs-to-fill-2018.aspx.

Stokes, G. S., Mumford, M. D., & Owens, W. A. (Eds.) (1996). *Biodata handbook: Theory, research, and use of biographical information in selection and performance appraisal.* Palo Alto, CA: CPP Books.

Wilhelmy, A., Kleinmann, M., Konig, C. J., Melchers, K. G., & Truxillo, D. M. (2016). How and why do interviewers try to make impressions on applicants? A qualitative study. *Journal of Applied Psychology, 101,* 313–332.

2

The Employment Value Proposition

Differentiating Yourself Among a Sea of Employers

William J. Shepherd
The Ohio State University

Employers are facing one of the most challenging staffing environments in recent history, with the recent COVID-19 pandemic causing potential hires to rethink changing companies, especially for a relocation. For hard-to-fill roles like experienced software developers, the competition for talent has sharpened, even in this environment, with employers from multiple organizations competing aggressively for the same employees. Many human resources (HR) teams have "attract and retain talent" as a core strategic goal, which leads them to initiatives around employee engagement, candidate experience, and employment branding. To meet the expectations of today's workforce, organizations must craft a compelling story of "why us?" for the critical talent segments they target. This employment value proposition (EVP) must resonate as appealing and authentic with both job candidates and current employees.

The quid pro quo relationship between an employer, which provides tangible and intangible rewards to the employee, and the employee, who provides effort and output to the employer, has been variously described as the employer value proposition, the employee value proposition, and the employment value proposition. The first term emphasizes the employer's role and the second term emphasizes the employee's role. I will adopt the third term because the nature of the relationship is not one-sided but rather is a "symbiotic, reciprocal relationship between the organization and the employee" (Shepherd, 2014, p. 580). The employment value proposition is the "psychological contract" (Argyris, 1960) between the two parties.

The proposition has been variously described as (1) "the full array of elements an organization delivers to employees in return for the contribution those employees make to the organization" (Davenport, 2013); (2) "the portfolio of tangible and intangible rewards an organization provides to employees in exchange for their job performance" (Shepherd, 2014, p. 580); and (3) "the total value an employer offers to their employees in return for their work" (Zojceska, 2018). An organization's EVP should be differentiated from its competitors: "it's the reason why an employee would want to work there as opposed to finding employment somewhere else" (Miller, 2016) and "the competitive strengths of a position within your company that separates it from other roles and similar roles offered by your competitors" (Murdock, 2018).

The EVP is different from the employment brand. The employment brand is the collective perceptions people have about the organization as an employer. The EVP will have an impact on the employment brand because the actual experiences of employees will become known to others through social media, personal interactions, and other communication vehicles. However, the employment brand is also affected by other factors, including the organization's employment brand marketing efforts through job advertisements, career websites, social media, job fairs, etc. The employment brand is also influenced through association with the overall reputation of the organization's products and services.

The structure of an EVP often contains common elements (Srivastava & Bhatnagar, 2010) that are historically connected to attractiveness to job candidates. These include financial results and company growth, product brand halos, word of mouth on social media, social responsibility, flexible work arrangements, hierarchy/autonomy, learning opportunities, compensation (now widely visible), and a perception of fun. If you are looking to build out an EVP in your organization, select one or more of these elements to emphasize.

Ideally, an organization would create an EVP within its budget constraints that would be highly appealing to all high-quality job applicants. The EVP would also be differentiated (and even unique), resulting in all high-quality applicants preferring to work at the organization over other organizations. However, this is difficult to achieve because not all high-quality job applicants have the same employment needs. Some will value one aspect of an organization's EVP (e.g., challenging work) over another (e.g., retirement benefits)—one size does not fit all. Any new EVP offering may be perceived as a positive by one employee segment and a negative by another. No organization will be able to fully satisfy all the employment needs of all employee types. Therefore, an organization needs to make choices about how to spend its EVP dollars. Organizations can make better-informed, data-driven choices by conducting an EVP study, which will provide insights about: (1) different types of employees and their respective EVP needs; (2) how to strategically prioritize and allocate limited resources to create the optimal EVP; and (3) key themes and messages to incorporate into employment brand marketing to attract, motivate, and retain talent.

Like much of talent acquisition, EVP research and employment branding can be informed and guided by the field of marketing. Marketing professionals conduct studies of consumers and segment them into target markets. Next, they conduct branding campaigns to influence consumers to buy their products. Similarly, HR professionals can conduct EVP studies of employees and segment them into target markets. They can conduct employment branding campaigns to improve the reputation of their organizations as an employer. This chapter will (1) review concepts from consumer product marketing, including target markets, the marketing mix, the total product offer, the marketing environment, and consumer behavior, and describe how to apply them to human resources; (2) describe the steps to completing an EVP study; (3) provide an example of an EVP research study conducted by a financial services organization; and (4) look to the future of the EVP.

Marketing Strategy

Marketing professionals are responsible for developing marketing strategies for an organization's products. A marketing strategy consists of two major components: (1) identifying the target market (a defined group of prospective customers) and (2) creating the marketing mix (the organization's market plan to appeal to the target markets). HR professionals can apply the same approach to developing marketing strategies for another type of organizational product—a job. For HR professionals who are developing marketing strategies for jobs, the first component is identifying the target market of the most qualified potential new hires. The second component is developing a marketing mix that will be appealing to workers from the target market and persuade them to apply for and accept the organization's jobs.

Target Marketing

Target marketing begins by identifying specific market segments within the overall market need. For consumer products, market segments are groupings of customers who have in common certain personal characteristics (geography, demographics, psychographic, etc.) as well as similar product needs. For example, consider the overall market for personal transportation. Within the overall market for personal transportation there are different target markets (e.g., married couples with children whose needs are met by minivans; retired couples whose needs are met by recreational vehicles). Applying this terminology to human resources and jobs, employee segments are groupings of job applicants who have similar personal characteristics (location, education, work values, etc.) and employment needs. The overall market need for employment contains a wide variety of employee segments (e.g., people who live in the Midwest with a law degree who wish to work for a nonprofit organization; college-age students who are seeking part-time work while attending classes). Organizations can invest in EVP research to determine how to attract and retain the workers they need to achieve their business objectives.

The objective of EVP research is to learn about the personal characteristics, employment needs, and preferences of workers from employee segments in the target market. The research may include collecting primary (focus groups, surveys, etc.) and secondary (white papers, research reports, etc.) data from current and prospective employees and conducting statistical analyses to group employees who have similar employment needs. After the research is completed, the next step is to focus on the marketing mix. This will include developing an employment brand marketing plan that effectively communicates the differentiated aspects of the organization's EVP.

Marketing Mix

The marketing mix is the organization's tactical plan for influencing the target market. The marketing mix has been described as consisting of four dimensions, sometimes referred to as the "4 Ps" and other times as the "4 Cs." The "4 Ps" are the more traditional view through the lens of the organization marketing the product. The "4 Cs" are a more recent model that views products through the eyes of the customer. Table 2.1 describes each of the 4 Ps.

Table 2.1 The Marketing Mix

The "4 Ps"	The "4 Cs"
Product—that meets the needs of customers	Customer—crafting a customized product for a niche market
Price—that is perceived as competitive	Cost—including the total cost of ownership
Promotion—to inform and persuade customers	Communication—two-way information exchanges with customers
Place—where the customer can access the product	Convenience—the ease of accessing the product

In human resources, the marketing mix for jobs is the operational plan for influencing qualified applicants from the target market to apply for employment with the organization. The marketing mix elements that are most relevant for employee staffing are product/customer and promotion/communication. In HR terms, they can be described as:

- **Product/customer**—designing an appealing job that will meet the specific employment needs of the prospective employees from the target market
- **Promotion/communication**—creating and executing a promotional campaign that communicates how the job will meet the target market's employment needs

The other two marketing mix elements could be contorted to apply to the concept of a job as a product, but it is a bit of a stretch. For example, a job's compensation levels could be considered as part of the price/cost element and the job's physical location could be considered as part of the place/convenience element. However, compensation and job location are part of job design, so for purposes of this chapter we will think of them as part of the product/customer element.

Product/Customer
Organizations should design jobs to include product/customer elements (job duties, pay, benefits, working conditions, development opportunities, etc.) that will fulfill the employment needs of job applicants from the organization's target market. If an organization can design the product/

customer elements of the job to include desirable attributes that are highly valued by workers from the target markets, it can provide a differentiated EVP, resulting in a higher-quality talent pool.

How can human resources professionals design their jobs to differentiate them in the employment marketplace? The marketing concept of the "total product offer" may provide a helpful framework. The total product offer specifies there are three levels of features and benefits that influence a customer's decision to buy a product:

- **Core product**—the underlying benefit of the product that motivates customers to buy
- **Actual product**—the physical embodiment of the product that delivers the benefits that meet customers' core needs and/or wants
- **Augmented product**—above and beyond the core and actual product, any additional real or perceived benefits that customers experience when using the product

For example, consider an automobile. The core product is the benefit of being able to transport oneself from one location to another. The actual product is the automobile constructed of steel, glass, rubber, etc. The augmented product includes the pleasure and pride one may receive from having a vehicle, especially if it is an enviable, expensive Italian sports car.

Similarly, consider a job. The core product is the benefit of earning income that can be exchanged for food and shelter. The actual product is the way the job is designed and experienced, including wages, hours, working conditions, supervisors, etc. The augmented product can be the satisfaction from working for a company with a positive reputation. HR professionals can differentiate their jobs at both the actual product and augmented product levels. The actual product of the job can be differentiated by designing the job to have unique or highly competitive EVP elements that are valued by the target market. The augmented product of the job can be differentiated by generating positive sentiment for the organization as part of the promotion/communication element of the marketing mix.

Promotion/Communication

The promotion/communication element of the marketing mix refers to the methods used to communicate and differentiate the advantages of products to customers and influence customers to purchase them. The overall strength of an organization's brand is driven by customers' perceptions of how well the organization's products meet their needs. Branding tactics include associating the product with unique words, names, phrases, and visuals (e.g., the term iPhone, the Amazon logo, or the shape of a Coca-Cola bottle) that identify the product and promote the brand. When organizations are successful in their branding efforts, customers have a positive association with the brand and become loyal to the brand (i.e., are more likely to purchase and re-purchase from the organization, are less likely to accept a substitute).

Prospective employees may have preexisting opinions about the general reputation of the organization, typically influenced by its product branding, product quality, and commitment to its community. The specific component of an organization's reputation as an employer is part of its employment brand (Lievens, 2007). One way to differentiate the employment brand is by associating it with the consumer brand. If customers have a positive association with the organization's products or services, they are more likely to have a positive impression of the organization as a place to work (e.g., "I like Apple products so I would like to work at an Apple store"). However, if the organization's products and services are unknown to job seekers, or worse yet have a negative reputation, the employment brand will suffer.

Academic research has examined how job seekers develop perceptions about organizations' attractiveness as employers (Cable & Turban, 2003; Chapman, Uggerslev, Carroll, Pisasentin, & Jones, 2005; Highhouse & Hoffman, 2001). Job seekers' perceptions are driven primarily by their familiarity with the potential employer, the image they have of the organization, and the reputation it has among job seekers' networks (Cable & Turban, 2003). Increased familiarity with an organization generally leads to more positive perceptions about the organization as a reputable, stable employer (Turban, 2001). Job seekers who have a generally positive image of the organization's products and services tend to have similarly positive perceptions of the organization's employment practices and culture (Lemmink, Schuijf, & Streukens, 2003). Organizations with better reputations tend to attract more, and in many cases higher-quality, applicants (Cable & Turban, 2000). Job seekers want to join a reputable organization that is respected by and impressive to their friends, families, and other important stakeholders in their life (Highhouse, Thornbury, & Little, 2007).

Employment Branding Campaigns

All organizations have employment brands; however, they may not be actively monitoring or managing them. The brand may be accurate or inaccurate, positive or negative, widely known or barely known. The findings from the academic literature support that organizations should measure how the public regards the organization as an employer. Organizations should also proactively promote their attractiveness as an employer through employment advertising, public relations, and personal selling. The HR function can differentiate its employment brand through job postings, employment advertisements, social media presence, press releases, and job fairs. The activities to promote the employment brand should be coordinated as part of an overall marketing campaign that will positively influence the public, especially prospective workers from their target markets, about the reputation of the organization as an employer. The branding may include consistent logos, slogans, language, color schemes, etc. Internal research at some large tech companies shows that their candidates respond best to videos describing the work and benefits of the employer, from the perspective of people like them—these videos result in significant increases in applications from targeted and diverse talent. To put together your own campaign, follow these steps:

1. **Determine marketing objectives**—Employment campaigns can have different goals, including increasing the number of job applications, increasing general awareness or reshaping existing perceptions of the employment brand, wooing job applicants from competitors, etc.
2. **Determine the budget**—Develop funding by connecting to the business need and objectives.
3. **Design the message**—Create advertising and communications that will appeal to the target market.
4. **Implement the promotional mix**—Deliver a consistent, integrated message about the product across all channels, including corporate social media sites (e.g., Facebook, LinkedIn), job fairs (posters, handouts), onsite ("help wanted" ads), pop-up web and mobile job opening advertisements, etc.
5. **Evaluate and adjust as needed**—Determine whether the campaign had the intended impact by tracking metrics such as the number/quality of job applicants, employee turnover, social media website ratings, and employee engagement scores.

The development of the employment branding campaign should also include an evaluation of the internal strengths and weakness of the HR function related to its employee recruitment capabilities. The organization should make a realistic assessment of its current hiring/staffing practices, processes, tools, and organizational structure. What capacity does the HR organization have to execute and act on the research? Does it have the right applicant tracking systems, recruiters, career site, in-house expertise, etc. to accomplish the goals? If not, what steps need to be taken? What is the available budget? The organization should consider the answers to these questions to ensure the proposed campaign can be properly executed.

On a final note, no amount of clever, well-executed employment branding will be effective if the actual job product doesn't live up to the hype. Mere association with a positive consumer brand will not create a strong, sustainable employment brand. The organization must create a truly differentiated EVP as part of the product/customer element of its marketing mix. The foundation of creating differentiation is market research. For that reason, we will return to the topic of EVP research in more detail.

EVP Research

The steps to conducting an EVP research study include (1) defining the focus; (2) identifying the target market; (3) gathering data; and (4) analyzing the data.

Defining the Focus

Typically, organizations embark on an EVP study because they are trying to address strategic human capital issues such as improving employee retention, job applicant flow, the quality of new hires, or organizational diversity. EVP research can address these strategic human capital initiatives by helping organizations (1) learn what existing and potential future employees value in a job; (2) apply that knowledge to evolve and improve their EVP; and (3) attract and retain a larger, more diverse, more qualified workforce. The underlying premise is that job applicants will seek employment and remain with organizations they perceive will meet their employment needs.

The scope of the EVP study can vary based on the budget, the timeframe, and the nature of the strategic human capital issue. The organization may conduct its research independently or partner with a research vendor (e.g., Burke, Inc.; Shaker Recruitment Marketing; Universum). Common research questions include:

- How attractive do current employees find the organization's EVP?
- What do non-employees and potential future employees know and feel about the organization's EVP?
- What changes to the organization's EVP would be valued by current or future employees?
- Are there segments of employees/job applicants who value certain aspects of an EVP more than other groups?

Identifying the Target Market

The objective at this stage of the research is to obtain a representative sample of people who are both able and motivated to perform the type of job being studied. Over time, organizations attract and retain an increasingly homogeneous workforce (Schneider, 1987). Such a workforce will have a commonality of knowledge, skills, abilities, and other characteristics, including their EVP needs. Organizations may default to seeking out the same type of employees and providing the same EVP that have led them to past success. However, changing business conditions and employee expectations will require the organization to adapt or become stagnant with "dry rot" (Argyris, 1960).

Changes in industry forces (Porter, 2008) require organizations to re-tool not only their strategies but also their workforces. Consider how the telecommunications industry changed in the 1990s from merely providing POTS ("plain old telephone service") for landline telephones to delivering high-speed internet access. This led to—at least in the short term—more heterogeneity in the workforce, including educational background, knowledge, experience, tenure, and skill. Telecommunications companies had to redesign jobs and recruit new types of employees with new types of technical skills who had different EVP needs.

Also, societal norms and individual worker expectations continue to evolve. Collective group attitudes about topics such as same-sex marriage, climate change, and work–life balance change over time. As a result, workers' individual expectations about same-sex employee benefits, corporate social responsibility, and job flexibility also change. Organizations must continually evolve their EVPs to continue to attract and retain talented employees.

Therefore, when identifying the target population for an EVP study, the organization should consider including (1) current employees; (2) typical job candidates; and (3) atypical job candidates who have not historically been part of the organization's recruitment efforts. The first two groups will provide insights into how the current EVP is meeting the needs of the current, typical employee segment. The third group provides insight into how the organization would need to evolve its EVP to attract new and different employee segments. There may be untapped pools of job applicants whom the organization has never targeted. Including this group provides insights about what these job applicants want and value in a job and whether it is different than what the organization currently offers. Recruiters talk about "fishing in the same pond" to describe how they continually target the same type of job candidates. If organizations can identify new pools of qualified job applicants they have not previously recruited, they can begin fishing in entirely new ponds, with potentially bigger, better, and more diverse fish.

For illustrative purposes, consider two fictional organizations:

- Mother Earth Recreation (MER) is an environmentally conscious camping and hiking retailer headquartered in Seattle. MER was founded in 1969 by two self-described "hippies" after they attended the Woodstock music festival. The organizational mission statement is "Enjoy Mother Earth, but do Her no harm." MER has 300 stores across the United States with approximately 10,000 employees. The company typically attracts and hires relatively young, inexperienced employees who have a passion for the outdoors and an attraction to the company's progressive ideals. The company offers flexible work hours and employee discounts on its equipment.
- Technology Maximized Consulting (TMC) is a consulting firm focused on helping organizations implement innovative, cutting-edge "big data" initiatives to generate increased profits. The company's motto is "The more you learn about people, the more you can earn from them." TMC is one of the largest employers of computer engineers in North America, with a total of over 5,000 employees. The company's workforce is composed primarily of workers with advanced degrees in computer science

and extensive prior work experience in information technology consulting. The company offers telecommuting as well as ongoing advanced technical skills training.

Current Employees

An organization's current employees, assuming they are performing well, are a critical employee segment to study as part of EVP research. The organization can gain insights about how well their current EVP is meeting the needs of the existing workforce. For example, the MER and TMC organizations described above could gather data about the degree to which their EVP current offerings (flexible work hours, discounts, telecommuting, technical skills training, etc.) are satisfying their employees. The organizations can use the EVP research results to (1) determine the extent to which current employees are satisfied with their organizations' EVPs and (2) monitor whether the workplace preferences of current employees are evolving.

The academic literature (Schneider, 1987; Schneider, Goldstein, & Brent, 1995) suggests there will be a commonality to the EVP preferences of current employees because (1) current workers were likely attracted to their jobs initially because of their pre-hire perceptions about the organization's EVP; (2) the organization hires workers whom they think will be a good cultural fit; and (3) employees who do not find their EVP needs being met leave the organization. As a result, the current employee segment becomes more homogeneous over time. But what about high-quality job applicants who do not yet work for the organization, have left the organization, or are not aware of or interested in the organization as an employer? Organizations should also study the EVP preferences of workers outside their current workforces to learn about how their EVP needs are the same and different from current employees.

Typical Job Applicants

The research should include the types of job applicants who have made up the historical core of successful new hires. These applicants typically have work experience in the organization's industry as well as industry-specific educational degrees or certifications. They often will have some degree of knowledge about the organization, its competitors, and its reputation as an employer. The data from this group can provide valuable information such as how well the organization is known, how favorably it is viewed as an employer, and what is most important when choosing one job over another within the industry. For example, the hypothetical MER organization might study the employment needs of high school and college students who attend schools from which MER has hired frequently in the past. TMC might gather data on the workplace preferences of experienced information technology professionals who work for its competitors and frequently attend leading-edge industry conferences.

Atypical Job Applicants

The research could also include potential job applicants who do not currently work in the organization's industry or have not been historically recruited by the organization. Consider the trend from the last two decades of retailers recruiting older workers for jobs that have previously been done by younger workers (Freudenheim, 2005). Atypical applicants may not have the standard work experience or education as the organization's current employees, but if they can successfully perform the job they provide a new source of talent for the organization. Organizations can learn how the employment needs of atypical applicants are the same and different from current employees and typical job applicants. They can also learn whether atypical job applicants have favorable impressions of the organization as an employer (or if they even have an impression at all). The organization can use these insights to determine how it might need to adapt, evolve, and/or promote its current EVP to attract and retain atypical job applicants. For example, MER might study applicants whom they have not historically recruited or hired, such as retirees. The TMC organization may decide to include in its employment research a sample of atypical students such as consultants who have worked in non-technical fields or early-career workers with liberal arts educations. Such atypical job candidates may bring new talent and innovation to the organization.

Gathering Data

Organizations can gather data for their EVP research from a wide variety of sources, including both secondary (websites with crowdsourced job reviews, social media, industry white papers, academic research, etc.) and primary (e.g., focus groups, surveys) sources.

Secondary Data Sources: Marketing Environment

As part of its EVP research, organizations should conduct an environmental scan of external opportunities and threats. HR organizations do not operate in a vacuum but rather within a marketing environment that includes many elements outside the organization's direct control, including competitive, sociocultural, economic, technological, global, and political/regulatory influences. For example, employee staffing and hiring can be impacted by non-controllable marketing environment influences such as (1) new competitors for employees (competitive); (2) low unemployment rates (economic); (3) changes in how applicants prefer to search and apply for jobs, such as on a mobile device (technological); (4) worker preferences for flexible "gig" employment (social and cultural); (5) local legislation raising the minimum wage (political, legal, and regulatory); and (6) declining interest from foreign workers in the organization's home country (global).

There are multiple sources organizations can consult as part of their environmental scan. Organizations can purchase industry white papers, review academic literature, and read popular press articles about changing worker preferences. Historically, these secondary data sources were written by industry experts, academics, and journalism professionals. However, the internet has created an entirely new secondary data source about employment brands. People in the workforce can voice—often anonymously—their opinions about employers online. Employees—both current and former—can share their personal experiences and attitudes about an organization as an employer via their own social media accounts (LinkedIn, Twitter, etc.) as well as sites that aggregate opinions, like Glassdoor. In today's online world, organizations must include these online secondary data sources as part of their EVP research.

In addition to consulting secondary sources about their own employment brands, organizations should also conduct research on their competitors to find out what EVPs they are offering the target markets. Competitor research can include examining competitors' proxy statements, career sites, press releases, and social media.

In summary, organizations can use secondary data to assess their current employee reputation, find opportunities to take advantage of weaknesses in competitors' EVP offerings, and identify threats from new competitive offerings.

Primary Data Sources—Focus Groups

Focus groups can be used as a formative data-gathering approach to develop initial insights, hunches, and hypotheses about what matters most to workers. Focus group participants should reflect the broader population of the employee segments being studied. Screening criteria may include age, gender, and ethnicity to ensure there is proportional representation compared to the full job applicant pool. Based on the research design and target markets, participants may also be required to be currently working in the organization's industry or willing to do so. Participants are typically paid incentives to participate.

The focus group should be led by a seasoned facilitator who can generate discussion to detect key EVP themes that are important to the target market. The small, interactive format allows the facilitator to probe for details and context about important EVP elements. The purpose of the focus group is to be exploratory in nature and to generate hypotheses to be tested and topics to be further explored during the subsequent EVP survey.

Primary Data Sources—Surveys

The organization needs to determine whom it will survey, how it will collect the data, and what data will be collected. The data can be collected independently by the organization or in partnership with a research vendor. The population can include current employees, typical applicants, and atypical applicants. The survey content should be based on theory and research in areas such as consumer behavior (Peterson, Albaum, & Beltramini, 1985), job satisfaction (Smith, Kendall, & Hulin, 1969), and person/organization (Ostroff, 1993). The survey content should also be tailored to the job, organization, industry, and employee segments being studied, as well as informed by other primary and secondary data sources. Potential survey topics could include personal information (demographics, psychographics, location, job history, etc.), job search behaviors, and on-the-job EVP preferences.

Data Collection

Surveys can be used to obtain a large amount of data from a representative sample of people from the target market. The sample can include current employees as well as those outside the organization (both typical and atypical applicants). Organizations can survey their current employees as part of their annual employee opinion survey process or have a separate EVP-specific survey. For non-employees, organizations can partner with market research vendors who have internet panels composed of people who have volunteered to participate in online surveys, typically in exchange for some sort of compensation. The organization and vendor should partner together to ensure the survey sample has the desired composition. One notable "do-it-yourself" alternative to using a research vendor is Amazon MTurk, an online marketplace where millions of "Turkers" agree to perform "HITs" (human intelligence tasks) for compensation. Organizations can utilize MTurk directly without the involvement of a third-party research vendor.

Consumer Behavior and Job Search

Consumers who are making a buying decision are influenced by multiple factors. For example, job seekers who are deciding whether to choose ("buy") a new job are impacted—consciously or not—by influences including personal (age, race, income, etc.); sociocultural (attitudes about work in general, work–life balance, etc.); psychological (attitudes about the company's reputation as an employer, current job satisfaction, etc.), and situational (current child/elder care commitments, personal health, etc.).

Consumers follow a consistent process when choosing a new product: (1) need recognition ("I want a new car"); (2) information search (compare online reviews of various makes and models of cars); (3) evaluation of alternatives (rate and rank different cars based on most important criteria); (4) purchase or no-purchase decision (to buy or not buy); and (5) post-purchase evaluation ("I'm glad I bought/didn't buy the new car"). Job seekers follow an analogous process when choosing a new job: (1) they say, "I need to get a job/get a new job;" (2) they search job boards and career sites and ask their friends about job openings; (3) they compare different job options against one another, including the current job if currently employed; and (4) they later form an opinion whether they made a good choice in taking ("buying") or not taking ("not buying") a new job.

Based on what we know about consumer behavior, the EVP survey should gather demographic, geographic, and psychographic information, as well as employment-specific information such as current job title, organizational tenure, job transfers, and recent promotions. The survey should ask respondents about how they search for information about jobs (e.g., job boards, career sites, social media, friends) and make decisions about which jobs to accept. In addition, the survey might ask about respondents' favorite mobile apps, social media platforms, and websites, as well as hobbies and other recreational interests. Their responses can be aggregated and used to inform subsequent job advertisement placement as well as post-hire recognition programs.

EVP Preferences

A typical survey might include 20 to 60 survey questions asking respondents to evaluate how much they value various EVP job attributes in categories such as:

- **The work itself**—a job that is challenging, independent, and secure with elements such as customer interaction, international assignments, flexible work hours, etc.
- **Compensation**—a job that offers competitive pay and benefits with programs such as 401(k) programs, sales incentive contests, stock options, medical benefits, etc.
- **Career growth**—a job that offers opportunities for training, development, and promotion through mentorship programs, cross-functional projects, fast-track management programs, etc.
- **People**—a job that offers competent, motivated coworkers and supportive managers who provide coaching and direction
- **Culture**—a job with an employer that values cultural elements such as diversity, recognition, innovation, quality, and environmental sustainability

The survey might also include questions that ask respondents to directly choose the relative attractiveness of two different EVP options or programs (e.g., "Would you prefer X% more vacation or X% more salary?").

Competitor Comparisons

As noted before, organizations should utilize secondary data sources (proxy statements, press releases, career sites, etc.) to track the EVP offerings of their competitors. In addition, surveys could be used to gather insights about how the workforce evaluates competitors' EVPs. The organization conducting the EVP study could identify a set of rival organizations against which it competes for talent. Rather than focusing on specific EVP job attributes, the survey questions would ask respondents to make organizational-level comparisons on general dimensions of employer attractiveness (Berthon, Ewing, & Hah, 2005). For example:

Based upon your perceptions of the organizations listed, please:
- Rank-order them based on where you would most want to work
- Rate how satisfied you think you would be working at the organization
- Rate how likely you would be to accept a job working at the organization
- Rate how attractive each organization is as an employer on each of the following attributes:
  - **Corporate brand**—"This is an organization with a positive reputation that offers quality products and job stability in a desirable industry."
  - **Culture**—"This is an organization that has values, norms, and standards similar to my own and allows me to be my true self at work."
  - **Compensation**—"This is an organization that provides competitive pay and benefits."
  - **People**—"This is an organization that has managers who care about you, treat you fairly, recognize good performance, and set appropriate performance goals, as well as coworkers who are competent, reliable, and enjoyable."
  - **Career growth**—"This is an organization that provides good professional development and advancement opportunities."

In addition, the survey design could ask respondents to pick which of two competitors they perceive have a more attractive EVP. The competitor comparison survey process could be repeated on a recurring basis to allow the organization to track its EVP competitiveness over time. This is similar to how many organizations track customers' brand perceptions about their products over time. The survey results will provide data about the extent to which an organization's EVP is viewed as competitive and differentiated to potential job applicants compared to competitors.

Analyzing Data

Employee Segmentation

The goal of segmentation is to create a relatively small, manageable number of distinctive employee segments that can be used to adapt, evolve, and promote an organization's EVP. The process of segmentation is a blend of art and science. Typically, cluster analytic techniques are used. Statistical sophistication is a prerequisite but should be combined with thoughtful application of theory and research on vocational interests, job attitudes, and worker motivation. The guiding principles of the data analysis are to (1) minimize differences within groups; (2) maximize differences between groups; and (3) balance what is not only most valued by a specific employee segment but also unique to the segment. Note: There are some aspects of an EVP that are generally universally valued across segments (e.g., most people care about base wages and would always value even higher compensation).

Naming Conventions

Each segment should be named. This goal of this "naming the baby" phase is to provide a moniker that reflects the primary EVP drivers of the people in the segment. The employee segments can be further understood by creating a singular persona who represents an archetype of the segment. For example, an employee segment name might be "Working College Student." A persona for the segment might be: "Carlos, a 20-year-old part-time college junior who is pursuing his business degree." The segment and persona names help bring the data to life, making it easier to remember and take action on the EVP research.

Selecting a Differentiated EVP Focus

The EVP research provides insights into the employment needs, wants, and preferences of workers from the targeted employee segments. However, organizations do not have unlimited time, resources, and budgets to develop an EVP that will fully satisfy all employees across all employee segments. Therefore, they need to make choices about where to invest. Some programs will have greater financial costs (e.g., a new onsite cafeteria) than others (e.g., relaxing the dress code). The EVP research results can be used to understand the extent to which different changes or interventions are likely to be valued by different employee segments.

Certain programs (e.g., tuition reimbursement) will be valued more by some employee segments (e.g., college-age employees) than others (e.g., those near retirement). Any given workplace intervention may result in increased employee engagement and retention for one segment of employees but may have no effect or negative effects for other segments. Organizations must pick and choose among different possibilities to identify the optimal portfolio of EVP programs that will provide the highest return on investment.

How should the organization use the insights from EVP research to guide its overall and relative investment in different EVP offerings? The organization may invest in a portfolio of programs that are equally appealing to each employee segment. Or it may choose to over-invest in one or more of the groups to drive increased job candidate flow and employee retention for that employee segment. For example, a retailer may realize that a disproportionate number of its employees are attending college and would greatly value a tuition reimbursement program. The retailer may choose to reduce spending on or forego altogether other programs that are less appealing to the college-age employee segment (e.g., retirement planning services) to be able to afford a more generous tuition reimbursement program.

Assume an organization has $1 million to invest in EVP enhancements (large organizations may budget more depending on their need for more applicants and the computed value per additional quality applicant). The organization has conducted an EVP study and knows different employee segments will differ in their value perceptions about potential enhancements. Consider the three potential allocations in Table 2.2: (1) equally invest in all its employee segments; (2) use a "some for all, but all for some" approach and invest a baseline amount for all but over-invest for one or more groups in relation to others; or (3) go "all in" and focus on one group to the exclusion of others.

Regardless of which allocation the organization chooses, it must be prepared to face possible motivation, engagement, and retention implications if certain employee segments feel the organization is under-investing in their EVP needs compared to other employee segments (Adams, 1965).

Much of the prior discussion has focused on what the employee wants and values. However, recall that the concept of EVP is reciprocal. The employer provides a portfolio of EVP benefits in exchange for employees performing their assigned work duties. The organization may be able to gather job performance data for their current employees who participate in an EVP study. The data analysis may reveal that certain employee segments perform better than others. If so, the organization may feel justified in investing more in elements of the EVP that are most valued by the higher-performing employee segments. The organization may also have other priorities, such as workplace diversity and inclusion, that will influence the allocation they choose.

Ultimately, the goal of the organization is to differentiate itself among a sea of employers and hire and retain workers from the identified employee

Table 2.2 EVP Segment Allocations

	EVP Segment 1	EVP Segment 2	EVP Segment 3	EVP Segment 4
Allocation 1	$250K	$250K	$250K	$250K
Allocation 2	$100K	$700K	$100K	$100K
Allocation 3	$0	$1 million	$0	$0

segments. Ideally, the organization can "own the market" on a particular EVP attribute by being the only one offering the attribute or providing it at a better, more satisfying level to the target market. However, this is difficult to do because competitors will quickly copy successful EVP offerings if they can.

Financial Services Case Study

The following case study helps illustrate some of the EVP research topics covered above. As part of its annual employee opinion survey program of over 10,000 employees, a financial services organization (Shepherd, 2013a, 2013b) presented current employees with a list of 26 EVP attributes. They were asked to identify the six attributes that were most important to them in an ideal work environment. They were also asked to identify the six attributes that were least important. Based on cluster analyses, four employee segments with common work preferences were identified and named by the researchers: (1) "Reward Me," (2) "Challenge Me," (3) "Don't Stress Me Out," and (4) "Take Care of Me" segments (Table 2.3).

Table 2.3 EVP Segment Descriptions

EVP Segments	More Important EVP Elements	Less Important EVP Elements
• Reward Me (23% of employees)	• Base wages • Opportunity for advancement	• Teamwork • Integrity/reputation of leaders • Learning and development
• Challenge Me (37% of employees)	• Challenging work • Competent management • Empowerment • Involvement in decision-making	• Base wages • Job security • Flexibility • Health and retirement benefits
• Don't Stress Me Out (20% of employees)	• Flexibility in work hours • Vacation • Balanced workload • Relaxed/fun atmosphere at work • Good friends at work	• Opportunity for advancement • Challenging work • Opportunities for incentive pay • Empowerment
• Take Care of Me (20% of employees)	• Health benefits • Job security • Retirement benefits • Vacation time	• Flexibility in work hours • Challenging work • Balanced workload

The "Reward Me" segment had a higher relative percentage of younger, shorter-tenured workers. The "Challenge Me" segment was composed of proportionally more mid-level and senior-level leaders. The "Don't Stress Me Out" segment had a higher percentage of women and entry-level workers. The "Take Care of Me" segment had a higher percentage of older, longer-tenured employees.

Job satisfaction ratings were also provided by the employees. The overall job satisfaction for the company was 78% (agree/strongly agree). However, the satisfaction levels for the "Take Care of Me" (84%) and "Challenge Me" (81%) employee segments were significantly higher than the "Don't Stress Me Out" (75%) or "Reward Me" (72%) segments. The employees were also asked to rate the extent to which the organization was delivering what they value in an ideal employer. Overall, 64% agreed the organization was delivering on its EVP. The "Take Care of Me" (70%) and "Challenge Me" (67%) employee segments were in stronger agreement than the "Reward Me" (53%) and "Don't Stress Me Out" (61%) segments. This indicated that the organization's EVP mix was evaluated more favorably by those who value employee benefits (especially valued by the "Take Care of Me" segment) than those who value high compensation (especially valued by the "Reward Me" segment). This illustrates that an organization's EVP may appeal differently to different segments of its workforce.

As part of the research, the organization hired a third-party marketing research agency to administer the same survey to an internet panel of non-employees who worked for competitor financial services organizations. This provided the organization supplemental insights about the degree to which typical workers from the industry perceived their competitors' EVPs.

The research also included text analytics of the open-ended comments provided by survey respondents. The "Reward Me" segment provided a significantly higher number of negative comments about the amount of "support" they received from the organization and the "workload and pace." The "Challenge Me" segment provided a significantly higher number of positive comments about "support" and their opportunity to engage in "meaningful work." The "Don't Stress Me Out" segment provided significantly more positive comments about "teamwork and collaboration" and more negative comments about "workload and pace." Finally, the "Take Care of Me" group also provided significantly more positive comments about "teamwork and collaboration" and negative comments about "workload and pace." The text analytics results provide additional insights into how the organization's EVP was meeting (or not meeting) the EVP needs of each segment.

Consider the following examples of people who would fall into each of the four employee segments:

- "Roberta" (in the "Reward Me" segment) has been recently promoted to branch manager; her goals are to earn more money and be promoted to district manager.
- "Che" ("Challenge Me") is an information technology professional in his mid-20s who recently graduated from college; his goals are to get an advanced degree and work on a variety of interesting projects.
- "Dante" ("Don't Stress Me Out") is a single parent with three young children who works in the customer call center; he wants a job with a work schedule that allows him the flexibility he needs to raise his children.
- "Tonya" ("Take Care of Me") is a vice president of finance who is nearing retirement; she cares most about the company's health and retirement benefits.

Table 2.4 provides examples of EVP programs these four people would find more or less desirable based on their EVP preferences.

Table 2.4 More and Less Desirable EVP Programs

Employee Description	More Desirable EVP Programs	Less Desirable EVP Programs
Roberta ("Reward Me")	• A new variable compensation incentive program • A "management fast-track" career advancement program	• A more generous tuition reimbursement program
Che ("Challenge Me")	• A more generous tuition reimbursement program • A "job rotation" program providing exposure to different business units	• An improvement to the company's long-term healthcare benefits
Dante ("Don't Stress Me Out")	• A new flexible work schedule and telecommuting policy • A new benefit to subsidize childcare costs	• A new variable compensation incentive program
Tonya ("Take Care of Me")	• An improvement to the company's long-term healthcare benefits • More generous company contributions to the retirement plan	• A new flexible work schedule and telecommuting policy

Table 2.5 Marketing Write-Ups for Employee Segments

Empower Me
Financial health: Get in shape fiscally.
You dream of financial security. But are you preparing now for the future that you deserve? You want it and we want it for you. Be deliberate and accountable by taking advantage of products and services designed just for you and life's uncertainties. You work hard. Now, plan hard for the fruits of your labor. We offer 401(k) retirement plans, health spending accounts, and LTD/life insurance.

Challenge Me
Professional health: Prepare for development.
An inclusive culture and employee engagement are what drive business success. High performance, teamwork, leadership, and communication are just a fraction of the succession planning process. We understand your aspirations. What's next for your career? The opportunities for growth are well within reach. We offer career development programs, job training, and tuition reimbursement.

Support Me
Personal health: Life is about balance.
We get it. Who doesn't want to enjoy a world outside of work? Volunteer, serve at a food pantry, participate in a fundraiser, and earn a degree. Take advantage of employee assistance, adoption assistance plans, paid time off, and holidays. Chicken soup for the employee soul can work wonders. We offer employee assistance programs, adoption assistance plans, PTO/holidays, and paid volunteer opportunities.

Encourage Me
Physical health: Focus on fitness holistically.
Become a corporate athlete. Just as you bring passion, ideas, and business solutions to work, that same energy and commitment is required of healthy choices. Try a triathlon of mind, body, and spirit. Reach higher to obtain your goals. With a focus on continuous improvement there's no better investment. We offer medical, dental, and vision insurance plus health and well-being programs.

The financial services organization utilized its internal corporate communications group and an external advertising agency to translate the EVP research results into employment branding materials that would appeal to all four segments. The communications and advertising professionals renamed some of the segments ("Reward Me" became "Empower Me," "Don't Stress Me Out" became "Support Me," and "Take Care of Me" became "Support Me"). They also wrote advertising copy (Table 2.5) that could be used in employee and job applicant–facing employment branding materials. The text was written specifically for each of the four segments and explicitly described the relevant EVP components that would appeal to each group.

Looking to the Future

The employer–employee relationship continues to be impacted by trends such as (1) a broadening of the scope of the EVP (the "employee experience");

(2) increasing focus on environmental and social responsibility; (3) the emerging concept of continuous listening; (4) a more heterogeneous workforce (increasing diversity, five generations in the workforce, nontraditional workers); (5) the external workforce (the rise of the "gig" economy); and (6) the power of employment-related social media (Glassdoor, Blind, Fairygodboss, etc.). As these trends evolve, so too must organizations evolve their approaches to researching, implementing, and monitoring their EVPs and employment brands.

Scope of the EVP

The historical focus for EVP research has been on organizational culture. More recently, organizations are expanding the scope to include the technological and physical environments (Morgan, 2016). This broader view can be defined as the total "employee experience" (or EX): "companies and their people working together to create personalized, authentic experiences that ignite passion and tap into purpose to strengthen individual, team, and company performance" (Dhingra, Emmett, & Samadani, 2018). The implications for the EVP include ensuring that workers have the right technology and the right working spaces for peak performance and engagement.

Environmental and Social Responsibility

Worldwide, organizations are becoming increasingly proactive not only on social issues, which has been a mainstay of corporate social responsibility, but also on environmental sustainability. Similarly, the workforce is paying increasing attention to not only an organization's stances and actions on social issues but also its commitment to addressing climate change. Organizations are seeking a unified and consistent way to quantify their efforts for public consumption (Cann, 2020). To maintain a competitive EVP, organizations will need to invest more time in developing and executing an environmental, social, and governance (ESG) strategy as part of attracting and retaining talent (Atkins, 2019).

Continuous Listening

Measuring and monitoring the EVP should not be a one-off effort but rather an ongoing continuous listening approach that integrates multiple data points and perspectives over time. Continuous listening is a relatively new concept that has been defined as a "coordinated and cross-functional effort to continuously collect and combine a variety of critical data sources to drive and enhance company performance—by applying the same customer-centric mindset, analytical techniques, and interventions to employees as those used in the field of marketing in relation to customers" (Stevens, 2018). Developing a successful continuous listening program requires cohesion and coordination across multiple functions, including HR, marketing, corporate communications, and operations. Organizations that can execute such a holistic approach will likely gain more robust, current data on their EVPs.

More Heterogeneous Workforce

Racial diversity is increasing in the workforce (Chappel, 2017). People are working longer; we now have five generations participating in the workforce together (Gourani, 2019). In addition, because pre-pandemic long-term low unemployment rates have made it difficult to find qualified hires, organizations have begun recruiting previously untapped applicant pools such as those with previous criminal backgrounds (Jackson, 2017; Kanno-Youngs, 2018). As a result, organizations have more heterogeneity of employee needs, which makes crafting an optimal EVP even more complex.

External Workforce

One macro-change happening in the labor market is the rise of the external workforce (or "gig" economy), which consists of people who are not directly employed by organizations. Examples might include independent contractors (e.g., an Uber driver), vendors (e.g., information technology professionals working on a software installation), temporary workers (e.g., administrative support brought in during peak times), or traditional full-time workers who work for a different employer that is deeply embedded into the supply chain of the organization (e.g., a warehouse worker who works in a facility that is entirely dedicated to processing orders for a single client). What, if any, EVP messaging should an organization send to external workers?

In the past, the employer–employee relationship was likened to a successful, long-term marriage that was built on loyalty and commitment from both sides. The employer would offer a traditional job with the associated compensation and benefits in return for employees dedicating most of their time and efforts to their sole employer. However, over time organizations have collectively demonstrated less loyalty to the relationship (more layoffs, decreasing job security, etc.). External employees are responding by viewing themselves not as married to a single employer but rather as free agents who may choose to work with multiple employers.

Organizations may operate under the assumption that external workers would prefer to work for them as full-time, traditional internal workers. However, recent research suggests that a significant portion of external workers prefer external work and the flexibility that goes along with it (SHRM & SAP Success Factors, 2019). An emerging question is the impact external workers will have on the attitudes of internal workers. Will internal workers envy the flexibility of external workers? What EVP implications will arise when internal and external workers work side by side? Organizations should also be mindful of potential legal ramifications (e.g., joint employer) when engaging with the external workforce. Organizations should consider creating a specific philosophy, strategy, and governance model specific to its external workforce (SHRM & SAP, 2019).

Employment-Related Social Media

Employees' social media postings may be positive and highlight recent work accomplishments, awards, or recognitions. Alternatively, they may be more damning exposures of negative employment experiences with managers, poor customer treatment, or ethical concerns. In addition, organizational outsiders, including customers and third-party organizations, may post positive (e.g., a great customer experience, sponsorship of a charitable organization) or negative (e.g., discriminatory treatment, questionable business practices) statements about the organization. A single social media post by one individual can go viral and have a significant impact—positive or negative—on the reputation of an employer. Individuals have more power than ever to influence organizations' employment brands. Organizations should be proactive in promoting their employment brands online. They can use their company websites, corporate social media accounts, and press releases to trumpet the positive aspects of their employees' experiences. An organization's current and future employment brand will be determined and modified by collective actions of management, employees and customers on the internet and in social media.

References

Adams, J. S. (1965). Inequity in social exchange. In L. Berkowitz (Ed.), *Advances in experimental social psychology* (Vol. 2, pp. 267–299). New York: Academic Press.

Argyris, C. (1960). *Understanding organizational behavior.* Homewood, IL: Dorsey.

Atkins, B. (2019). How your company should embrace environmental, social and governance issues. https://www.forbes.com/sites/betsyatkins/2018/11/21/how-your-company-should-embrace-environment-social-and-governance-issues/#39e44ab7af8a.

Berthon, P., Ewing, M., & Hah, L. L. (2005). Captivating company: Dimensions of attractiveness in employer branding. *International Journal of Advertising, 24*(2), 151–172.

Cable, D. M., & Turban, D. B. (2000). Establishing the dimensions, sources, and value of job seekers' employer knowledge during recruitment. *Research in Personnel and Human Resources Management, 20*, 115–163.

Cable, D. M., & Turban, D. B. (2003). Firm reputation and applicant pool characteristics. *Journal of Organizational Behavior, 24*, 733–751.

Cann, O. (2020). Measuring stakeholder capitalism: World's largest companies support developing core set of universal ESG disclosures. https://www.weforum.org/press/2020/01/measuring-stakeholder-capitalism-world-s-largest-companies-support-developing-core-set-of-universal-esg-disclosures.

Chapman, D. S., Uggerslev, K. L., Carroll, S. A., Pisasentin, K. A., & Jones, D. A. (2005). Applicant attraction to organization and job choice: A meta-analytic review of the correlates of recruiting outcomes. *Journal of Applied Psychology, 90*(5), 928–944.

Chappel, B. (2017). Census finds a more diverse America, as whites lag growth. https://www.npr.org/sections/thetwo-way/2017/06/22/533926978/census-finds-a-more-diverse-america-as-whites-lag-growth.

Davenport, T. O. (2013). The 4 stages of the employee value proposition. https://www.tlnt.com/the-4-stages-of-the-employee-value-proposition/.

Dhingra, N., Emmett, J., & Samadani, M. (2018). Employee experience: Essential to compete. https://www.mckinsey.com/business-functions/organization/our-insights/the-organization-blog/employee-experience-essential-to-compete.

Freudenheim, M. (2005). More help wanted: Older workers please apply. https://www.nytimes.com/2005/03/23/business/more-help-wanted-older-workers-please-apply.html.

Gourani, S. (2019). Leading multiple generations in today's workforce. https://www.forbes.com/sites/soulaimagourani/2019/04/25/leading-multiple-generations-in-todays-workforce/#1d46e3fa4636.

Highhouse, S., & Hoffman, J. R. (2001). Organization attraction and job choice. *International Review of Industrial and Organizational Psychology, 16*, 37–64.

Highhouse, S., Thornbury, E. E., & Little, I. S. (2007). Social-identity functions of attraction to organizations. *Organizational Behavior and Human Decision Processes, 103*, 134–146.

Jackson, A. (2017). An Ohio restaurant owner hires former criminals on purpose.https://www.businessinsider.com/hot-chicken-takeout-fried-chicken-restaurant-ohio-2017-10.

Kanno-Youngs, Z. (2018). "I thought I was done for": Tight job market opens doors for ex-convicts. https://www.wsj.com/articles/i-thought-i-was-done-for-tight-job-market-opens-doors-for-ex-convicts-11545215400.

Lemmink, J., Schuijf, A., & Streukens, S. (2003). The role of corporate image and company employment image in explaining application intentions. *Journal of Economic Psychology, 24*, 1–15.

Lievens, F. (2007). Employer branding in the Belgian Army: The importance of instrumental and symbolic beliefs for potential applicants, actual applicants, and military employees. *Human Resource Management, 46*(1), 51–69.

Miller, B. (2016). What is an employee value proposition? https://hrdailyadvisor.blr.com/2016/01/18/what-is-an-employee-value-proposition/.

Morgan, J. (2016). What is employee experience? https://www.forbes.com/sites/jacobmorgan/2016/04/22/what-is-employee-experience/#41e8f0607386.

Murdock, P. K. (2018). The importance of an employment value proposition for recruiting in 2018 and beyond. https://www.forbes.com/sites/forbeshumanresourcescouncil/2018/01/09/the-importance-of-an-employment-value-proposition-for-recruiting-in-2018-and-beyond/#7abf44ac6690.

Ostroff, C. (1993). Relationships between person-environment congruence and organizational effectiveness. *Group & Organization Management, 18*(1), 103–122.

Peterson, R. A., Albaum, G., & Beltramini, R. F. (1985). A meta-analysis of effect sizes in consumer behavior experiments. *Journal of Consumer Research, 12*(1), 97–103.

Porter, M. E. (2008). The five competitive forces that shape strategy. *Harvard Business Review 86*(1), 78–93.

Schneider, B. (1987). The people make the place. *Personnel Psychology, 40*, 437–454.

Schneider, B., Goldstein, H. W., & Brent, D. (1995). The ASA framework: An update. *Personnel Psychology, 48*(4), 747–773.

Shepherd, W. J. (2013a, April). Applications of employee value propositions: Delivering what matters most. Paper presented at the 28th Annual Society for Industrial and Organizational Psychology conference, Houston.

Shepherd, W. J. (2013b, April). Developing an employment value proposition: Discovering what matters most. Paper presented at the 28th Annual Society for Industrial and Organizational Psychology conference, Houston.

Shepherd, W. (2014). The heterogeneity of well-being: Implications for HR management practices. *Industrial and Organizational Psychology, 7*(4), 579–583.

SHRM & SAP Success Factors. (2019). Want your business to thrive? Cultivate your external talent. https://www.shrm.org/hr-today/trends-and-forecasting/research-and-surveys/pages/external-workers.aspx.

Smith, P. C., Kendall, L., & Hulin, C. L. (1969). *The measurement of satisfaction in work and retirement.* Chicago: Rand McNally.

Srivastava, P., & Bhatnagar, J. (2010). Employer brand for talent acquisition. *Vision: The Journal of Business Perspective, 14*, 25–34.

Stevens, L. (2018). The 4 guiding principles of a successful continuous listening program. https://www.linkedin.com/pulse/4-guiding-principles-successful-continuous-listening-program-phd/.

Turban, D. B. (2001). Organizational attractiveness as an employer on college campuses: An examination of the applicant population. *Journal of Vocational Behavior, 58*, 293–312.

Zojceska, A. (2018). Employee value proposition (EVP): Magnet for attracting candidates. https://www.talentlyft.com/en/blog/article/105/employee-value-proposition-evp-magnet-for-attracting-candidates.

3

Sourcing

David Dorsey
HumRRO
Matt Allen
University of Nebraska at Omaha

This chapter describes what sourcing is, why it is done, and how to do it efficiently and effectively. To aid practitioners, we highlight proven tactics and strategies cited by top field recruiters, organizational researchers, and recruiting analytic specialists. We describe how sourcing serves as the essential first step in building a talent pipeline and how core elements from the previous two chapters, such as the employee value proposition (EVP) and the workforce plan (WFP), serve as a foundation for sourcing. We further discuss intelligent resource allocation for sourcing and related cost drivers. We review other key components of an effective sourcing strategy such as referrals, realistic job previews, and emerging technology drivers. We conclude with a larger, big-picture discussion of elements that will likely impact sourcing in the future. Throughout the chapter, we highlight examples to show effective practices as actually implemented. See Table 3.1 at the end of this chapter for a practical, user-friendly checklist for those building a sourcing plan and system.

Introducing Sourcing and Defining Key Terms

In ordinary conversation, we use the adage "plenty of fish in the sea" to denote a wealth of choices, for everything from finding the right mate to identifying the ideal employee. Yet behind these analogies, a larger question looms: How does one know where to fish? In the current chapter, we address the fundamental issue of talent "sourcing"—or, stated another way, knowing where to fish.

David Dorsey and Matt Allen, *Sourcing* In: *Becoming a Talent Magnet*. Edited by: Mark A. Morris, Oxford University Press.
© Oxford University Press 2024. DOI: 10.1093/oso/9780190938512.003.0003

Table 3.1 A Sourcing Practitioner's Checklist

Topic	Detail	Present (yes/no)
Sourcing strategy	*Construct a written strategy that identifies:* • *Key stakeholders* • *Goals* • *Mechanisms of action* • *Resources*	
WFP	*Build a WFP, to include:* • *Internal and external scanning* • *Analysis of the current workforce* • *Analysis of future workforce needs* • *Gap analysis* • *Action planning*	
EVP	*Implement a compelling, realistic, and differentiating EVP, to include information about:* • *Purpose* • *Values and company culture* • *Jobs and careers* • *People and leadership* • *Compensation/benefits*	
Sourcing tools	*Evaluate and deploy a set of sourcing tools:* • *Referrals* • *Company website* • *Social media* • *Job boards* • *RJPs* • *Campus recruiting* • *Other*	
Analytics	*Implement sourcing analytics, including:* • *Overall sourcing success (% of new hires from each source that last one year or longer, % of new hires per source with good performance ratings, promotion rate by source organization, etc.)* • *Compensation & EVP (e.g., % of offers accepted, intern conversion ratios, % of offers with compensation exceptions, average # offers per filled requisition)* • *Formative sourcing process measures* • *Measures related to diversity, inclusion, and bias*	
Focus on the future	*Plan for changes in sourcing strategies and processes (e.g., changes in technology, changes in jobs, nontraditional applicant pools)*	

The Society for Human Resource Management (SHRM) defines sourcing as "the proactive search for qualified job candidates for current or planned open positions" (SHRM, 2019). Accordingly, sourcing is not simply a reactive function of reviewing résumés and applications; instead, sourcing professionals proactively seek to identify groups of qualified candidates. The idea of "sourcing" is closely related to the idea of talent "pipelines," which Brymer, Chadwick, Hill, and Molloy (2018) define (based on a rigorous review of over 100 studies) as "the sequenced flow and development of individuals repeated over time, disproportionately from specific labor sources into particular positions within firms, occupations, and geographies" (p. 7). Sourcing is typically part of a recruiting function within human resources (HR) organizations, but line managers and other professionals within a company often play key roles. Sourcing typically includes both passive (those not actively looking for a job) and active (those actively searching) candidates. Despite the obvious importance of this concept to organizational functioning, numerous researchers and practitioners have called out the dearth of research on this topic (e.g., Phillips & Gully, 2015; Ployhart & Cragun, 2017).

Inherent to sourcing activities is the fundamental reality that organizations and potential applicants often have little information on each other. Thus, decisions around choice and matching often take place in a relatively poor information environment—barring an intervention to counteract this information deficit. Moreover, purposeful information distortion can take place; for example, job seekers may purposely embellish résumés, and/or organizations may mislead job seekers about the organization (Bergh, Connelly, Ketchen, & Shannon, 2014). Weller, Hymer, Nyberg, and Ebert (2019) argue that credible signals (e.g., required education credentials), realistic job previews (RJPs), referral networks, and labor market intermediaries (e.g., "headhunters") can remedy the information deficit and increase the quality of applicant–organization matches. In the following sections, we elaborate on some of these interventions and mechanisms, and we define additional components of sourcing, such as the EVP and the WFP. Before moving on, we should highlight one last feature of sourcing, which is essential: Sourcing involves the targeting of specific types of labor sources, which can be conceived of at multiple levels of analyses, to include specific individuals, specific groups of candidates, or even entire entities (such as rival organizations) that may contain high-value talent. One useful source available online for free is the Talent Intelligence Collective Battlecards, available in their document library. This real-time interactive website allows the recruiting team to pick a country and view likely sourcing pools, even including five Hofstede cultural criteria. Staffing teams can use resources like these to provide useful context on global sourcing and outsourcing decisions.

Constructing a Sourcing Strategy

As with any human capital initiative, constructing a sourcing strategy requires that organizations align sufficient resources and infrastructure to support the plan. A first step is identifying key stakeholders and defining their roles. The following stakeholders are frequently involved in the development and execution of sourcing and recruitment initiatives:

1. *Recruiters*—Both internal and external recruiters can be involved in the sourcing process.
2. *Hiring managers*—Hiring managers are the customers in the sourcing process and thus a key source of input and, potentially, a key resource in developing talent sources.
3. *Senior leaders*—As described in Cappelli (2019), surveys suggest that hiring is a top concern of executives throughout the C-suite. Thus, they have a vested interest in improvement sourcing initiatives. As described later, senior leader involvement in the planning phases of any new large-scale talent management initiative is critical to success. Budget for headcount is also typically approved at senior levels of the organization, as are new executive roles and new organizations that are tied to strategic decisions.
4. *HR technology support*—A change in sourcing strategy may require changes or new uses of HR technology, such as applicant tracking systems. Consequently, support is needed from the technology professionals who maintain these systems to ensure successful implementation. They are also a key source of input on (a) the capabilities of current systems and (b) potential alternative systems that may better suit organizational sourcing and hiring needs.
5. *Other stakeholders*—Other key stakeholders may include (a) Equal Employment Opportunity (EEO) offices, (b) general counsel, (c) finance, and/or (d) human capital analytics/human capital strategy offices.

Project leads should identify team leads, team members, and sponsors/champions of the initiative from among these stakeholder groups to ensure successful project completion. Once the project team has been assembled, goals should be set to define success, with the fundamental underlying question being how the workforce will look different upon full implementation of the new initiatives. This implies an underlying talent philosophy that governs corporate strategy toward human capital, such as whether the organization generally buys or builds in new strategic areas, whether human capital decision-making is centralized versus decentralized, whether promotions are more performance-based or more tenure-based, the philosophy for handling poor and star performers, and so forth. As an example, Effron (2018) suggests that a talent management philosophy is defined by five elements:

1. Performance (consequences of high/low performance),
2. Behaviors (how much they matter in career),
3. Differentiation (compensation philosophy for levels of performance),
4. Transparency (openness in communicating processes), and
5. Accountability (management responsibility in managing their teams).

He further suggests that project leads can define these elements through facilitated discussion with the senior leadership team.

Once a strategy team has specified an overarching talent management philosophy, they need to further identify the resources required to fund key elements of new systems and their implementation. For example, if the talent management philosophy suggests more differentiation in pay between acceptable and star performers, the increased base pay for those performers will need to be resourced. In terms of sourcing, this can have significant cost implications, as increases in the base pay for new employees may also impact base pay rates for current employees (e.g., due to equity considerations). Another example is technology. Many changes to human capital management systems require accompanying changes to the underlying HR information technology infrastructure. For example, increased base pay for new-hire star performers may require increases in the rigor of the hiring process (to include, for example, pre-employment assessments) where star performers are being targeted for key roles. Project planners should consider the following types of direct (e.g., payments to vendors, salary increases) and indirect (e.g., time off task for current employees) costs when estimating needed resources:

- Compensation and benefits-related costs,
- Direct costs for new programs (e.g., training),
- Technology costs,
- Design costs (e.g., costs for consultants to design a new human capital system), and
- Costs to communicate changes to the workforce.

Implementation planning is the critical last step in making changes to human capital systems, to include changes to sourcing and hiring systems. As discussed elsewhere, implementation often surpasses design in importance in human capital systems (Hedge & Pulakos, 2002). As such, developers of these new systems must fully think through (a) governance, or who will be responsible for what aspects of the new system, (b) ownership, or who will be accountable for successful execution of the new plan, and (c) maintenance, or who will be responsible for continuously evaluating whether the new system is working and making changes as necessary.

A shared understanding of an organization's talent management philosophy, the stakeholders that should be involved, and associated resource requirements can inform two specific human capital initiatives critical to the development of a sourcing strategy—the WFP and the EVP. We briefly describe both in the next sections; interested readers should also consult Chapters 1 and 2 in the current volume for more information.

Building a WFP

An organization's talent management philosophy is a key input to developing another critical element in an effective sourcing strategy—the WFP (see Chapter 1 for more). At the most basic level, a WFP represents an organization's projected workforce needs in the context of strategic objectives (e.g., Emmerichs, Marcum, & Robbert, 2004; Panda & Sahoo, 2013; Pynes, 2004). However, the WFP process has become much more complex, corresponding to broader changes in the economy due to globalization, technology changes, and demographic shifts. These economic changes have shifted the composition of the modern workforce to include more contracted workers and workers on alternative work arrangements, with contracted workers coming in many forms, such as full-time, onsite contractors, contracted experts, temporary employees, and "gig" workers (Chartered Institute of Personnel Development, 2018; Deloitte, 2018; Mankins, 2017; Younger & Smallwood, 2016). One industry survey estimates that 40% of employees work on an alternative work arrangement (Deloitte, 2018; see also Maurer, 2015), a figure no doubt poised to rise since the onset of the pandemic in 2020.

Given these rapid changes to the external environment, there is a perception that deliberate planning is too slow, resource-intensive, or lacking in utility to be worth the resource investment (Cappelli, 2009). Survey research suggests that many companies do not have a WFP, or if they do, the companies do not deliberately tie such plans to human capital management strategies (Human Capital Institute, 2014 [in Maurer, 2015]). Previous organizational planning research suggests that well-constructed plans will include prognosis, scenario development, and contingency planning that is adaptable to changing environmental conditions and positively related to organizational performance (Miller & Cardinal, 1994; Mumford, Schultz, & Osburn, 2002; Wolf & Floyd, 2017). Indeed, research and industry recommendations suggest that this increased complexity makes workforce planning *more* of a necessity rather than less. By accounting for environmental changes, a well-constructed WFP has the potential to provide a competitive advantage by making talent management more proactive rather than reactive (Louch, 2014; Mankins, 2017).

Although the exact approach will change depending on specific organizational needs, models of WFP generally involve some variation of the following five steps:

1. Internal and external environmental scanning,
2. Analysis of the current workforce,
3. Analysis of future workforce needs,
4. Gap analysis, and
5. Action planning (e.g., Chartered Institute of Personnel Development, 2018; Emmerichs et al., 2004; Louch, 2014; Panda & Sahoo, 2013; Pynes, 2004).

The first step involves examining internal and external factors that impact current and future workforce needs. As referenced previously, the organization's talent management strategy is one key internal input, as is the organization's strategic business plan (Effron, 2018; Panda & Sahoo, 2013). The latter information informs the potential future needs, while the former informs the organization's philosophy toward fulfilling those growth needs. The organization's operating model—such as processes, information systems, location, and partners—can also be an informative part of the internal environmental scan as variables that may impact current labor supply and future demand (Chartered Institute of Personnel Development, 2018).

In terms of external environmental factors, the primary focus of the scan should be the external labor market and how it is changing in key industries of interest. For critical talent pools, organizations should examine where there are skill shortages and surpluses to account for in subsequent planning steps (SHRM, 2016a). For example, in the critical and growing area of cybersecurity, the talent pool is facing severe shortages that organizations will have to account for in their WFP (Dreibelbis, Martin, Coovert, & Dorsey, 2018). In addition to global shortage/surplus, labor markets can go through shifts in demographics, experience generational shifts (Louch, 2014), or be fundamentally changed by "shocks" such as those experienced by organizations during the COVID-19 pandemic. These shifts can have profound implications on various human capital strategies, including sourcing. A final external factor is changes to labor market competitors (Chartered Institute of Personnel Development, 2018): What other organizations hire the types of talent you are seeking? What are those competitors' offerings?

The second step in developing a WFP involves an analysis of the current workforce. The ultimate goal of this step is to identify talent segments that are most critical to the organization and drive its success (cf. Maurer, 2015). A key component in achieving this objective is organizational data. Organizations with more mature (e.g., discoverability, quality; Ryu, Park, & Park, 2006) human capital data will be at an advantage in this phase of the process as it simplifies collection and analysis. When examining the current workforce, two types of information are of most interest: (a) jobs and (b) people. An examination of jobs includes identifying key job functions, job families, and job roles critical to organizational success. Job analysis information can supplement this information if available (Pynes, 2004), which includes the knowledge, skills, abilities, and other characteristics (KSAOs) critical to successful performance. A data file containing job analysis information also allows for the development of job clusters, grouped by key KSAOs.

In terms of people, organizations can start with basic information within key talent segments, such as demographics, qualifications (e.g., experience, education), and individual KSAO information (if available). Total composition of the types of workers in the organization should also be examined, to include not just regular full-time employees but also part-time employees, contractors, and external experts. Companies often fail to adequately account for workers with these types of nontraditional relationships, despite their growing prevalence in organizations (Deloitte, 2018; Younger & Smallwood, 2016).

The third step in developing a WFP is forecasting future needs. This activity can begin with a very basic forecast model. For example, if there were no major environmental changes, reorganizations, or other major organizational change initiatives, an organization would still need to determine future workforce needs due to turnover (e.g., separations, retirements) and incremental growth. Once analysts build a basic forecasting model, they can refine it with information from the environmental scan, such as growth projections based on the business strategy and projected labor shortfalls or surpluses in key areas. For example, an increasing number of organizations have diversity and inclusion objectives (Bourke, Garr, van Berkel, & Wong, 2017). There is some research that suggests demographic and individual difference diversity can predict organizational outcomes such as innovativeness when linked to organizational objectives (e.g., Allen, Dawson, Wheatley, & White, 2008; Mohammadi, Browstöm, & Franzoni, 2017; Richard, 2000). Recruitment professionals can identify future diversity needs in relation to strategic organizational objectives and make these explicit during this phase of the forecasting process. Given that human beings struggle with accurately forecasting the future (Moore, Kurtzberg, Fox, & Bazerman, 1999; Önkal, Yates, Simga-Mugan, & Öztin, 2003), these models should account for uncertainty, either through quantitative approaches such as sensitivity analysis (Cappelli, 2009) or qualitative approaches such as scenario planning (Bunn & Salo, 1993; Chartered Institute of Personnel Development, 2018).

The fourth step in developing a WFP is gap analysis—identifying the gap between the current workforce and future needs. These gaps can be described quantitively or qualitatively depending on the nature of the information gathered from previous steps, but quantitative gap identification can lead to more specificity in identifying the costs and level of effort associated with filling those gaps. Once gaps have been identified, they should be prioritized by workforce segment and fed into the action plan. In very large organizations such as the U.S. Department of Defense, it may make sense for this gap analysis to occur at the business-unit level rather than the organizational level, provided that the segments are concentrated in one or two functional units (RAND, 2006).

The final step in workforce planning is to develop a strategy to resolve the gaps. While this volume focuses on sourcing and recruitment, labor gaps can also be resolved using a number of strategies, such as retaining a higher percentage of current employees (Allen, 2008; Hom, 2011), growing your own talent (Aguinis & Kraiger, 2009), or eliminating the need for labor through processes such as automation (Chartered Institute of Personnel Development, 2018). The success of these approaches will depend on a variety of factors, such as time, resources, current internal depth, and internal workforce dynamics (Pynes, 2004). As referenced previously, an organization's strategy should also consider the role of nontraditional employees, such as those on alternative work arrangements. Often, these individuals are not vetted or treated in the same way as full-time employees (Younger & Smallwood, 2016), though their role should be considered deliberately as part of an organization's overall talent management system.

Successful implementation of a WFP depends on a variety of factors, such as (a) the quality and integrity of extant data, (b) availability of analytic skills to develop effective forecast models, (c) senior leadership support and participation, and (d) clear ownership of the WFP process (Emmerichs et al., 2004; Louch, 2014). Once it has been implemented, the WFP should be continuously updated with new information and regularly maintained. Owners of the WFP development process should check for changes in assumptions to costs (e.g., have some interventions cost more than expected?), success (e.g., are the chosen strategies succeeding in closing gaps?), labor market changes (e.g., has the market rate for talent in certain locations changed?), and changes to forecasting model assumptions (e.g., is the company growing faster or slower than expected?). These updates create opportunities to improve forecast models based on new data and input from stakeholders. Greater investments in WFP development on the front end will pay dividends in subsequent years as plans can be more easily updated once the infrastructure is in place.

Developing and Deploying an EVP

Another critical component in developing a sourcing strategy involves the creation of a clear and compelling EVP (see Chapter 2). An EVP is typically described as a statement that summarizes the value a member receives by working for the organization (e.g., Heger, 2007). The "value proposition" terminology is typically associated with marketing (i.e., "customer value proposition") as a concrete reflection of the employer brand. Recently, however, value propositions have been described by academic researchers in terms of reciprocal relationships among stakeholders and the organization, where they are continuously evaluated and updated (Ballantyne, Frow, Varey, &

Payne, 2011; Frow et al., 2014; Payne, Frow, & Eggert, 2017). This recognition is particularly resonant in our current technology age, where perceptions of an EVP are impacted by other stakeholders such as current employees, competitors, and external applicants, in addition to an organization's own employer branding efforts. For example, current employees, company alumni, and applicants can provide ratings on a company's desirability on dimensions typically included in an EVP (e.g., work–life balance, compensation) through sites such as Glassdoor.com and Indeed.com. Social media sites such as Twitter also allow outside actors, such as competitors, to influence brand perceptions through responses to posts (or tweets). Given these realities, following Frow and colleagues (2014), we define an EVP as a dynamic mechanism for determining how resources are shared between an organization and employees in an employment ecosystem.

A review of academic literature, corporate websites, and industry publications suggests that there are several elements frequently included in an EVP. However, there can be wide variation in how these elements are communicated to be compelling to current or potential employees. For example, certain elements may be more salient in the EVP than others depending on factors such as the business strategy. Based on our review, the most common elements in an EVP include the following (see, for example, Chambers, Foulon, Handfield-Jones, Hankin, & Michaels, 1998; Eaton, 2015; Heger, 2007; Keller & Meaney, 2017; Mercer, 2018; Moseley, 2015; Sengupta, Bamel, & Singh, 2015; Sibson, 2009; Srivastava & Bhatnagar, 2010; Towers Watson, 2014):

1. *Purpose*—EVPs often contain statements of corporate purpose, often linked to broader societal goals. For example, Clayton (2018) describes how outdoor apparel retailer Patagonia incorporates environmentalism into its EVP and carries it through in its human capital systems. She further cites this as a primary reason for positive organizational outcomes, such as turnover at Patagonia that is lower than the broader retail industry. This statement of purpose may also include current business goals or priorities that are particularly relevant for certain segments of the workforce.

2. *Values and company culture*—Indicators of corporate values and culture are also frequently included in EVPs. Inclusion of values and culture send a signal to potential like-minded employees that they will "fit" with the company—a strong predictor of attraction and selection of an

organization (Cable & Judge, 1996; Carless, 2015; Chapman, Uggerslev, Carroll, Piasentin, & Jones, 2005). For example, a company may tout cultures and values that encourage innovation (or stability), relaxation (or a hard-charging attitude), or a strong work–life balance.

3. *Job and career*—Another common element of an EVP involves signaling information about the work itself. Drawing on work motivation literature, these signals may include motivating information about the specific job opportunity (e.g., autonomy, task significance; Hackman & Oldham, 1976). Employers may also tout their career opportunities, such as opportunities for career growth, training and development, leadership, international travel, and so on. For example, retail coffee company Starbucks has information about career paths as one of the first items on its corporate careers landing page.[1]

4. *People and leadership*—In addition to values and culture, EVPs will often signal exactly the types of people they are looking for to join the organization. For example, online retailer Amazon's careers website says it is a "company of pioneers" and goes on to enumerate the leadership principles sought in potential applicants, such as "customer obsession," "ownership," "bias for action," and "deliver results."[2]

5. *Compensation/benefits*—EVPs will often include information about compensation and/or benefits. These may reinforce aspects of the other elements listed above. For example, a company that touts family values may have parental leave policies that are more generous than similarly situated competitors.

EVP development can be accomplished in four phases: (a) research, (b) development, (c) deployment, and (d) delivery. Development of an effective EVP begins with an understanding of a WFP linked to business strategy. Next, developers often conduct research to serve as inputs to the EVP. Current employees serve as a key resource input for EVPs. Multiple researchers (Chambers et al., 1998; Keller & Meaney, 2017) suggest that practitioners interview top performers to determine key motivators and drivers of their performance. Information regarding key drivers of employee engagement (or, on the flip side, turnover) in the organization can also serve as inputs into the EVP (Allen, 2008; Bersin, 2018; Hom, 2011; O'Boyle & Adkins, 2015), as

---

[1] https://www.starbucks.com/careers/
[2] https://www.amazon.jobs/en/working/working-amazon

well as input from other stakeholders, such as senior leaders and marketing professionals.

A critical part of this research is employee segmentation—identifying key personas or profiles in critical areas of talent need (Chambers et al., 1998; Keller & Meaney, 2017; Mankins, 2017). While the WFP identifies key employee segments, research should uncover any differential motivators for those segments. As illustrated by Beiker (2016), organizations (particularly large organizations) are not monolithic entities and may have different drivers for key staff. As an example, Beiker describes how automakers are employing more Silicon Valley technologists. These technologists often value work styles such as flexibility and creativity, while the culture of these companies often emphasizes other factors, such as stability and legacy. In these cases, EVPs must be tailored to these different segments of core talent, ideally by having unifying EVP themes with different emphases for different segments.

Once this research is complete, an EVP can be drafted to include the previously described elements. Our review of extant resources and research suggests the following as characteristics of an effective EVP:

1. *Compelling*—The EVP should be compelling to the intended audience. Input from key stakeholders (incumbent employees, executives, recruiters) and corporate marketing team involvement will help to craft and iterate a message that resonates.
2. *Realistic*—An EVP should be clear and contain information that accurately reflects the work environment. When not grounded with incumbent input, it is easy for an EVP to come across as aspirational and unrealistic (Keller & Meaney, 2017). Survey research by Weber Shandwick and KRC Research (2014; see also Clayton, 2018) on a global sample of workers suggests that only 53% of respondents agree with the statement "What my employer portrays about itself publicly matches what it's like to work there." Their research further went on to suggest that "aligned" organizations were more likely to have stronger business outcomes, such as recruitment, advocacy, retention, and productivity. Several streams in the research literature reinforce this point. For example, lack of alignment between an EVP and the actual work experience would violate implicit psychological contracts, an outcome that is linked to lower organizational commitment and other factors (Coyle-Shapiro & Kessler, 2000; Robinson & Rousseau, 1994; Turnley

& Feldman, 2000). On the flip side, alignment between an EVP and the work environment would provide a realistic preview of the job, which is positively related to employee commitment and performance (Earnest, Allen, & Landis, 2011; Guest & Conway, 2002; Premack & Wanous, 1985).

3. *Differentiating*—Multiple industry publications suggest that an EVP should clearly differentiate the company from competitors (e.g., Chadha, 2017; Keller & Meaney, 2017). In most cases, companies differentiate using symbolic factors such as culture rather than instrumental factors such as pay—factors that are also more likely to attract someone to an organization (Lievens & Highhouse, 2003). Differentiating on non-compensation and benefits factors is also more likely to lower the premium to pay for new talent. However, instrumental factors can be differentiating if they illustrate a larger purpose. For example, a company that includes innovation and work–life balance might include an unusual benefit, such as sabbaticals, in its benefits package to clearly reinforce the EVP.

Upon completion of the EVP, the next step is to incorporate it into the organization's employer branding. For recruitment purposes, the EVP should be incorporated into corporate websites (e.g., applicant tracking systems), job advertisements, and social media activities related to recruitment and employer branding. However, leadership should also advertise and communicate the EVP internally to current employees. The reciprocal relationship between employees and organizations in the employment ecosystem means that effective recruitment starts with an engaged and committed workforce, making the employees themselves into advertisers and evangelists for your employer brand (Chadha, 2017). Organizations can lean into this new trend of employee activism (Clayton, 2018; Weber Shandwick, 2014) by asking employees to contribute directly to the manifestation of the EVP. Research suggests that potential hires are more likely to trust what employees have to say about working at the organization, in comparison to other resources such as recruiters and corporate websites (Mosely, 2015). Research by Gallup (O'Boyle & Adkins, 2015) suggests that only a small percentage of employees are currently brand ambassadors, representing an untapped resource for communicating a compelling EVP.

The final step in EVP development is to keep the promise—the EVP should be reinforced by aligning its message with current human capital systems (e.g., performance management, compensation, benefits, communications), including communications from senior executives internally and externally, and corporate programs, such as corporate social responsibility (CSR) initiatives. While many organizations develop EVPs and change their branding, they often neglect to ensure the veracity of their EVP internally (Frow & Payne, 2011; Towers Watson, 2014). Failure to deliver on the promise of an EVP will do considerable damage to the organization's reputation, while delivering on them offers significant benefits.

Choosing Tools to Drive Effective Sourcing

Once the WFP and EVP are in place, the sourcing professional faces a set of choices around the specific tools to put in place to realize elements of their sourcing strategy. Here, there are two main questions: (a) whom to source and (b) how best to source them. We focus this section on the second issue. Our tools review is by no means exhaustive, but it does summarize tools that are (a) most frequently used and (b) best supported by extant research. Research by SHRM (2016b) suggests that the top tools organizations use to source candidates are (a) employee referrals (83% of organizations surveyed), (b) company websites (81%), (c) social media websites (67%), and (d) paid/free job boards (66% and 63% respectively).

Referrals

Sourcing through referrals is ubiquitous, with two industry surveys finding that roughly a third of current positions were filled through referrals (Frank, 2018; SilkRoad, 2018). Based on the extant research, it is easy to see why this is the case. Across multiple disciplines (psychology, sociology, economics), there is remarkable consistency in research supporting the positive effect of employee referral programs. Previous research has consistently found that referred candidates are (a) more likely to be offered a job, (b) more likely to accept a job offer, (c) more likely to be satisfied once hired, and (d) less likely to leave than candidates sourced through other means (Breaugh, 2012; Brown, Setren, & Topa, 2012; Burks, Cowgill, Hoffman, & Housman, 2015; Dustmann, Glitz, Schönberg, & Brücker, 2015; Gannon, 1971; Mani, 2012; Weller, Holtom, Matiaske, & Mellewigt, 2009; Zottoli & Wanous, 2000).

Referrals also have lower cost per hire and higher yield ratios (i.e., the percentage of hires from applicants sourced through that method; Burks et al., 2015; Mani, 2012; Rafaeli, Hadomi, & Simons, 2005). Additionally, previous research found that referred employees are more productive than non-referred employees, though these results are somewhat mixed across studies and the differences dissipate over time (Brown et al., 2012; Burks et al., 2015; Castilla, 2005; Dustmann et al., 2015; Weller et al., 2009). Increased use of referrals can also increase profitability, primarily due to lower costs associated with recruiting and turnover (Burks et al., 2015).

Despite the above, there are several caveats to the benefits of employee referrals. First, research suggests that the primary mechanism through which referred employees outperform non-referred employees is through their working relationship with the referrers (Castilla, 2005; Pallais & Sands, 2015). Thus, when the referrer leaves, performance can drop either to the level of non-referred individuals or even lower (Castilla, 2005). Second, one study found that knowledge by a candidate that a referrer was receiving a monetary bonus damaged the credibility of that message, with credibility being a partial mediator between antecedents and organizational attractiveness (Stockman, Van Hoye, & Carpentier, 2017). Finally, if not properly designed or incentivized, employee referral programs can hurt organizational diversity by reinforcing the existing workforce makeup (Breaugh, 2012; Caldwell & Spivey, 1983; Frank, 2018). It is typical to obtain 25% to 30% of experienced salaried hires from referrals, but this can vary due to the rarity of skills or requirements. Referral rates for hourly or lower-base-rate jobs can be higher than 40% in some locations (e.g., small towns with few other options) or when EVPs are very compelling.

Company Website

Researchers have conducted substantial research on the characteristics of employee websites that are positively related to antecedents of application intentions. In terms of aesthetics and usability, research suggests that these factors are positively predictive of outcomes related to pursuit, such as organizational attraction (Braddy, Meade, & Kroustalis, 2008; Cober, Brown, Levy, Cober, & Keeping, 2003; Thompson, Braddy, & Wuensch, 2008; see Uggerslev, Fassina, & Kraichy, 2012, for a meta-analysis). Higher-quality website aesthetics can also increase the time individuals spend on the website, increasing content recall (Dineen, Ling, Ash, & DelVecchio, 2007). In terms of content, research suggests that websites should include substantial and specific information about both the organization and the job (Allen, Mahto, & Otondo, 2007; Williamson, King, Lepak, & Sarma, 2010). To take one study as an example, positive perceptions of organizational/job information predicted positive attitudes toward the website and the organization, and attitudes of the organization predicted employment intentions (Allen, Dawson, Wheatley, & White, 2008).

This research is consistent with our previous suggestion that the goal of a website should be to communicate the EVP to key talent segments in a manner that is compelling, realistic, and differentiating. One way to enhance differentiation and realism is customization that allows applicants to explore aspects of fit (e.g., fit with the organization, fit with the job) that are most relevant to their needs (Dineen & Noe, 2009). As mentioned previously, perceptions of fit, particularly person–organization fit (Uggerslev et al., 2012), are related to application decisions and enhance the quality of the applicant pool by discouraging lower-fit applicants from applying (Dineen & Noe, 2009). Many organizations, both in the private and the public sector, have added fit assessments to their websites for this purpose (see Ryan & Delany, 2017, for one list). We elaborate on this point in the RJP section below. A caveat to these recommendations is that some research has found that increased media richness in company websites is negatively related to the retention of factual information related to recruitment (Badger, Kaminsky, & Behrend, 2014; Lievens & Slaughter, 2016).

Social Media

Although being used by more companies, research into the use of social media in recruiting is still fairly sparse (Lievens & Slaughter, 2016; Ryan & Delany, 2017). The advent of social media changed the recruiting landscape, as more companies began sourcing *passive* candidates (e.g., job boards; Phillips-Wren, Doran, & Merrill, 2016). McFarland and Ployhart (2015) define social media as "digital platforms that facilitate information sharing, user-created content, and collaboration across people" (p. 1653). This definition covers a wide range of different platforms, platforms that are constantly changing. This makes the study of social media in relation to recruiting difficult, as each platform has its own pros, cons, and considerations for best practices (for a review of these considerations, see Phillips-Wren et al., 2016). To provide one concrete example, Wazed and Ng (2015) proposed a three-step process for recruitment on Facebook that involves (a) attracting prospective applicants, (b) developing compelling content to continue engagement, and (c) calling to action (e.g., by asking for applications to new positions) when the need arises. These authors also describe a number of tools (e.g., promoted posts) available to companies to facilitate recruitment.

There are two primary advantages to using social media in recruitment. First, social media allows companies to advertise job postings through word-of-mouth and virtual referrals (Kluemper, Mitra, & Wang, 2016; Van Hoye & Lievens, 2017). As described earlier, referrals can be very effective, and social media allows for these word-of-mouth referrals to be distributed quickly, and on a large, geographically distributed scale (McFarland & Ployhart, 2015). Consistent with our previous discussion, candidates find online word-of-mouth content more attractive and credible than organizational testimonials posted on a company website (Van Hoye & Lievens, 2017).

Second, social media allows for the communication of a corporate EVP in personal ways at scale, while also allowing for audiovisual and cognitive complexity (Kissel & Büttgen, 2015; Kluemper et al., 2016). The sometimes-personal nature of social media interactions means that potential candidates may be interacting with organizational members or representatives, such as recruiters. Thus, the previous research finding that personable and competent recruiters can increase organizational attraction (and vice versa) is also potentially relevant in a social media context (e.g., Saks & Uggerslev, 2010; see Breaugh, 2012, and Lievens & Slaughter, 2016, for reviews).

The best-practice research to date on the use of social media in recruiting suggests that simply having a strong presence on social media and enough information available for potential applicants to ascertain key organizational and job information increases corporate image/brand perceptions, reputation, and application intentions (Kissel & Büttgen, 2015; cf. Lievens & Slaughter, 2016). According to Kluemper and colleagues (2016), a well-designed social media recruiting strategy will allow applicants to find information about the company, will allow for interactivity, and will reveal information about the corporate culture. As described previously, a major "con" for the use of social media is that its content cannot be controlled (Kissel & Büttgen, 2015; McFarland & Ployhart, 2015), making authenticity in messaging and alignment with corporate realities critical to successful application.

Job Boards

There is not a lot of academic research on job boards, and much of the extant research tends not to account for new developments in job board technology. Traditional job boards have been largely replaced by job aggregators such as Indeed.com (Phillips-Wren et al., 2016), which now dominates the marketplace in one industry survey (SilkRoad, 2018). These new websites have several features that help to mitigate issues found in earlier research. For example, previous research has found that job boards tend to yield a high number of unqualified applicants (see, for example, the Breaugh [2012] review). While this still may be the case, sites such as LinkedIn.com and ZipRecruiter.com are producing innovative ways to mitigate this issue, such as algorithmic matching between jobs and candidates. Previous findings that targeted postings on geographic or industry-specific boards yield higher-quality candidates (e.g., Jattuso & Sinar, 2003) are likely still to hold, particularly when hiring in more niche industries. Regardless of technology, writing an effective job advertisement is key to success on job boards. The topic of job advertisements and job boards is covered in detail in Chapter 4 of the current volume, so we will not discuss it further here.

RJPs

Across the recruitment and sourcing literature, one of the most consistent findings is that perceived fit to the job and the organization is linked to outcomes such as organizational attraction (Uggerslev et al., 2012). To increase possible perceived fit, organizations are increasingly using RJPs. RJPs allow a candidate to see what a job is actually like (e.g., a day in the life), thus allowing potential applicants to better evaluate their opportunities. While there is a wealth of literature on the use of RJPs, researchers are still debating their conceptualization, operationalization, and evaluation (Shibly, 2019). Moreover, RJPs cross many elements of a recruiting process, including pre-recruitment, post-recruitment, and even marketing (Shibly, 2019).

A recent trend is that companies are beginning to make RJPs (a) more interactive and (b) able to collect information about the applicants through virtual job tryouts (VJT). VJTs present a realistic activity for potential candidates to "try out" the job. The activity may include questions that also assess, from the organization's side, their fit for the organization or position.

Leading companies such as Bank of America are using VJTs to assist with both recruitment and selection. Related to VJTs, some companies are relying on other innovative techniques that combine recruitment and selection, such as competitions or games. For example, the U.S. Army uses the game *America's Army* to inspire folks to apply for enlistment.[3] Although there has been a mad rush among companies to "gamify" many aspects of recruiting and hiring processes, evaluation research yields mixed results, and some of its presumed value remains unclear (Landers, 2019).

Campus Recruiting and Other Traditional Sourcing Approaches

While becoming less common, sourcing through less digital means such as college campuses, career centers, recruitment events, and alumni networks can still be highly effective. As summarized by Breaugh (2012, 2016), the keys to success in these endeavors include:

- Honing the recruitment message (e.g., its specificity),
- Adequately preparing recruiters (e.g., being informative),
- Being prepared to meet with the right individuals (e.g., connecting with influential stakeholders), and
- Timing recruitment events strategically.

As discussed by Breaugh (2012), these critical success factors have been linked to outcomes such as the quality of job applicants and ultimate employee retention.

A theme across many of these success factors is relationship building. Building relationships and maintaining a presence in communities of interest is critical to sustaining a steady pipeline of qualified applicants through these means. For example, in the authors' practice experience, we have anecdotally witnessed several fruitful sourcing relationships emerge via building relationships with local career centers (e.g., colleges, universities, state and local government outlets, military transition centers).

Beyond the tools mentioned above, there is a host of tools that serve the needs of professional recruiters themselves, as they deal with intake requests

---

[3] https://www.americasarmy.com/

from hiring managers and other parties. These can range from intake forms to job description/design aids. Because many of these tools are outside the scope of the current sourcing discussion, we do not describe these tools in detail. However, many online resources are available that describe such tools (e.g., see LinkedIn's Recruiting Toolbox[4]). Future sourcing may be more likely to leverage existing alumni and applicant databases either owned by the company or purchased from a third party who may even pull subsets of candidates for a client based on job requirements.

Leveraging Measurement and Analytics

Like every other area in the modern human capital landscape, sourcing professionals are increasingly turning to "big data," analytics, and other forms of measurement to optimize results. Entire volumes have been written about the impact of technology on recruitment at large (e.g., Wolfe, 2017). In addition, the field of professional recruiting has been good about consolidating best practices around metrics that are useful (although often hard to collect); see for example, McIntosh's (2015) list of standard recruiting metrics, published on the ERE website. For our current purpose, we focus here only on a few of the highest-value uses of analytics for sourcing, namely:

1. Measuring overall sourcing success (e.g., quality of applicants), particularly for the highest-value jobs/work,
2. Generating sourcing process measures (e.g., time/cost to generate high-quality applicants; applicant reactions), and
3. Measuring diversity, inclusion, and bias among sources.

The first of the analytic uses mentioned above, measuring sourcing success, corresponds to a need among companies to define and measure the relative value of sources in term of producing high-quality applicants. Imagine a scenario where a company is using a combination of modern sources, as described above, including job postings, social media, job fairs, referrals, networking, outsourcing, and crowdsourcing. Upon implementation, stakeholders typically start to ask the following types of questions: Which of

---

[4] https://business.linkedin.com/content/dam/me/business/en-us/talent-solutions/resources/pdfs/2018-ultimate-recruiting-toolbox-en.pdf

these provided the greatest "yield" (conversion of prospects to candidates)? What was the relative cost of sourcing candidates from these sources? Which source(s) yielded the highest-quality applicants, etc.? By answering such questions using modern analytic methods, a firm can create a sourcing "dashboard," showing the relative value of sources over time and segments of the workforce. In measuring the relative value of sources, sourcing professionals are well served to focus more effort on those segments of the workforce, and particular jobs, that deliver differential value to the company. Organizational scientists have long argued (e.g., Huselid, Beatty, & Becker, 2005) that not all jobs are of equal value; thus, differential sourcing success should factor in differential job/work value. Measuring sourcing success can be complicated by the fact that outcomes are multivariate—we are often seeking to optimize more than one outcome. For example, a specific sourcing channel might be expected to generate a given mix of active versus passive candidates. As with any modern analytic area, development of effective sourcing success measures will likely proceed through stages of maturation, namely:

1. Level 1: operational reporting, using data to understand and reflect on what happened in the past;
2. Level 2: advanced reporting, reporting that is proactive, routine, or even automated;
3. Level 3: strategic analytics, conducting analyses that inform causal understanding and variable relationships; and
4. Level 4: predictive analytics, using data to make reliable and valid predictions (Waters, Streets, McFarlane, & Johnson-Murray, 2018).

After deciding upon some key indicators of sourcing success, stakeholders in the sourcing process are also well served to consider formative indicators around the sourcing process itself. Although some of these metrics extend beyond sourcing into other parts of the recruiting system, process measures can include items such as (1) total time to fill key positions, (2) time to produce job offers, (3) number of applicants required to successfully fill positions, (4) total costs by source, (5) various applicant reaction and acceptance measures, (6) and a "funnel" or "pipeline" view, showing where valued applicants might fall out of a recruiting/application process. By using and setting goals around such process metrics, sourcing professionals can dramatically increase conversion rates for successful applicants.

Increasingly, we have seen a more intense focus on the issues of diversity, inclusion, and bias among sources—a topic that can go hand in hand with the use of advanced analytics. Across occupations from surgeons (Gardner, 2018) to computer scientists (Whitney & Taylor, 2018), sourcing professionals are looking for innovative and implementable ways to ensure fair access to job opportunities. Among the various discussions of interventions, some common themes and applications emerge, namely:

1. *Emphasizing earlier exposure (i.e., K–12) to career opportunities.* Along these lines, numerous organizations have made profound changes in increasing school students' access to professional information. As just one example, in the area of computing, see the Code.org curriculum.[5]
2. *Increasing leader accountability.* Across most interventions in the human capital space, researchers frequently cite the involvement of top leaders and their support as critical success factors (e.g., Lee, Park, & Baker, 2018).
3. *Evaluating the effectiveness of diversity efforts.* As discussed by Dobbin and Kalev (2016), too often companies accept the mere presence of diversity programs and efforts as evidence of effectiveness without looking more closely at actual evidence of return on investment.
4. *Evaluating and remedying the presence of bias in recruiting tools.* For example, some companies have analyzed the language of their job descriptions and revised them to be more neutral, and organizations have evaluated and changed the fundamental sources where they recruit, thereby increasing participation from women and underrepresented minorities (Whitney & Taylor, 2018). Recently, researchers have also begun using big data and related analytic methods to detect and to ultimately remedy gender-related bias in jobs ads. As one example, Tang and colleagues (2017) studied the effects of potential gender-biased terminology in job listings, and their impact on job applicants, using a large historical corpus of 17 million listings on LinkedIn spanning 10 years. They developed and validated algorithms to detect and quantify gender bias, specifying the degree of bias in job listings over time. Currently, commercial companies such as Textio[6] are leveraging this kind of big data research to offer services around optimizing job ads to produce more diverse applicant populations.

[5] https://code.org
[6] Textio.com

Big-Picture Elements and the Possible Future of Sourcing

In this last section we will summarize themes throughout this chapter and point to future needs. First, based on the current review, we believe that the field of recruiting and sourcing will need to broaden its understanding of applicant behaviors and motivations. Increasingly, potential candidates view their recruitment experience as a value judgment about a company itself. Thus, we need identify what candidates value most during the hiring process and ensure that these valued attributes are emphasized, even at the beginning of building a sourcing strategy. Moreover, companies are well served to understand the weakest links in a candidate experience. Given ready access to almost any company in the world via the internet, impressions are formed (and lost) quickly. Even though calls for additional research on these broader facets of applicant motivation have existed for 20-plus years (e.g., Rynes, Bretz, & Gerhart, 1991), there is still little extant research to guide sourcing professionals in this area.

Second, companies are increasingly considering the importance of hiring for the whole organization (e.g., culture, broader careers), not just a particular job. While this too is not a new idea (e.g., see Bowen, Ledford, & Nathan, 1991), few organizations have the research-based tools needed to build companies and cultures starting at sourcing and selection.

Concomitant with the need to expand our understanding of applicants and look at building sourcing systems for whole organizations, companies will have to continue to accommodate specific job requirements in a fast-changing world. Accommodating such changes can start at the level of sourcing—knowing where to find the candidates of the future. Yet, despite its obvious importance, we are aware of almost no research looking at the effects of sourcing success on companies' ability to adapt over time. This is true despite a wealth of literature on individual-level and organization-level adaptability (e.g., Dorsey et al., 2017; Ployhart, Turner, & Chan, 2014).

In addition to the above themes and trends, there is little doubt that next-generation technologies will continue to emerge that disrupt sourcing and recruiting practices. Emerging technologies that appear in current popular discussions of recruiting and sourcing include (Sabel, 2019):

- *AI-driven assessments.* An increasing number of AI-driven pre-hire assessments are on the market today.

- *Candidate rediscovery.* Existing candidate databases can be effectively "mined" to rediscover possible candidate-to-job connections.
- *Job description optimization.* Job description optimizers provide text changes that make job ads more attractive to a wider group of applicants.
- *Job market forecasting.* Market forecasting software analyzes potential pools of talent for different types of jobs, experiences, locations, etc.
- *Candidate relationship management.* Candidate relationship management software can lead to a personalized experience that assists candidates through an entire sourcing-to-hire process.
- *Chatbots.* Chatbots can provide an interface to assist candidates in locating jobs.
- *Social candidate discovery.* Social candidate discovery software analyzes social media and other online platforms to find passive candidates.

Of course, many of these technologies remain in the "emergent" stage, and little rigorous research is available to measure their relative value.

As mentioned previously, companies are likely to experience continued pressure to state and to meet diversity and inclusion goals. From a sourcing perspective, one fruitful and important topic for continued research to support such goals will be approaches for locating and tapping nontraditional applicant pools. For example, when looking for computer scientists, particularly those with coding skills, comparisons suggest that coding "bootcamps" produce more diverse applicant pools than those typically found in computer science university programs (e.g., 36% women vs. 19% women).[7] Older workers represent another very important potential nontraditional pool. As summarized by Breaugh (2016), older workers potentially bring job-relevant knowledge and experience, may be willing to work flexible hours, may require fewer benefits (because of factors like Medicare), and can demonstrate lower levels of absenteeism and turnover. As also profiled by Breaugh (2016), organizations such as Home Depot and H&R Block specifically target the hiring of experienced older workers. Other nontraditional groups worthy of sourcing consideration include workers with disabilities, individuals with criminal records, and individuals transitioning from the military (Breaugh, 2016). Here again, little academic research is available on potential sources

---

[7] See https://www.modelexpand.com/blog/non-traditional-candidates for a description of these data and findings.

of nontraditional pools. As mentioned throughout the current chapter, numerous avenues for continued research and development are open in the area of sourcing, and sourcing professionals could benefit greatly from such efforts.

To conclude the current chapter, we present a practical, user-friendly checklist for those building a sourcing plan and system (Table 3.1). This checklist pulls together themes, interventions, and actions from across the chapter. We hope that this checklist and the information presented here has enlightened sourcing and recruiting professionals and researchers and painted a way forward to improving sourcing for organizations and their potential employees.

References

Aguinis, H., & Kraiger, K. (2009). Benefits of training and development for individuals and teams, organizations, and society. *Annual Review of Psychology, 60*, 451–474. http://10.1146/annurev.psych.60.110707.163505.

Allen, D. G. (2008). Retaining talent: A guide to analyzing and managing employee turnover. Society for Human Resource Management. https://www.shrm.org/hr-today/trends-and-forecasting/special-reports-and-expert-views/Documents/Retaining-Talent.pdf.

Allen, D. G., Mahto, R. V., & Otondo, R. F. (2007). Web-based recruitment: Effects of information, organizational brand, and attitudes toward a web site on applicant attraction. *Journal of Applied Psychology, 92*, 1696–1708. http:/ 10.1037/0021-9010.92.6.1696.

Allen, R. S., Dawson, G., Wheatley, K., & White, C. S. (2008). Perceived diversity and organizational performance. *Employee Relations, 30*, 20–33. http:/ 10.1108/01425450810835392.

Badger, J. M., Kaminsky, S. E., & Behrend, T. S. (2014). Media richness and information acquisition in internet recruitment. *Journal of Managerial Psychology, 29*(7), 866–883. http:/ 10.1108/JMP-05-2012-0155.

Ballantyne, D., Frow, P., Varey, R., & Payne, A. (2011). Value propositions as communication practice: Taking a wider view. *Industrial Marketing Management, 40*, 202–210. http:/ 10.1016/j.indmarman.2010.06.032.

Beiker, S. (2016, July). How automakers can get the most value from Silicon Valley. McKinsey & Company. https://www.mckinsey.com/business-functions/operations/our-insights/how-automakers-can-get-the-most-value-from-silicon-valley.

Bergh, D. D., Connelly, B. L., Ketchen, D. J., & Shannon, L. M. (2014). Signaling theory and equilibrium in strategic management research: An assessment and a research agenda. *Journal of Management Studies, 51*(8), 1334–1360. http:/ 10.1111/joms.12097.

Bersin, J. (2018, December 10). The alternative workforce: It isn't so alternative any more. https:// joshbersin.com/2018/12/the-alternative-workforce-it-isnt-so-alternative-any-more/.

Bourke, J., Garr, S. S., van Berkel, A., & Wong, J. (2017). Diversity and inclusion: The reality gap. In *Rewriting the rules for the digital age: 2017 Deloitte Global Human Capital Trends*. Deloitte University Press. https://www2.deloitte.com/content/dam/Deloitte/global/Documents/HumanCapital/hc-2017-global-human-capital-trends-gx.pdf

Bowen, D. E., Ledford Jr, G. E., & Nathan, B. R. (1991). Hiring for the organization, not the job. *Academy of Management Perspectives, 5*(4), 35–51. http:/ 10.5465/ame.1991.4274747.

Braddy, P. W., Meade, A. W., & Kroustalis, C. M. (2008). Online recruiting: The effects of organizational familiarity, website usability, and website attractiveness on viewers' impressions of organizations. *Computers in Human Behavior, 24*(6), 2992–3001. http:/ 10.1016/j.chb.2008.05.005.

Breaugh, J. A. (2012). Employee recruitment: Current knowledge and suggestions for future research. In N. Schmitt (Ed.), *The Oxford handbook of personnel assessment and selection* (pp. 68–87). New York: Oxford University Press. http:/ 10.1093/oxfordhb/ 9780199732579.013.0005.

Breaugh, J. A. (2016). Talent acquisition: A guide to understanding and managing the recruitment process. Society for Human Resource Management Foundation. https:// www.shrm.org/hr-today/trends-and-forecasting/special-reports-and-expert-views/ documents/talent-acquisition-recruitment.pdf.

Brown, M., Setren, E., & Topa, G. (2012). *Do informal referrals leads to better matches? Evidence from a firm's employee referral system* (Staff Report, No. 568). New York: Federal Reserve Bank. http:/ 10.2139/ssrn.2130009.

Brymer, R. A., Chadwick, C., Hill, A., & Molloy, J. (2018). Pipelines and their portfolios: A more holistic view of human capital heterogeneity via firm-wide employee sourcing. *Academy of Management Perspectives, 33*(2), 207–233. http:/ 10.5465/amp.2016.0071.

Bunn, D. W., & Salo, A. A. (1993). Forecasting with scenarios. *European Journal of Operational Research, 68*(3), 291–303. http:/ 10.1016/0377-2217(93)90186-q.

Burks, S. V., Cowgill, B., Hoffman, M., & Housman, M. (2015). The value of hiring through referrals. *Quarterly Journal of Economics, 130*(2), 805–839. http:/ 10.2139/ ssrn.2253738.

Cable, D. M., & Judge, T. A. (1996). Person-organization fit, job choice decisions, and organizational entry. *Organizational Behavior and Human Decision Processes, 67*(3), 294–311. http:/ 10.1006/obhd.1996.0081.

Caldwell, D. F., & Spivey, W. A. (1983). The relationship between recruiting source and employee success: An analysis by race. *Personnel Psychology, 36*(1), 67–72. http:/ 10.1111/j.1744-6570.1983.tb00503.x.

Cappelli, P. (2009). A supply chain approach to workforce planning. *Organizational Dynamics, 38*(1), 8–15. http:/ 10.1016/j.orgdyn.2008.10.004.

Cappelli, P. (2019, May–June). Your approach to hiring is all wrong: Outsourcing and algorithms won't get you the people you need. *Harvard Business Review.* https://hbr. org/2019/05/recruiting#your-approach-to-hiring-is-all-wrong.

Carless, S. A. (2015). Person-job fit versus person-organization fit as predictors of organizational attraction and job acceptance intentions: A longitudinal study. *Journal of Occupational and Organizational Psychology, 78*, 411–429. http:/ 10.1348/ 096317905x25995.

Castilla, E. J. (2005). Social networks and employee performance in a call center. *American Journal of Sociology, 110*(5), 1243–1283. http:/ 10.1086/427319.

Chadha, S. (2017). The journey from experience to engagement. *Human Capital, 21*(5), 14–19.

Chambers, E., Foulon, M., Handfield-Jones, H., Hankin, S., & Michaels, E. (1998) The war for talent. *McKinsey Quarterly, 3*(3), 44–57.

Chapman, D. S., Uggerslev, K. L., Carroll, S. A., Piasentin, K. A., & Jones, D. A. (2005). Applicant attraction to organizations and job choice: A meta-analytic review of the correlates of recruiting outcomes. *Journal of Applied Psychology, 90*(5), 928–944. http:/10.1037/0021-9010.90.5.928.

Chartered Institute of Personnel Development (CIPD). (2018, May). Workforce planning practice. https://www.cipd.co.uk/Images/workforce-planning-guide_tcm18-42735.pdf.

Clayton, S. (2018, May 16). How to strengthen your reputation as an employer. *Harvard Business Review*. https://hbr.org/2018/05/how-to-strengthen-your-reputation-as-an-employer.

Cober, R. T., Brown, D. J., Levy, P. E., Cober, A. B., & Keeping, L. M. (2003). Organizational web sites: Web site content and style as determinants of organizational attraction. *International Journal of Selection and Assessment, 11*, 158–169. http:/ 10.1111/ 1468-2389.00239.

Coyle-Shapiro, J., & Kessler, I. (2000). Consequences of the psychological contract for the employment relationship: A large-scale survey. *Journal of Management Studies, 37*(7), 904–930. http:/ 10.1111/1467-6486.00210.

Deloitte. (2018, March 28). The rise of the social enterprise: 2018 global human capital trends. https://www2.deloitte.com/insights/us/en/focus/human-capital-trends/2018/ introduction.html.

Dineen, B. R., Ling, J., Ash, S. R., & DelVecchio, D. (2007). Aesthetic properties and message customization: Navigating the dark side of web recruitment. *Journal of Applied Psychology, 92*(2), 356–372. http:/ 10.1037/0021-9010.92.2.356.

Dineen, B. R., & Noe, R. A. (2009). Effects of customization on application decisions and applicant pool characteristics in a web-based recruitment context. *Journal of Applied Psychology, 94*(1), 224–234. http:/ 10.1037/a0012832.

Dobbin, F., & Kalev, A. (2016). Why diversity programs fail. *Harvard Business Review, 94*(7), 14.

Dorsey, D. W., Cortina, J. M., Allen, M. T., Waters, S. D., Green, J. P., & Luchman, J. (2017). Adaptive and citizenship-related behaviors at work. In J. L. Farr & N. T. Tippins (Eds.), *Handbook of employee selection* (2nd ed., pp. 448–475). New York: Routledge. http:/ 10.4324/9781315690193-21.

Dreibelbis, R. C., Martin, J., Coovert, M. D., & Dorsey, D, W. (2018). The looming cybersecurity crisis and what it means for the practice of industrial and organizational psychology. *Industrial and Organizational Psychology, 11*(2), 346–365. http:/ 10.1017/iop.2018.3.

Dustmann, C., Glitz, A., Schönberg, U., & Brücker, H. (2015). Referral-based job search networks. *Review of Economic Studies, 83*(2), 514–546. http:/ 10.1093/restud/rdv045.

Earnest, D. R., Allen, D. G., & Landis, R. S. (2011). Mechanisms linking realistic job previews with turnover: A meta-analytic path analysis. *Personnel Psychology, 64*(4), 865–897. http:/ 10.1111/j.1744-6570.2011.01230.x.

Eaton, D. (2015). Making the shift: Leading first with who we are, not what we do. *People+ Strategy, 38*(3), 46–49.

Effron, M. (2018). What's your talent philosophy? https://www.talentstrategygroup.com/ application/third_party/ckfinder/userfiles/files/What's%20Your%20Talent%20Phil osophy_.pdf.

Emmerichs, R. M., Marcum, C. Y., & Robbert, A. A. (2004). *An operational process for workforce planning*. Santa Monica, CA: RAND Corp. https://www.rand.org/content/ dam/rand/pubs/monograph_reports/2005/MR1684.1.pdf.

Frank, L. (2018, March 15). How to use employee referrals without giving up workplace diversity. *Harvard Business Review*. https://hbr.org/2018/03/how-to-use-employee-referrals-without-giving-up-workplace-diversity.

Frow, P., McColl-Kennedy, J. R., Hilton, T., Davidson, A., Payne, A., & Brozovic, D. (2014). Value propositions: A service ecosystems perspective. *Marketing Theory*, *14*(3), 327–351. http:/ 10.1177/1470593114534346.

Frow, P., & Payne, A. (2011). A stakeholder perspective of the value proposition concept. *European Journal of Marketing*, *5*(1/2), 233–240. http:/ 10.1108/03090561111095676.

Gannon, M. J. (1971). Sources of referral and employee turnover. *Journal of Applied Psychology*, *55*(3), 226–228. http:/ 10.1037/h0031151.

Gardner, A. K. (2018). How can best practices in recruitment and selection improve diversity in surgery? *Annals of Surgery*, *267*(1), e1–e2. http:/ 10.1097/sla.0000000000002496.

Guest, D. E., & Conway, N. (2002). Communicating the psychological contract: An employer perspective. *Human Resource Management Journal*, *12*(2), 22–38. http:/ 10.1111/j.1748-8583.2002.tb00062.x.

Hackman, J. R., & Oldham, G. R. (1976). Motivation through the design of work: Test of a theory. *Organizational Behavior and Human Performance*, *16*, 250–279. http:/ 10.1016/0030-5073(76)90016-7.

Hedge, J. W., & Pulakos, E. D. (2002). *Implementing organizational interventions: Steps, processes, and best practices.* San Francisco: Jossey-Bass.

Heger, B. K. (2007). Linking the employment value proposition (EVP) to employee engagement and business outcomes: Preliminary findings from a linkage research pilot study. *Organization Development Journal*, *25*(2), 121–132. http:/ 10.5392/jkca.2013.13.07.369.

Hom, P. W. (2011). Organizational exit. In S. Zedeck (Ed.), *American Psychological Association (APA) handbook of industrial and organizational psychology, Vol. 2. Selecting and developing members for the organization* (pp. 325–375). Washington, DC: APA. http:/ 10.1037/12170-011.

Huselid, M. A., Beatty, R. W., & Becker, B. E. (2005). "A players" or "A positions"? *Harvard Business Review*, *83*(12), 110–117.

Jattuso, M. L., & Sinar, E. F. (2003). Source effects in internet-based screening procedures. *International Journal of Selection and Assessment*, *11*(2–3), 137–140. http:/ 10.1111/1468-2389.00236.

Keller, S., & Meaney, M. (2017, November). Attracting and retaining the right talent. McKinsey & Company. https://www.mckinsey.com/business-functions/organization/our-insights/attracting-and-retaining-the-right-talent.

Kissel, P., & Büttgen, M. (2015). Using social media to communicate employer brand identity: The impact on corporate image and employer attractiveness. *Journal of Brand Management*, *22*, 755–777. http:/ 10.1057/bm.2015.42.

Kluemper, D. H., Mitra, A., & Wang, S. (2016). Social media use in HRM. *Research in Personnel and Human Resources Management*, *34*, 153–207. http:/ 10.1108/S0742-730120160000034011.

Landers, R. N. (2019). Gamification misunderstood: How badly executed and rhetorical gamification obscures its transformative potential. *Journal of Management Inquiry*, *28*(2), 137–140. http:/ 10.1177/1056492618790913.

Lee, J. Y., Park, S., & Baker, R. (2018). The moderating role of top management support on employees' attitudes in response to human resource development efforts. *Journal of Management & Organization*, *24*(3), 369–387. http:/ 10.1017/jmo.2017.37.

Lievens, F., & Highhouse, S. (2003). The relation of instrumental and symbolic attributes to a company's attractiveness as an employer. *Personnel Psychology*, *56*(1), 75–102. http:/ 10.1111/j.1744-6570.2003.tb00144.x.

Lievens, F., & Slaughter, J. E. (2016). Employer image and employer branding: What we know what we need to know. *Annual Review of Organizational Psychology and Organizational Behavior, 3*, 407–440. http:/ 10.1146/annurev-orgpsych-041015-062501.

Louch, P. (2014). Workforce planning is essential to high-performing organizations. Society for Human Resource Management. https://www.shrm.org/resourcesandtools/hr-topics/technology/pages/louch-workforce-planning.aspx.

Mani, V. (2012). The effectiveness of employee referral as a recruitment source. *International Journal of Management Sciences and Business Research, 1*(11), 12–25.

Mankins, M. (2017, September 6). How leading companies build the workforces they need to stay ahead. *Harvard Business Review.* https://hbr.org/2017/09/how-leading-companies-build-the-workforces-they-need-to-stay-ahead.

Maurer, R. (2015). Tying workforce planning to business strategy still a challenge for most. Society for Human Resource Management. https://www.shrm.org/resourcesandtools/hr-topics/talent-acquisition/pages/workforce-planning-business-strategy.aspx.

McFarland, L. A., & Ployhart, R. E. (2015). Social media: A contextual framework to guide research and practice. *Journal of Applied Psychology, 100*(6), 1653–1677. http:/ 10.1037/a0039244.

McIntosh, R. (2015, September 4). A standard set of recruiting metrics. https://www.ere.net/a-standard-set-of-recruiting-metrics/.

Mercer. (2018). Strengthening your employee value proposition.https://www.mercer.com/our-thinking/career/unlock-workforce-potential-with-total-rewards-and-a-strong-evp.html.

Miller, C. C., & Cardinal, L. B. (1994). Strategic planning and firm performance: A synthesis of more than two decades of research. *Academy of Management Journal, 37*(6), 1649–1665. http:/ 10.2307/256804.

Mohammadi, A., Browstöm, A., & Franzoni, C. (2017). Workforce composition and innovation: How diversity in employees' ethnic and educational backgrounds facilitates firm-level innovativeness. *Journal of Product Innovation Management, 34*(4), 406–426. http:/ 10.1111/jpim.12388.

Moore, D. A., Kurtzberg, T. R., Fox, C. R., & Bazerman, M. H. (1999). Positive illusions and forecasting errors in mutual fund investment decisions. *Organizational Behavior and Human Decision Processes, 79*(2), 95–114. http:/ 10.1006/obhd.1999.2835.

Moseley, R. (2015, May 11). CEOs need to pay attention to employer branding. *Harvard Business Review.* https://hbr.org/2015/05/ceos-need-to-pay-attention-to-employer-branding.

Mumford, M. D., Schultz, R. A., & Osburn, H. K. (2002). Planning in organizations: Performance as a multi-level phenomenon. In F. J. Yammarino & F. Dansereau (Eds.), *Research in multi-level issues: The many faces of multi-level issues* (Vol. 1, pp. 3–63). Bingley: Emerald. http:/ 10.1016/s1475-9144(02)01026-3.

O'Boyle, E., & Adkins, A. (2015). Super Bowl ads don't make a brand. Gallup. https://news.gallup.com/businessjournal/181358/super-bowl-ads-don-brand.aspx.

Önkal, D., Yates, J. F., Simga-Mugan, C., & Öztin, S. (2003). Professional vs. amateur judgment accuracy: The case of foreign exchange rates. *Organizational Behavior and Human Decision Processes, 91*(2), 169–185. http:/ 10.1016/S0749-5978(03)00058-X.

Pallais, A., & Sands, E. G. (2015). *Why the referential treatment: Evidence from field experiments on referrals* (Working Paper No. 21357). Cambridge, MA: National Bureau of Economic Research. http:/ 10.3386/w21357.

Panda, S., & Sahoo, C. K. (2013). Workforce planning and talent acquisition: An exploration. *Productivity, 54*(1), 77–84.

Payne, A., Frow, P., & Eggert, A. (2017). The customer value proposition: Evolution, development, and application in marketing. *Journal of the Academy of Marketing Science, 45,* 467–489. http:/ 10.1007/s11747-017-0523-z.

Phillips, J. M., & Gully, S. M. (2015). Multilevel and strategic recruiting: Where have we been, where can we go from here? *Journal of Management, 41*(5), 1416–1445. http:/ 10.1177/0149206315582248.

Phillips-Wren, G., Doran, R., & Merrill, K. (2016). Creating a value proposition with a social media strategy for talent acquisition. *Journal of Decision Systems, 25*(1), 450–462. http:/ 10.1080/12460125.2016.1187398.

Ployhart, R. E., & Cragun, O. R. (2017). Collective human capital complementarities. In D. Collings, K. Mellahi, & W. F. Cascio (Eds.), *The Oxford handbook of talent management.* New York: Oxford University Press. http:/10.1093/oxfordhb/9780198758273.013.1.

Ployhart, R. E., Turner, S. F., & Chan, D. (2014). Organizational adaptability. In D. Chan (Ed.), *Individual adaptability to changes at work: New directions in research* (pp. 73–91). New York: Routledge. http:/ 10.4324/9780203465721.

Premack, S. L., & Wanous, J. P. (1985). A meta-analysis of realistic job preview experiments. *Journal of Applied Psychology, 70*(4), 706–719. http:/ 10.1037//0021-9010.70.4.706.

Pynes, J. (2004). The implementation of workforce and succession planning in the public sector. *Public Personnel Management, 33*(4), 389–404. http:/ 10.1177/ 009102600403300404.

Rafaeli, A., Hadomi, O., & Simons, T. (2005). Recruiting through advertising or employee referrals: Costs, yields, and the effects of geographic focus. *European Journal of Work and Organizational Psychology, 14*(4), 355–366. http:/ 10.1080/13594320500183709.

RAND. (2006). *Civilian workforce planning in the Department of Defense: Different levels, different roles.* Santa Monica, CA: RAND Corporation. https://www.rand.org/content/ dam/rand/pubs/monographs/2006/RAND_MG449.pdf.

Richard, O. C. (2000). Racial diversity, business strategy, and firm performance: A resource-based view. *Academy of Management Journal, 43*(2), 164–177. http:/ 10.5465/1556374.

Robinson, S. L., & Rousseau, D. M. (1994). Violating the psychological contract: Not the exception but the norm. *Journal of Organizational Behavior, 15,* 245–259. http:/ 10.1002/job.4030150306.

Ryan, A. M., & Delany, T. (2017). Attracting candidates to organizations. In J. L. Farr & N. T. Tippins (Eds.), *Handbook of employee selection* (2nd ed., pp. 165–181). New York: Routledge. http:/ 10.4324/9781315690193.

Rynes, S. L., Bretz, R. D., & Gerhart, B. (1991). The importance of recruitment in job choice: A different way of looking. *Personnel Psychology, 44,* 487–521.

Ryu, K., Park, J., & Park, J. (2006). A data quality management maturity model. *ETRI Journal, 28*(2), 191–204. http:/ 10.4218/etrij.06.0105.0026.

Sabel, J-M. (2019). AI in recruiting: What it means for talent acquisition in 2019. https:// www.hirevue.com/blog/ai-in-recruiting-what-it-means-for-talent-acquisition.

Saks, A. M., & Uggerslev, K. L. (2010). Sequential and combined effects of recruitment information on applicant reactions. *Journal of Business and Psychology, 25,* 351–365. http:/ 10.1007/s10869-009-9142-0.

Sengupta, A., Bamel, U., & Singh, P. (2015). Value proposition framework: Implications for employer branding. *Decision, 42*(3), 307–323. http:/ 10.1007/s40622-015-0097-x.

Shibly, S. A. (2019). Mapping the holistic impact of realistic job preview—pre-recruitment phase, post-recruitment phase and marketing spillover effect. *Journal of Organizational Psychology, 19*(1), 70–78. http:/ 10.33423/jop.v19i1.1091.

SHRM. (2016a). *The new talent landscape: Recruiting difficulty and skills shortages*. Alexandria, VA: Society for Human Resource Management. https://www.shrm.org/ hr-today/trends-and-forecasting/research-and-surveys/pages/talent-landscape.aspx.

SHRM. (2016b, April). *Talent acquisition: Recruitment*. Alexandria, VA: Society for Human Resource Management. https://www.shrm.org/hr-today/trends-and-forecast ing/research-and-surveys/Documents/Talent-Acquisition-Recruitment.pdf.

SHRM. (2019, April 24). Recruiting: What is sourcing? https://www.shrm.org/resourcesa ndtools/tools-and-samples/hr-qa/pages/whatissourcing.aspx.

Sibson. (2009). Rewards of work study. The Segal Group. https://www.sibson.com/media/ 1609/2009row.pdf.

SilkRoad (2018). Sources of hire 2017: Where the candidate journey begins (Report No. RPT-SOH2017-052217). SilkRoad Technology, Inc. https://www.silkroad.com/blog/ 2017-sources-of-hire-report/.

Srivastava, P., & Bhatnagar, J. (2010). Employer brand for talent acquisition: An exploration towards its measurement. *Vision: The Journal of Business Perspective, 14*, 25–34. http:/ 10.1177/097226291001400103.

Stockman, S., Van Hoye, G., & Carpentier, M. (2017). The dark side of employee referral bonus programs: Potential applicants' awareness of a referral bonus and perceptions of organizational attractiveness. *Applied Psychology: An International Review, 66*(4), 599–627. http:/ 10.1111/apps.12100.

Tang, S., Zhang, X., Cryan, J., Metzger, M. J., Zheng, H., & Zhao, B. Y. (2017). Gender bias in the job market: A longitudinal analysis. *Proceedings of the ACM on Human-Computer Interaction, 1*, 99. http:/ 10.1145/3134734.

Thompson, L. F., Braddy, P. W., & Wuensch, K. L. (2008). E-recruitment and the benefits of organizational web appeal. *Computers in Human Behavior, 24*(5), 2384–2398. http:/ 10.1016/j.chb.2008.02.014.

Towers Watson. (2014, January). Building a compelling employee value proposition and delivering on it. *HR Matters, 2*, 10–11. https://www.towerswatson.com/en/Insights/ Newsletters/Europe/HR-matters/2014/01/HR-Matters-January-2014.

Turnley, W. H., & Feldman, D. C. (2000). Re-examining the effects of psychological contract violations: Unmet expectations and job dissatisfaction as mediators. *Journal of Organizational Behavior, 21*, 25–42. http:/ 10.1002/ (SICI)1099-1379(200002)21:1<25::AID-JOB2>3.0.CO;2-Z.

Uggerslev, K. L., Fassina, N. E., & Kraichy, D. (2012). Recruiting through the stages: A meta-analytic test of predictors of applicant attraction at different stages of the recruiting process. *Personnel Psychology, 65*, 597–660. http:/ 10.1111/j.1744-6570.2012.01254.x.

Van Hoye, G., & Lievens, F. (2017). Investigating web-based recruitment sources: Employee testimonials vs. word-of-mouse. *International Journal of Selection and Assessment, 15*(4), 372–382. http:/ 10.1111/j.1468-2389.2007.00396.x.

Waters, S. D., Streets, V. N., McFarlane, L., & Johnson-Murray, R. (2018). *The practical guide to HR analytics: Using data to inform, transform, and empower HR decisions*. Alexandria, VA: Society for Human Resource Management.

Wazed, S., & Ng, E. S. (2015). College recruiting using social media: How to increase applicant reach and reduce recruiting costs. *Strategic HR Review, 14*(4), 135–141. http:/ 10.1108/SHR-02-2015-0017.

Weber Shandwick. (2014, April). Employees rising: Seizing the opportunity in employee activism. https://www.webershandwick.com/news/employee-activism-the-next-front ier-of-employee-engagement/.

Weller, I., Holtom, B. C., Matiaske, W., & Mellewigt, T. (2009). Level and time effects of recruitment sources on early voluntary turnover. *Journal of Applied Psychology, 94*(5), 1146–1162. http:/ 10.1037/a0015924.

Weller, I., Hymer, C. B., Nyberg, A. J., & Ebert, J. (2019). How matching creates value: Cogs and wheels for human capital resources research. *Academy of Management Annals, 13*(1), 188–214. http:/ 10.5465/annals.2016.0117.

Whitney, T., & Taylor, V. (2018). Increasing women and underrepresented minorities in computing: The landscape and what you can do. *Computer, 51*(10), 24–31. http:/ 10.1109/mc.2018.3971359.

Williamson, I. O., King, J. E., Lepak, D., & Sarma, A. (2010). Firm reputation, recruitment web sites, and attracting applicants. *Human Resource Management, 49*(4), 669–687. http:/ 10.1002/hrm.20379.

Wolf, C., & Floyd, S. W. (2017). Strategic planning research: Toward a theory-driven agenda. *Journal of Management, 43*(6), 1754–1788. http:/ 10.1177/0149206313478185.

Wolfe, I. S. (2017). *Recruiting in the age of Googlization: When the shift hits your plan.* Melbourne, FL: Motivational Press.

Younger, J., & Smallwood, N. (2016, February). Aligning your organization with an agile workforce. *Harvard Business Review.* https://hbr.org/2016/02/aligning-your-organizat ion-with-an-agile-workforce.

Zottoli, M., & Wanous, J. (2000). Recruitment source research: Current status and future directions. *Human Resource Management Review, 10*(4), 353–382. http:/ 10.1016/ s1053-4822(00)00032-2.

4

Job Postings, Ads, and the Age
of the Aggregator

Valerie N. Streets
Dell

The first point of contact most organizations have with a potential candidate is through a job advertisement. Job ads have long created the first impression in job seekers' eyes, and thus play a crucial role in attracting or deterring individuals from the broader recruitment and selection process. While job ads have long been used, the modern recruitment landscape is molding ads to become more interactive, customized, and engaging. Along with those changes comes a host of new issues for practitioners and researchers alike. In this chapter, I present an overview of the evolution of job advertisements along with some guiding principles and best practices on recruiting via job ads. Finally, I introduce some of the emerging topics and issues when it comes to modern job advertisements.

A Brief History of Job Advertisements

Some of the earliest research on recruitment countered economic theory and widely held assumptions that people were well informed about job openings and made rational job decisions. Instead, early recruitment researchers found that individuals were largely ignorant of job openings and relied on their close personal networks to acquire such information (Myers & MacLaurin, 1943; Parnes, 1954). These findings marked the beginning of both a scientific and a practical focus on the recruitment function within an organization. As this focus emerged, job advertisements began playing a larger role in the selection process. Historically, print advertisements were shared with employment centers and then physically distributed to potential applicants. While that process remained static for decades, it began to rapidly evolve in the 1990s.

Valerie N. Streets, *Job Postings, Ads, and the Age of the Aggregator* In: *Becoming a Talent Magnet*. Edited by: Mark A. Morris, Oxford University Press. © Oxford University Press 2024. DOI: 10.1093/oso/9780190938512.003.0004

The widespread adoption of email in the 1990s created an environment in which recruiters could directly contact potential applicants much more readily than in the past. From there, recruiters looked for online approaches to their traditional means of attracting job candidates. One of the first major efforts in this vein was the online job board.

The first notable online job board, the Online Career Center, debuted in 1992. The Online Career Center, and many subsequent job boards, followed a generalist model in which jobs across a range of industries and geographies were featured (Dickey-Chasins, 2012). Within less than a decade, online job boards supplanted more traditional methods (e.g., physical job boards in employment centers, newspaper advertisements; Li, Charron, Roshan, & Flemming, 2002). For the first time in roughly 50 years, the recruitment function shifted and became substantially more efficient. This pattern continued into the 2000s, as customization tools evolved, equipping job seekers with the ability to tailor their searches by region, industry, and position (Maurer & Liu, 2007). The evolution of employee recruitment led to a new, more modern approach to attracting potential applicants: electronic recruiting, or "e-recruiting." Online recruiting steadily became preferential to traditional methods, as online methods often yield larger applicant pools at relatively low costs (Breaugh, 2008).

The Current State of Job Advertisements

Although job advertisements are still commonly featured on online job boards, the state of e-recruitment and online job advertisements is considerably more complex today than when it first emerged. Today's recruitment landscape features a plethora of advertising media, including employer websites, job ad aggregators, and social media. Recruiting strategy is more involved than ever before, and an added layer of complexity stems from today's highly savvy yet often passive candidates.

The State of the Recruitment Function

The early stages of recruitment, primarily those surrounding candidate generation, are where e-recruitment has had the quickest and most notable impact. Online employee recruitment is now an established practice for organizations, and posting job advertisements on job boards and corporate websites is largely regarded as table stakes (Acikgoz & Bergman, 2016; Raphael, 2011). The most popular e-recruiting methods are still online job boards and corporate websites (Chapman & Godollei, 2017), but organizations are expanding beyond these media.

With the rising popularity of social media, organizations are beginning to realize the potential social networking sites offer to their recruitment efforts. Social media usage can vary by the type and size of the recruiting organization. For example, if an organization has a large, active following on Facebook or Twitter, it may be successful in posting available jobs there. Recruiters can also leverage social networking to take a more targeted approach. Sites like LinkedIn and Facebook allow recruiters to tailor their job advertisements to attract desired applicants and distribute them accordingly (Chapman & Godollei, 2017; Walker & Hinojosa, 2014). Recruiters are using a blend of more static job postings and customized outreach via social networking. In the United States, LinkedIn is used by over 90% of recruiters, while Facebook and Twitter are used by over half of recruiters (JobVite, 2019). Similar patterns have been found among European employers (Zanella & Pais, 2014).

The State of the Candidate

Post-pandemic job seekers are more likely to ask about remote work options. Recent local requirements require more finesse when assessing compensation fit. Current job seekers are also accustomed to advanced technology and thereby expect rapid communication and digitally sophisticated recruitment messages (Dineen & Allen, 2014). Job seekers can be more interactively involved today by creating online profiles, using interactive search engines, and completing online fit assessments and games. They also have the freedom to choose between synchronous job search methods such as web chats with recruiters and webinars, or asynchronous methods such as email. Additionally, job seekers can now access information from inside sources through large-scale platforms such as Glassdoor and segment-specific sites such as FairyGodBoss or compensation information (for a tech example, see levels.fyi). Skills-based communities (e.g., GitHub, StackOverFlow) also provide candidates with a new perspective on jobs and employers, giving virtually anyone access to previously privileged information (Gartner, 2019).

The surplus of information and individual sources has altered the way many individuals learn about employment opportunities. Job ad aggregators are now a common starting point for many job seekers (Gartner, 2019; JobVite, 2019). Job ad aggregators are search engines specifically designed to pull job postings from corporate career sites and online job boards (e.g., Indeed, SimplyHired, Google for Jobs). Such tools funnel dispersed information into a single source, allowing candidates to better eliminate noise and locate opportunities that are likely to be a fit. This shift in candidate behavior affords employers the ability to bypass expensive job boards without sacrificing visibility (Dickey-Chasins, 2012).

Despite the boom in technology and information, the core process job candidates follow is relatively slow to evolve. A 2020 survey (CareerArc, 2021) of 667 active job seekers found that the most frequently used recruitment sources were: social media (92% used this, with Facebook #1 and LinkedIn & Glassdoor virtually tied for #2), referrals (87%), online job boards (used by approximately 82% of respondents), followed by company career sites (used by 69% of respondents). The use of social media by job seekers has nearly tripled since 2016 (Acikgoz & Bergman, 2016). Furthermore, a searching pattern is evident where most job seekers begin their search in job boards and/or aggregators and move to company-specific resources (i.e., company-owned social media sites, company website) to further their research (JobVite, 2019).

While active job seekers' behaviors may not be rapidly changing, many employers are currently filling roles with passive job seekers. In many cases, the strongest applicants are content with their current employers (Chapman & Godollei, 2017). In such circumstances, social networking, most notably LinkedIn, is the most common way individuals learn about potential opportunities (JobVite, 2019). Additionally, passive job candidates conduct most of their interactions with potential employers "on the go," making mobile friendly advertisements and applications highly desirable (Glassdoor, 2019).

Making the Most of Your Job Ads: Guiding Principles

Given the limited empirical research on job advertisements and e-recruitment, recruiters who create job ads often must rely on trial and error.

However, there is still guidance in the extant literature. To effectively employ e-recruiting for your organization, it is important to understand the mechanisms underlying candidate attraction. By drawing on the concepts that explain how candidates perceive and interact with job ads, recruiters can craft their strategy and materials to better attract attention, appeal to desired candidates, and draw in a diverse candidate pool.

Understanding How Job Ads Work

Much of candidate reactions and behaviors can be understood through signal theory. According to this theory, job seekers look to a variety of environmental cues to make inferences about organizational values and job attributes (Spence, 1973). At the earliest stages of the job search, job seekers likely know very little about potential jobs or employers. When direct and specific information is lacking, individuals then look to informational cues as signals of salient job and organizational attributes (Highhouse & Hoffman, 2001). For example, the inclusion of a salary range may signal to candidates that the organization values transparency.

Signal theory helps explain how candidates make sense of recruitment materials. Social identity theory then helps explain how candidates relate to those materials. Social identity theory argues that one's self-concept consists of a *personal identity*, or the perception of the self in terms of one's characteristics (e.g., personality, abilities), and a *social identity*, or the perceptions of the social group to which one belongs (Tajfel, 1982). When viewing job advertisements, potential applicants look for the degree of match between their salient social identities and the perceived identity of the organization (Herriot, 2004). Engaging in this process leads to the formation of person–environment fit perceptions. Specifically, the job requirements and job description indicate how compatible one's skills, abilities, and interests are likely to be with the demands of the job (i.e., person–job fit). This information, along with descriptions of the work environment, signals the likely degree of match between one's values and those of the organization (i.e., person–organization fit; Lauver & Kristof-Brown, 2001; Schneider, Goldstein, & Smith, 1995). This theory is upheld in recruitment contexts, as job seekers report higher intentions to pursue employment with organizations when they feel their social identity will be affirmed (Avery et al., 2013). Job seekers are differentially attracted to employment opportunities based on perceived person–job and person–organization fit; this attraction significantly influences job seekers' application intentions, as potential candidates are ultimately seeking a place where they will belong (Carless, 2005; Chapman et al., 2005; Nolan, Gohlke, Gilmore, & Rosiello, 2013).

Attracting Candidate Attention

When it comes to initial attraction, much of the research has focused on aesthetic properties of recruiting messages. Especially early in the decision-making process, individuals rely on thinking that is fast, instinctive, and emotional rather than slow, deliberate, and logical thought (Kahneman, 2000). Therefore, it makes sense to emphasize the visual appeal of job advertisements.

While much of the research on visual appeal and e-recruitment is related to company websites, the general principles readily translate to job ads. The presentation of a recruitment message is crucial for attracting and maintaining attention. It is the first thing job seekers experience and creates a first impression about the overall organization (Tractinsky, Katz, & Ikar, 2000). Unlike company websites, job advertisements are limited in terms of interactivity and navigation requirements. Thus, aesthetics are the foremost component of visual appeal and audience interest. Aesthetics include the use of color, fonts, images, and spacing. Stylistic tastes tend to change over time and generation (Djamasbi, Siegel, & Tullis, 2010), but some general guidelines for aesthetic appeal have emerged from the literature.

Unity
Unity describes the extent to which all of the components of a given display or message are visually connected in a meaningful way (Tractinsky et al., 2000). A consistent style in terms of fonts, colors, and images is associated with more favorable reactions and increased comprehension of information (Cober, Brown, Keeping, & Levy, 2004; Williams, 2004). Unity also entails the degree of consistency between the design elements and content of a given message (Zusman & Landis, 2002). For example, an image portraying a demographically diverse workforce helps reinforce an organization's diversity-oriented values that are described via text.

Contrast

Contrast focuses on the distinct elements of a given display or message. When design elements are distinct, they must be made obviously so. In recruitment messaging, this is often achieved through color. Colors that look purposely different (e.g., red and blue) create visual excitement and emphasize the desired components of the job advertisement (Chen & Wells, 1999; Williams, 2004).

Location

User experience and website design research revealed that individuals respond negatively when they struggle to find desired information (Cober et al., 2003; Selden & Orenstein, 2011). Specific to employee recruitment, eye-tracking studies have found that applicants spend much of their time looking for URLs to click (Allen, Biggane, Pitts, Otondo, & Van Scotter, 2013). Application links as well as links to employee websites should be easily recognizable to help focus attention and maintain candidate interest through possible application completion.

Media Richness

With the adoption of e-recruitment has come advanced media richness. A medium is considered rich when it is particularly vivid and/or interactive (e.g., containing images, videos, animations; Lengel & Daft, 1988). More vivid advertisements attract more attention and can have a greater effect on candidate judgment than strictly text-based messages (Nolan et al., 2013). Job seekers generally prefer ads that include company logos, video testimonials, and pictorial depictions of the workforce (Avery & McKay, 2006; Nolan et al., 2013).

Appealing to Desired Candidates

Visual elements of job advertisements are important for attracting initial attention and for reinforcing aspects of the job opening or organization. However, when it comes to appealing to a potential candidate, particularly one who is likely to be a good fit, verbal content is most critical (Gartner, 2019). Verbal information can be broken into two major categories: instrumental and symbolic. *Instrumental* information describes employers in terms of factual and objective attributes. *Symbolic* information instead describes employers in terms of subjective, intangible attributes, allowing candidates to make their own inferences (Lieven, Van Hoye, & Anseel, 2007).

Online job ads contain substantially more instrumental than symbolic information. A content analysis of online job advertisements revealed that all ads contain instrumental information while 13% of ads entirely lack symbolic information (Nolan et al., 2013). These findings are unlikely to be surprising, given that the most common features of job ads fall under this category (e.g., pay, benefits, location, and job duties). However, symbolic information allows job seekers to better evaluate a job in terms of fit with their social identity. In fact, experimental research has indicated that symbolic information about an organization contributes above and beyond instrumental information to individuals' attraction and likelihood of applying to an organization (e.g., Van Hoye & Saks, 2011). While instrumental information such as job responsibilities and benefits are important—and perhaps even table stakes—including content that signals organizational values (e.g., prestige, empathy, impact) can go a long way in encouraging a potential candidate to move forward with the application process. A recent Gartner (2019) study of job seekers revealed that a combination of instrumental and symbolic factors is important to candidates. Specifically, five pieces of information increase the probability an individual will apply to a job by 23%: job duties and responsibilities, organizational culture, the direct supervisor's management style, the career path of the given role, and defining characteristics of success in the role. Based on these findings, Figure 4.1 presents an organizing framework for thinking about your own job advertisements as they relate to common job seeker questions.

Whether conveyed via instrumental or symbolic information, an important area of emphasis is how the organization and job opportunity will meet the candidate's needs. Often, job advertisements focus on the demands of the position and the corresponding abilities a successful candidate must possess. Role demands are important ways of communicating the core elements of a job and helping job seekers to self-select out of any roles for which they are under- or over-qualified. However, information that appeals to candidates' needs has been shown to be much more effective in attracting applications from higher-quality candidates (Schmidt, Chapman, & Jones, 2015). It is likely the case that higher-quality applicants can be more selective in where they apply and thus focus on employers that speak to how their needs will be met. Often, the framing of statements can change an idea from a demands statement to one that appeals to candidates' needs. Examples of common job demands and candidate needs statements are listed in Table 4.1.

Position Title

Section 1: Job Duties
- What type of work will the job entail?
- What will my average day look like?

Section 2: The Organizational Context
- What is the culture like?
- What kind of management style can I expect?
- What is the team dynamic?

Section 3: The Desired Candidate
- What characteristics do I need to be successful here?
- What career paths are likely for me in this role?

Figure 4.1 Organizing your job ad around candidate concerns

Table 4.1 Job Description Framing Based on Demands Versus Needs

Example Job Demands Statement	Example Candidate Needs Statement
Individuals will be required to show initiative in prioritizing tasks and executing on them.	The job will provide you with autonomy, as you will be required to prioritize and complete tasks with minimal supervision.
Successful candidates will enthusiastically support and cooperate with teammates.	You will have many opportunities to collaborate with talented individuals.
We are looking for individuals who are interested in constantly expanding their skill set and developing their potential.	Employees are given constructive feedback and many opportunities for advancement within the organization.
The successful applicant must be able to handle working on a variety of tasks that will require the use of several different skills.	You will have the opportunity to work on a variety of tasks and develop your skills in many areas.

Drawing in a Diverse Candidate Pool

In later stages of the hiring process, diversity is usually rigorously scrutinized. Selection methods and tools come with a host of important considerations surrounding adverse impact (see *The Uniform Guidelines* on *Employee Selection Procedures* [U.S. General Accounting Office, 1982] for more detail). However, recruitment research does not usually take adverse impact into consideration (Tippins, 2010). Given that recruitment messages, such as job advertisements, are often the first touchpoint for a potential candidate and employer, their appeal and impact on diverse groups merits attention.

Some organizations employ targeted recruiting strategies to ensure they are reaching out to underrepresented groups when positions become available. However, the results of such efforts are mixed (Avery, 2003). Therefore, researchers and practitioners are beginning to turn their attention to the content of recruitment messages, such as the required personality traits and skills. The advantage of focusing on content rather than sourcing or other targeted strategies is that it emphasizes deep-level attributes rather than just surface-level diversity. For instance, Casper, Wayne, and Manegold (2013) found that advertising company policies like work–family balance is more effective for attracting a diverse pool of applicants than is targeting surface-level demographics.

One key consideration when it comes to diversity and recruitment is that of language. Many studies have found that meta-stereotypes, one's beliefs about how out-group members perceive in-group members, can influence both job attractiveness and intent to apply (Purdie-Vaughns, Steele, Davies, Ditlmann, & Crosby, 2008; Vorauer et al., 2000; Wille & Derous, 2017). Meta-stereotypes can be triggered by the characteristics outlined in a job ad. Born and Taris (2010) found that women were less inclined to apply for a masculine than a feminine job profile. Masculine jobs were indicated by traits such as strong, competitive, and assertive, while feminine job profiles included traits like concerned, polite, and nurturing. Figure 4.2 displays examples of masculine and feminine candidate traits along with more gender-neutral alternatives. Furthermore, the way traits are communicated often sends a signal that can elicit meta-stereotypes. Verbs, which describe more concrete behaviors or mental processes, tend to mitigate stereotyping effects, while adjectives convey more abstract and stable dispositions that can raise candidate concern (Semin & Fiedler, 1991). The effect of language choice has been upheld in studies of women and ethnic minorities, indicating that behaviorally based language should be used in favor of trait-based statements (Wille & Derous, 2017, 2018). Table 4.2 presents examples of trait and behavioral statements.

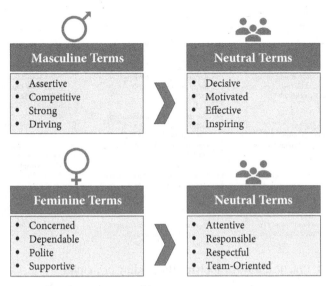

Figure 4.2 Gendered versus neutral language

Table 4.2 Trait Versus Behavioral Statements

Example Trait Statement	Example Behavioral Statement
The candidate must be reliable.	The desired candidate must protect confidential information.
The desired candidate is even-tempered.	Successful candidates demonstrate an ability to remain calm in stressful situations.
You are extraverted.	You enjoy interacting with others.

Putting It All Together

Most of the above principles can be thought of as guidelines for designing or revising your job advertisements. These recommendations can help you craft stronger job postings, but what might this look like in reality? While not comprehensive, Figure 4.3 offers some practical suggestions for better attracting candidate attention, appealing to desired candidates, and drawing in a diverse candidate pool.

Attracting Candidate Attention	Appealing to Desired Candidates	Drawing In a Diverse Candidate Pool
• Use videos of current employees applying their skills to supplement a written job description. • Create a infographic summarizing responsibilities, qualifications, and competencies of the role. • Integrate your brand colors and logo to reinforce your employer brand. • Leverage social media platforms like Instagram to showcase day-to-day life at your organization.	• Keep postings concise; length of the ad doesn't necessarily convey importance. • Use creative language. Headings such as "Could You Be a Fit?" carry a more welcoming tone than the standard " Candidate Qualifications." • Mention specific projects to give clearer context and help the person picture themselves in the role. • Highlight recent qualification of the team to better clarify the role.	• When feasible, emphasize professional capabilities (e.g., ability to balance multiple timelines) over minimum education requirements to attract non-obvious candidates. • Be explicit about available support; share information about accessibility to encourage diverse candidate to apply. • Broaden listed skills and experiences to increase the diversity of candidates that opt into the application process.

Figure 4.3 Practical ways of applying the guiding principles

What's Next for Online Job Advertisements

Practice has long exceeded the pace of research with regard to job advertisements and e-recruitment in general. Given that, there are many new recruiting practices that have yet to receive research attention. In this final section, I present a few emerging trends among recruiting professionals and follow with some suggested avenues for future research.

New Directions for Practice

While technology continues to advance, there are more traditional e-recruitment approaches that remain important. Research on job seeker attitudes and behaviors indicate that organizations should maintain a presence on online job boards, as they are impactful during the first phase of the recruitment process (Acikgoz & Bergman, 2016). Job seekers report official lines of communication, such as the company's website, as the most trusted and valued sources of recruitment information (Acikgoz & Bergman, 2016; Gartner, 2019). These findings indicate that organizations should take a broad recruitment strategy of using multiple recruitment sources and distribute the message across those sources based on when job seekers use them. For example, a cost-effective approach would be sharing basic information about the role on online job boards and offering a rich presentation of the organization and position on the company website. Once the broad strategy is set, there is a growing number of new considerations recruiting organizations can make surrounding vendors and information integration.

Vendors

With the growth of social media and social networking has come a niche market centered around employee recruitment. Even within a focused area, vendors are popping up to cover several aspects of e-recruiting and advertising job openings. Some vendors focus on identifying potential candidates while others aim to better attract candidate attention and interest. Many also provide consultation on employer branding and online image. While the rise of social recruiting vendors provides organizations with a host of new resources for advancing their recruitment practices, vendor proliferation is an emerging challenge talent acquisition professionals must navigate.

Information Integration

Data scraping is showing early promise for recruiters. In many cases data scraping is being used to inform the development and location of job advertisements. For example, data from job descriptions, employee skill profiles, and career pathing documentation can be pooled to flesh out an advertisement for an open role. Externally, job scraping is a means of gathering data from outside of one's organization to better understand job markets and competitors. With the amount and complexity of location and browsing data available today, it's plausible to envision online job ads in the future that are curated based on the viewer's information. For example, a job seeker who often searches for and views content related to physical fitness may be directed to information about an organization's on-site gym when they visit the company's website. The advancements in data availability and integration are opening the doors for richer, more targeted recruitment messaging. However, as advancements continue, so will the pressure on organizations to consider privacy and ethical implications.

New Directions for Research

Because recruitment research, particularly that surrounding job advertisements and other early-stage activities, has long lagged behind practice, there is ample future opportunity. Two major areas of opportunity lie in diversity and research methods.

Diversity and Recruitment

Much of the existing literature considers overall group reactions to recruitment content. Whether the subject is visual appeal or informational content, most job advertisement studies examine the overall job seeker experience (e.g., Dineen & Noe, 2009; Schmidt et al., 2015). Such findings are important for informing best practices in recruitment, but a deeper understanding of the role of individual differences in job seeker reactions is needed. Some research has explicitly targeted the effects of recruitment messaging on underrepresented demographic groups (e.g., Walker et al., 2009; Wille & Derous, 2018), but these studies often target specific pieces of information related to stereotypes or diversity and inclusion policies. A more holistic examination of how potential candidates process and react to job ads, especially regarding applicant behavior, would better equip practitioners to ensure their messaging resonates with a diverse pool of potential applicants. One possible tool for doing so, the application impact ratio (AIR) was proposed by Wille and Derous (2017). The AIR is the ratio of application rates of qualified minority groups to majority groups and may be a viable way for checking the mass appeal of job ads.

Research Methods and Job Ads

Several methodologies that are applicable to recruitment research are seldom used. For example, eye-tracking devices can allow researchers to better understand what job seekers are looking at when they view job ads and other recruitment messages (Allen et al., 2013). Click-through ratios allow for the examination of job ad effectiveness in a minimally invasive manner (e.g., Schmidt et al., 2015). Technological advancements continue to bring about new means of studying human behavior, so it is likely innovative research methods to understand audience interaction will continue to evolve. However, recruitment research could also benefit from the use of designs that do not rely as heavily on technology. Longitudinal studies would provide a far deeper view of the job search process in the early stages. Diary studies and qualitative interviews or focus groups would also provide rich detail on applicant perceptions and intentions. Expanding beyond survey designs will allow researchers to assess different aspects of the recruitment process and gain a more thorough understanding of job seekers' attitudes and behaviors.

Conclusion

While formal job advertisements have been a common recruiting practice for decades, relatively little empirical research exists to guide practitioners. Fortunately, theories related to attention, information processing, and user experience lend themselves to general principles that can inform effective job postings. Based on the general guidelines and research findings presented here, the following outline provides a series of general practices to guide you in creating your own job advertisements.

1. Open with a selling statement that captures the role in a succinct and memorable way.
   a. Candidates are likely to encounter job ads at a high volume, meaning any given advertisement could be easily forgotten. Attract attention from the beginning by identifying one or two features that distinguish your role from others.
   b. For example: *Join a sales team that consistently works with the company's Corporate Executive Office and has a proven history of promoting from within.*
2. Begin the body of the ad by putting the position in context. Write a brief introductory paragraph or statement that explains the reporting structure of the role, how the role fits in with the broader organizational structure and strategy, and the expected performance objectives.
   a. This introduction helps potential applicants understand the experience of being in the role, not just the main responsibilities.
   b. For example: *Reporting to the Regional Sales Director, the person in this role will support our enterprise-wide initiative of growing business by 10% in 2021 by regularly meeting and exceeding their own personal sales goals.*
3. List out daily responsibilities and elaborate on those duties with details to help bring the job to life.
   a. Highlight which responsibilities take up most of the time. For example: *Generate new leads to build new business, which typically accounts for about 90% of time spent in the role.*
   b. Indicate likely customers, vendors, etc. to provide a more accurate preview of the role. For example: *Generate new C-suite leads to build new business, which typically accounts for about 90% of time spent in the role.*

   c. Expand on tasks with techniques that are commonly used to better articulate day-to-day responsibilities. For example: *Generate new C-suite leads via networking events and cold-calling techniques, which typically accounts for about 90% of time spent in the role.*

4. Describe qualities of the ideal applicant.

   a. Listing characteristics that will lead to success in the role enables possible candidates to more accurately gauge their level of fit.

   b. Be explicit about which qualifications are required and which are preferred. Statements such as *A successful candidate will . . .* and *A successful candidate may . . .* both discourage poor-fit candidates from applying and encourage top candidates to move forward despite not meeting all listed qualifications.

5. Review and proof your advertisement.

   a. Remove any jargon or organization-specific language that may create candidate misunderstandings. Check for:

     i. Non-standard department names

     ii. Unexplained acronyms

     iii. Terms specific to your organization's culture and operations

   b. Check for writing mistakes, including:

     i. Spelling errors

     ii. Parallel structure

     iii. Repetitive word choice

   c. Share the ad with a diverse group to ensure that language is clear, representative of the role, and as inclusive as possible.

References

Acikgoz, Y., & Bergman, S. M. (2016). Social media and employee recruitment: Chasing the runaway bandwagon. In R. N. Landers & G. B. Schmidt (Eds.), *Social media in employee selection and recruitment* (pp. 175–195). Switzerland: Springer International Publishing.

Allen, D. G., Biggane, J. E., Pitts, M., Otondo, R., & Van Scotter, J. (2013). Reactions to recruitment web sites: Visual and verbal attention, attraction, and intentions to pursue employment. *Journal of Business and Psychology, 28,* 263–285.

Avery, D. R. (2003). Reactions to diversity in recruitment advertising—Are differences black and white? *Journal of Applied Psychology, 88,* 672–679.

Avery, D. R., & McKay, P. F. (2006). Target practice: An organizational impression management approach to attracting minority and female job applicants. *Personnel Psychology, 59,* 157–187.

Avery, D. R., Volpone, S. D., Stewart, R. W., Luksyte, A., Hernandez, M., McKay, P. F., & Hebl, M. R. (2013). Examining the draw of diversity: How diversity climate perceptions affect job-pursuit intentions. *Human Resource Management, 52,* 175–194.

Born, M., & Taris, T. W. (2010). The impact of wording of employment advertisements on students' inclination to apply for a job. *Journal of Social Psychology, 150*, 485–502.

Breaugh, J. A. (2008). Employee recruitment: Current knowledge and important areas for future research. *Human Resource Management Review, 18*(3), 103–118.

CareerArc (2021). Future of Recruiting Study 2021. Retrieved from https://social.career arc.com/2021-future-of-recruiting-study/

Carless, S. A. (2005). Person-job fit versus person-organization fit as predictors of organizational attraction and job acceptance intentions: A longitudinal study. *Journal of Occupational and Organizational Psychology, 78*, 411–429.

Casper, W. J., Wayne, J. H., & Manegold, J. G. (2013). Who will we recruit? Targeting deep- and surface-level diversity with human resource policy advertising. *Human Resource Management, 52*, 311–332.

Chapman, D. S., & Godollei, A. F. (2017). E-recruiting: Using technology to attract job applicants. In G. Hertel, D. L. Stone, R. D. Johnson, & J. Passmore (Eds.), *The Wiley Blackwell handbook of the psychology of the internet at work* (pp. 213–230). Hoboken, NJ: Wiley & Sons.

Chapman, D. S., Uggerslev, K. L., Carroll, S. A., Piasentin, K. A., & Jones, D. A. (2005). Applicant attraction to organizations and job choice: A meta-analytic review of the correlates of recruiting outcomes. *Journal of Applied Psychology, 90*, 928–944.

Chen, Q., & Wells, W. D. (1999). Attitude toward the site. *Journal of Advertising Research, 5*, 27–37.

Cober, R. T., Brown, D. J., Keeping, L. M., & Levy, P. E. (2004). Recruitment on the net: How do organizational web site characteristics influence applicant attraction? *Journal of Management, 30*, 623–646.

Cober, R. T, Brown, D. J., Levy, P. E., Keeping, L. M., & Cober, A. B. (2003). Organizational websites: Website content and style as determinants of organizational attraction. *International Journal of Selection and Assessment, 11*, 158–169.

Dickey-Chasins, J. (2012, December). Job board evolution. HR Examiner. https://www.hrexaminer.com/job-board-evolutio/.

Dineen, B. R., & Allen, D. G. (2014). Internet recruiting 2.0: Shifting paradigms. In K. Y. T. Yu & D. M. Cable (Eds.), *The Oxford handbook of recruitment* (pp. 382–401). New York: Oxford University Press.

Dineen, B. R., & Noe, R. A. (2009). Effects of customization on application decisions and applicant pool characteristics in a web-based recruitment context. *Journal of Applied Psychology, 94*, 224–234.

Djamasbi, S., Siegel, M., & Tullis, T. (2010). Generation Y, web design, and eye tracking. *International Journal of Human-Computer Studies, 68*, 307–323.

Gartner. (2019). The decisive candidate: Redesigning the hiring process to drive candidate decisions. Gartner Research. https://www.gartner.com/en/human-resources/trends/redesigning-the-hiring-process.

Glassdoor. (2019). 50 HR and recruiting stats for 2019. https://www.glassdoor.com/employers/resources/hr-and-recruiting-stats/.

Herriot, P. (2004). Social identities and applicant reactions. *International Journal of Selection and Assessment, 12*, 75–83.

Highhouse, S., & Hoffman, J. R. (2001). Organizational attraction and job choice. In C. L. Cooper & I. T. Robertson (Eds.), *International review of industrial and organizational psychology* (Vol. 16, pp. 37–64). Chichester, England: Wiley & Sons.

JobVite. (2019). 2019 job seeker nation survey: The strength of the job market is one-sided. https://www.jobvite.com/wp-content/uploads/2019/04/2019_Job_Seeker_Nation.pdf.

Kahneman, D. (2000). A psychological point of view: Violations of rational rules as a diagnostic of mental processes. *Behavioral and Brain Sciences, 23*, 681–683.

Lauver, K. J., & Kristof-Brown, A. (2001). Distinguishing between employees' perceptions of person-job and person-organization fit. *Journal of Vocational Behavior, 59*, 454–470.

Lengel, R. H., & Daft, R. L. (1988). The selection of communication media as an executive skill. *Academy of Management Perspectives, 2*, 225–232.

Li, C., Charron, C., Roshan, S., & Flemming, G. N. (2002). Online recruitment grows up. *Forrester Research*. Retrieved from https://www.forrester.com

Lievens, F., Van Hoye, G., & Anseel, F. (2007). Organizational identity and employer image: Towards a unifying framework. *British Journal of Management, 18*, S45–S59.

Maurer, S. D., & Liu, Y. (2007). Developing effective e-recruiting websites: Insights for managers from marketers. *Business Horizons, 50*, 305–314.

Myers, C. A., & MacLaurin, W. R. (1943). *The movement of factory workers*. New York: Wiley & Sons.

Nolan, K. P., Gohlke, M., Gilmore, J., & Rosiello, R. (2013). Examining how corporations use online job ads to communicate employer brand image information. *Corporate Reputation Review, 16*, 300–312.

Parnes, H. S. (1954). *Research on labor mobility*. New York: Social Science Research Council.

Purdie-Vaughns, V., Steele, C. M., Davies, P. G., Ditlmann, R., & Crosby, J. R. (2008). Social identity contingencies: How diversity cues signal threat or safety for African Americans in mainstream institutions. *Journal of Personality and Social Psychology, 94*, 615–630.

Raphael, T. (2011, February 15). UPS says it's now delivering hires, not just fans and followers. ERE. https://www.ere.net/articles/ups-says-its-now-delivering-hires-not-just-fans-and-followers.

Schmidt, J. A., Chapman, D. S., & Jones, D. A. (2015). Does emphasizing different types of person-environment fit in online job ads influence application behavior and applicant quality? Evidence from a field experiment. *Journal of Business and Psychology, 30*, 267–282.

Schneider, B., Goldstein, H. W., & Smith, D. B. (1995). The ASA framework: An update. *Personnel Psychology, 48*, 747–773.

Selden, S., & Orenstein, J. (2011). Government e-recruiting web sites: The influence of e-recruitment content and usability on recruiting and hiring outcomes in US state governments. *International Journal of Selection and Assessment, 19*, 31–40.

Semin, G. R., & Fiedler, K. (1991). The linguistic category model, its bases, applications and range. *European Review of Social Psychology, 2*, 1–30.

Spence, M. (1973). Job market signaling. *Quarterly Journal of Economics, 87*, 355–374.

Tajfel, H. (1982). Social psychology of intergroup relations. *Annual Review of Psychology, 33*, 1–39.

Tippins, N. T. (2010). Adverse impact in employee selection procedures from the perspective of an organizational consultant. In J. L. Outtz (Ed.), *Adverse impact: Implications for organizational staffing and high stakes selection* (pp. 201–225). New York: Routledge.

Tractinsky, N., Katz, A. S., & Ikar, D. (2000). What is beautiful is usable. *Interacting with Computers, 13*, 127–145.

U.S. General Accounting Office. (1982). *Uniform guidelines on employee selection procedures*. Washington, D.C.

Van Hoye, G., & Saks, A. M. (2011). The instrumental-symbolic framework: Organizational image and attractiveness of potential applicants and their companions at a job fair. *Applied Psychology, 60*, 311–335.

Vorauer, J. D., Hunter, A., Main, K. J., & Roy, S. A. (2000). Meta-stereotype activation: Evidence from indirect measures for specific evaluation concerns experienced by members of dominant groups in intergroup interaction. *Journal of Personality and Social Psychology, 78*, 690–707.

Walker, H. J., Feild, H. S., Giles, W. F., Armenakis, A. A., & Bernerth, J. B. (2009). Displaying employee testimonials on recruitment web sites: Effects of communication media, employee race, and job seeker race on organizational attraction and information credibility. *Journal of Applied Psychology, 94*, 1354–1364.

Walker, H. J., & Hinojosa, A. S. (2014). Recruitment: The role of job advertisements. In K. Y. T. Yu & D. M. Cable (Eds.), *The Oxford handbook of recruitment* (pp. 269–283). New York: Oxford University Press.

Wille, L., & Derous, E. (2017). Getting the words right: When wording of job ads affects ethnic minorities' application decisions. *Management Communication Quarterly, 3*, 533–558.

Wille, L., & Derous, E. (2018). When job ads turn you down: How requirements in job ads may stop instead of attract highly qualified women. *Sex Roles, 79*, 464–475.

Williams, R. (2004). *The non-designer's design book*. Berkeley, CA: Peachpit Press.

Zanella, S., & Pais, I. (2014). The Adecco global study 2014: Job search, digital reputation and HR practices in the social media age. Adecco Group. https://blog.adeccousa.com/social-recruiting-study/

Zusman, R. R., & Landis, R. S. (2002). Applicant preferences for Web-based versus traditional job postings. *Computers in Human Behavior, 18*, 285–296.

5

Recruiting Technology

Mark A. Morris

Amazon

This chapter will address the core elements of technology used in talent acquisition (TA), along with future directions and trends, with emphasis
on where practitioners will want to evaluate potential additions to their
recruiting technological arsenal. First, I will cover a recent survey of senior
TA leaders across the United States and offer some guiding principles for
human resources (HR) leaders making technology decisions. Next I will
deep dive into two vital areas of recruiting technology. First, the applicant
tracking system (ATS), which forms the core of recruiting technology for
most firms, will be covered, with attention to innovative ATS add-ons that
offer potential incremental value. The second area for a deep dive will involve
artificial intelligence (AI), such as ChatGPT and other tools; AI represents
a rapidly emerging area of technology with significant implications for
enhancing productivity, accelerating actions, and changing processes in TA.
Other topics that will be dealt with more briefly include social media tools,
virtual interviews, and other types of technological tools used throughout the
hiring lifecycle. Recommendations on when to use each type with different
industries/candidates/HR systems will be made and risks identified. Because
this chapter discusses current practice and technology, I will include the
names of specific representative tools to assist users in their research, but the
inclusion of a proprietary product or service should not be construed as an
endorsement. It is my assumption that some of the tools cited in this chapter
could soon be superseded or become obsolete in this rapidly changing field.

Current State of Practice

Whether as part of a human capital system that runs all of HR (such as
Workday or ADP) or as a stand-alone system, most companies continue to

Mark A. Morris, *Recruiting Technology* In: *Becoming a Talent Magnet*. Edited by: Mark A. Morris, Oxford University Press.
© Oxford University Press 2024. DOI: 10.1093/oso/9780190938512.003.0005

rely on their ATS as the core of their recruiting technology. The ATS allows organizations to track candidates as they move through the recruiting process; some authors (e.g., Bersin & Enderes, 2021) and companies already envision a powered-up ATS that actively matches people to opportunities. According to Bersin and Enderes (2021), the average TA leader in the Fortune 50 is contacted by 10 vendors every day seeking to sell technology solutions, often AI-based, that are often niche solutions designed to bolt onto or work with the ATS. To explore the use of ATS in current recruiting efforts, a survey was conducted in March 2020 of 30 experienced agency founders and senior-level recruiting leaders on LinkedIn. Respondents ($n = 17$) included 41% from agencies/search firms (e.g., Korn Ferry) and 59% internal TA leaders (director and above) from large firms in a variety of industries, including aerospace, logistics, consumer goods, automotive, and hospitality. Respondents were asked (during the early stages of the COVID-19 pandemic) to look around corners for the recruiting technology likely to make the biggest impact on the recruiting field in the next few years. The four top responses were ATS/candidate relationship management (CRM) tools, virtual interviews, AI, and social media. The most common answers for the recruiting technology that will have the biggest impact over the next few years were as follows[1]:

1. *Powerful ATS and CRM tools*, cited by 41% of respondents. ATS (e.g., iCims)can search internal and external databases of candidates, and have improved integration with other HR systems, like online assessments from external vendors: With recruiters still spending on average 23 hours screening résumés for each open professional requisition (Cocca, 2019), there is still a big opportunity for ATS vendors to automate posting, interviewing, screening, and offer creation processes, and few have yet seized the chance to tie in succession and workforce planning. However, progress is being made. Since 2018, as Cerrato and Freyermuth (2020) noted, CRM is increasingly integrated into ATS platforms.
2. *Virtual interviews* (cited by 41%), including Zoom, Google Hangouts, Slack, etc., to conduct and record live interviews, with integrated scheduling and onboarding (see Chapter 7 for more): HireVue's (2022) survey of 1,657 hiring leaders found that 77% have implemented virtual

---

[1] Please note that some respondents cited more than one innovation.

interviews in the past year. The pandemic accelerated a rapid cost-saving trend toward virtual interviewing, and it is now the standard for many jobs due to speed, more familiarity with tools like Zoom, and savings in travel costs. Companies should track candidate experience by virtual versus onsite personal interviews to ensure consistency.

3. *AI* (cited by 29%) offers many potential benefits that will be covered in more detail below; examples include AI-based machine learning for sourcing, selection, and talent flow, to reduce time to fill and add insights. AI also allows the personalization of recruiting approaches and improved lead generation. One potential use case with AI involves scraping together data on passive candidates to build detailed profiles that enable better candidate engagement (see HiringSolved and hireEZ as examples of this technology). Having more information on a candidate allows more targeted recruiting approaches to passive candidates. AI can compute the likelihood that a candidate will be at a stage where they are ready to consider or be open to a new role (variables could include pension eligibility, stock vesting schedules, recent promotions, etc.). Based on the data available to most companies, many users may find that the initial usage of AI for recruiting may be on the front end of the hiring funnel, through sourcing and screening versus improving acceptance rates. Improvements to selection for hiring through the use of AI in assessment and interviewing already exist but, depending on the maturity of the selection process, may be smaller scale in impact as they may only increment existing approaches or be used for subsets of jobs. One potential indirect approach for AI to improve sourcing is by helping to drive socialization and engagement in online communities. Most organizations can anticipate challenges around managing the high volume of data collected (e.g., every text, post, chat message, and email if you want to do organizational network analysis). The data must be organized, stored, and cleaned to support trend identification by business intelligence, data science, and industrial/organizational (I/O) psychologist teams to spot patterns and opportunities (e.g., did new hires onboarded during the pandemic form social connections just as fast as previous hires?). Some AI tools include hundreds or thousands of features/variables with few internal rules or criteria around selection or review of predictors once their correlations with outcomes are understood. AI users will need to decide, for example, how many compensation variables you should retain versus engagement survey

items versus tenure, or whether you should keep everything that adds predictive power in an atheoretical approach. How do you weight the impact of diversity in the AI's training set and recommendations?

4. *Social media* (cited by 29%), such as LinkedIn, which is especially popular for salaried positions: LinkedIn has made an investment to grow its intelligence services for recruiters. These services (for sale as an add-on to corporate recruiting accounts) allow a recruiting team to view statistics on percentage and counts of talent flowing out from their company to see the top destinations for departing employees, as well as people who are top sources of talent, by company and job title. Social media can also harness internal employees to get the word out about opportunities (think posting or referrals on your LinkedIn page) to draw in more candidates. Others cited were X (formerly Twitter) and Glassdoor.

5. *CRM/marketing tools* were cited by 12%. An example tools is TextRecruit, which allows recruiters to send batches of texts or campaigns to candidates while being able to view or report on the status of all candidates, the last time they were contacted, by whom, status, etc.: CRM tools like Salesforce also can often be integrated with the company's ATS. The next iteration in this space could work like a dating app where candidates swipe right based on the job profile or hiring managers swipe right on a good candidate. Such an app could contain résumés, social media links, work timelines, etc. and could tell recruiters whom to engage with personally.

6. *Personalized career sites* (such as Phenom People), cited by 6%, can offer different content based on who is visiting and what number of visits it is for that person. This creates a different candidate experience for a sales candidate than an engineering candidate. This content can be curated based on where candidates engage or go on versus where they drop out.

7. *Online databases*, cited by 6%, including examples such as D&B Hoovers, contain information on industry, growth rate, number of employees, location of headquarters, revenue, debt, profit, and other important characteristics of the company that candidates and recruiters can use to identify potential talent sources or employers where their skills may fit.

8. *Metrics*: Survey respondents pointed out that there is opportunity here because TA needs better data on the return on investment (ROI) of a recruiting change. Right now, social media sites like Glassdoor

or X (formerly Twitter) are not sufficiently reliable when you can hire people to respond a certain way to shape perceptions. A common measure is unique page views, but a better measure might include click-throughs to a career site or percentage of shares. There is also an opportunity to report on hiring trends, efficiency, etc. (cited by 6%). See Chapter 6 in this book for more ideas on future trends.

9. *Mobile reference checking platforms*, cited by 6%, examples like Checkster or SkillSurvey, allow a recruiter to automate reference checking without having to call references on the phone. They can also generate additional names/leads for new potential candidates.

10. *Virtual career fairs* (cited by 6%) can be held with webcasts, webinars, or live interactive broadcasts using a company's internal tools or vendors like Communiqué Conferencing. Just like a live career fair, employers and job seekers can meet, discuss opportunities, and make connections.

11. *Virtual onboarding and self-guided facility tours* (cited by 6%): These activities take place once the new hire has obtained company technology, such as a laptop or tablet, and has access to company internet sites. It can include walk-through videos, interactive exercises, virtual meet-and-greets with buddies, a schedule for the first 30 days with links to learn about the company history, strategy and key leaders, etc. Research is not complete on what gets lost versus in-person onboarding.

Virtual Jobs/Virtual Hiring

These survey responses provide useful insight from TA practitioners into the path ahead as the world emerges from the COVID-19 pandemic more dependent than ever on technology to manage hiring brands and interactions without sacrificing candidate experience. Organizations are experimenting with what lessons to learn and evaluating what new approaches to retain as employees stay remote, return to the office, or move to a hybrid model. A 2021 survey (Shufran, 2021) reported that 88% of recruiters are using a fully virtual recruiting and hiring process with no onsite or in-person meetings between the candidate and the hiring organization, and nearly all expect it to stay that way. While quantitative research on predictive validity is still being established, anecdotally it appears that hiring managers can do more hiring events per month, but without access to company facilities, candidates have fewer opportunities to assess culture. Preliminary findings in education (showing reduced learning of math and language) and in clinical psychology (showing that patients appear more comfortable in the safe space of their own homes) may suggest avenues for future research. To the extent that virtual interviews (and remote work) stick around, this will open the funnel for organizations and candidates, offering new opportunities with fewer geographic constraints, but it does create a greater dependence on technology to do more, from sourcing to selection to onboarding. The same survey reported that 72% of recruiters are now considering out-of-area talent and expect this to benefit diverse fills as well. There may be significant resistance to returning to a physical office, so some degree of remote work is likely to stick for jobs that can primarily be done virtually. For example, internal surveys (Axon, 2021) of companies like Apple show that 90% of respondents ($n = 1,749$) "strongly agree" that "location-flexible working options are a very important issue for me." And 68% agreed "that the lack of location flexibility would likely cause me to leave Apple."

In this environment it is tempting to look to automate remote recruiting practices. Automation is indicated when you have repeatable processes that are headcount intensive. In HR departments the most frequently outsourced and automated work in HR has been self-service functions, especially benefits and compensation administration. Recruiting and TA appear to be good candidates for automation as they are often among the largest departments within HR in terms of headcount at most large corporations, and this is even more lopsided at fast-growth companies. Large high-tech companies in growth mode may have as many as 1,000-plus full-time recruiters and additional part-time contractors, and as of this writing during the "Great Resignation" we are seeing very high attrition of recruiters, especially technical recruiters who might have a good network of technology talent. The combination of a need to process high volumes of candidates and the infusion of many new staff getting up to speed creates even more pressure to automate to create a consistent and positive candidate experience. See Chapter 2 for more on how to blend advances in recruiting technology with companies' talent branding/employee value proposition.

During the COVID-19 pandemic that began in 2020, many companies canceled face-to-face interviews, accelerating a cost-saving trend toward virtual interviews, which are done remotely via web-based video or audio. In some cases jobs can now be done remotely anyway, so this was a good chance to evaluate a candidate's comfort with the technology and ability to interact interpersonally across Zoom, Skype, Slack, Discord, or related tools. In LinkedIn's October 2020 survey of 1,500 talent professionals, 81% expected virtual recruiting to continue after the pandemic. Job designs have also changed, and recruiters who cannot offer remote work are at a disadvantage in pursuing sought-after talent. Sethi (2020) reported a PwC study showing that 78% of global CEOs expect remote collaboration is here to stay, and Heger (2024) reports that even years after the pandemic 27% of companies are mandating full time in office policies with 72% applying a 3 days/week hybrid model or fully remote work. Companies like Amazon are moving to a hybrid model with some days in the office and some remote, depending on the role and task. Virtual interviews offer the chance to do some assessment-center–related tasks as well and allow candidates or interviewers to upload or read documents or files in real time. Given the reduction in travel expenses and reduced time footprint for candidates, virtual interviews could be here to stay.

Virtual Interviews: Good Practices for HR Teams

- Provide preparatory materials to candidates on attire, expected questions, and links to company culture and values. Some companies go beyond the standard and include guidance on how to prepare for interview questions or the interview loop experience. Guidelines for candidate preparation are standard at companies like Amazon to give all candidates a level playing field and make good use of the interviewer's valuable time.
- Ensure that the home network or location is quiet and well lit and has good connectivity, with a backup plan. Some companies offer reimbursement for a good home USB speaker for their laptop, supply options to dial in via cellphone, or provide headsets.
- Be mindful of time-zone differences when scheduling.
- Set up testing systems for candidates to ensure their apps/camera/audio will work well, with a backup plan for FaceTime or cell calls.
- If interactivity is needed during the interview, provide a tool that allows a candidate to work out problems on a shared whiteboard, upload files, or react to shared files (such as problems to be solved, scenarios, exercises, etc.).

What We Can Learn from Cutting-Edge Research

Unfortunately, few academics are publishing in this space, and company legal departments rarely approve data sharing in this highly competitive area. Most large-sample studies in the public domain are from recruiting and job-posting companies who have a clear interest in promoting their product or services. In confidential benchmarking and internal discussions with HR executives it is common to hear that cutting-edge research is focused on balancing the efficiency pressures of automation of applicant processing with the need for bias reduction to support diversity, equity, and inclusion (DEI) efforts. DEI business partners at some large technology companies advocate for taking more time to hire to improve diversity rates of new hires, while time to fill, cost, and quality of hire must be maintained. Automation efforts can encounter criterion challenges when the algorithm is being trained and evaluated against a performance rating criterion that is not equally distributed among protected groups. Companies considering machine learning (ML) algorithms should be sure to assess adverse impact in their sourcing and filtering, as bias can be introduced in the datasets used to train them.

Post-pandemic investments in recruiting technology are expected to increase. A 2023 survey from the Society for Human Resource Management (SHRM), and Harvard Business Review asked 500 senior executives about future plans for remote work and reported that only 28% of workdays were remote in 2023, down from 50% in 2020 during the heart of the pandemic. In addition, the survey reports signification increases in research and patents for remote working technology (Bloom, Barrero, Davis, Meyer, & Mihaylov, 2023). In a tight labor market, such as the one experienced from fall 2021 to spring 2022, these investments focused on making it easier to identify and sell candidates on a company's value proposition while tracking compensation to inflation. Another investment cited in the survey by 34% of the same HR professionals in the United States is in improving remote collaboration tools to accelerate virtual assimilation into company culture. A survey of 2,800 senior managers in the United States by Robert Half (Popovic, 2020) reported that during the first year of the pandemic the percentage of respondents conducting virtual interviews went from 12% to 75%. COVID-19 required millions of Americans to work from home for extended periods of 2020, enabling widespread familiarity with video conferencing and meeting tools like Zoom and Teams. Video-based interviewing became the norm for many jobs.

While virtual hires may be engaged and feel productive working remotely, they may also have fewer affective commitments to an organization where they've never met anyone in person or visited any physical facility. As the pandemic effects ebb this will be interesting data to inspect, particularly around the risk of attrition as remote workers form fewer and weaker social connections and are less likely to have a geographic commitment.

Improving DEI

Many organizations show differences in attrition, promotion, and hiring rates based on demographics. To vaccinate managers against potential bias in a remote or in-person hiring model, some leading organizations are surfacing and challenging unconscious thought patterns, even among allies, by refreshing leaders with unconscious bias primers as part of the hiring process. TA asks panel interviewers to read these primers right before debriefs and seek to create a space where people can "call out" others who are showing bias. Raising awareness in this way will use priming techniques to reduce bias.

Guiding Principles for Selecting Recruiting Technology

This section specifies principles that are recommended for TA leaders or HR executives seeking to create or enhance their recruiting technology. A discussion follows the principles with more attention to the ATS, as that will form the usual foundation of recruiting technology for most organizations.

1. **Review talent strategy**: Identify the most important strategic priorities for talent in your organization, such as staffing, top technical talent, senior leadership, source from targeted competitors, retention of critical role players, etc., and ensure that technology investments are appropriately allocated to address them. While this chapter focuses on TA technology investments, it is wise to consider job and process redesign approaches to simplify and improve the candidate and employee experience.
2. **Ensure that metrics are in place**: Track accurate metrics of cost per hire, quality of hire, and time to fill as a group to ensure you aren't

trading off quality to quickly fill requisitions. Quality of hire need not be highly sophisticated to be effective; a simple question for the hiring manager ("How likely would you be to rehire person xx?") 90 days after hire gives you a starting point in addition to retention rates to balance speed of hire, compensation, etc.

3. **Focus on technology integration**: Recruiting technology should be integrated with learning technology, compensation technology, assessments, and online branding technology to get the most ROI. Pushing data obtained during the hiring process into learning can speed up onboarding and reduce time to productivity while increasing retention of new hires.

4. **Build a simple user interface**: User interfaces need to be simple and intuitive—a frustrated hiring manager, recruiter, or candidate can hurt credibility, cause high dropout rates during the application process, and eventually doom an ATS.

5. **Balance high-touch and high-tech tradeoffs**: Be intentional about which parts of the hiring process need to be personal and which can and should be automated to drive velocity. High touch is indicated when it will be an expectation of the candidate (e.g., in executive recruiting) or when the company's value proposition alone is not sufficient to obtain good talent. Automation is indicated when cost-reduction opportunities are high and risk to candidate experience is low.

6. **Integrate Processes**: Workforce and succession planning should both feed into and pull from your recruiting technology. As mentioned in Chapter 1, the workforce plan is tied into headcount planning, staffing ratios, etc. Succession plans identify future workforce needs and bench gaps for TA to begin sourcing to fill.

7. **Define Recruiter productivity**: These expectations should be tied to a requisition's degree of difficulty. A hard-to-fill requisition for cybersecurity or mobile app development might take three to six months to fill versus hourly staffing, which can be much easier.

Deep Dive: ATS

The core data-management tool for most TA departments remains the ATS, also sometimes called the applicant management system (AMS) to highlight the candidate experience aspect. ATS services include standardized employment assessment, job posting integration, interview note storage, competency and job description integration, background checking, and compliance with General Data Protection Regulation (GDPR) and global regulatory requirements as well as the chance to collect information about eligibility for government incentives. New technologies like social media–based job posting (e.g., SmashFly by Symphony Talent, CareerArc), chatbots for initial screening, and machine learning algorithms that scrape LinkedIn to find high-probability passive candidates also offer new paths forward for recruiting as a field.

With 90% of large companies and 68% of small and mid-size businesses estimated to use an ATS (Mondal, 2021), ATS represents the biggest category of recruiting software. The ATS/AMS remains the central hub of core hiring processes like interview debriefing, dashboards, and candidate flow, triggering automatic actions like notifications to the next step of workflow (e.g., time to schedule a screening call in Outlook, auto-enroll a strong candidate in a talent network to notify of future suitable openings).

Common ATS tools include SAP Success Factors, IBM Kenexa's BrassRing, Oracle's Taleo, iCims, and Workday. Generally, ATS tools have similar capabilities but vary in terms of price, learning curves, and ease of use, and customer preferences fluctuate. A recent Ongig survey (2020) of 1,063 companies found the market share was fragmented, with about 22% using Workday, 15% Taleo, 12% SAP Success Factors, 9% iCims, and 5% IBM Kenexa (disclosure: Jeff Bezos owns stock in Workday). Major HR software players like Oracle, SAP, and IBM have moved into this market as they see the potential to add assessment, learning, succession, and other add-on modules to the central ATS platform, which could potentially become the hub of strategic talent management even as it becomes more mobile friendly. In a sample of 12 million job seekers, Glassdoor (Zhao, 2019) reported that 58% now search for jobs using their phones and 35% prefer this method, although they report that applications take twice as long on mobile phones (median of 10 minutes vs. 5 minutes). This "mobile tax" results in fewer applications completed and implies that shorter, simpler mobile-optimized applications or autofilled (from LinkedIn profiles) applications would be appealing and would draw more applications from mobile users.

While widespread, an ATS is not the solution of choice for all organizations. Mid-size firms ($100m–$500 million in revenue) may choose the simplicity of a single integrated HR system that does all or many elements of HR work beyond just an ATS (such as Workday). Smaller companies that don't have large HR departments or economies of scale that justify the expense of a large central HR information system (HRIS) backbone may gravitate to low-cost subscription models (e.g., software as a service [SaaS]). A SaaS approach leveraging the cloud requires less expensive hardware and can allow scaling as a small company grows, in addition to flexibility around adding new recruiting technology.

Some ATS platforms allow other tools to be integrated as plug-ins or add-ons, such as social media–based CRM software that can be used for initially attracting, engaging, and sourcing candidates. Common features include content marketing where brand-right content is pushed to a talent network of interested candidates, integrated referral and virtual interviewing tools, social media integration, search engine optimization, ML, and detailed dashboards. Vendors here include Avature, Symphony Talent's SmashFly, and Talemetry and are often cloud-based.

The trend of building out from and adding onto the base ATS has been consistent since ATS tools entered the market in the late 1990s and quickly became widely used due to their ability to automate manually intensive tasks like storing, managing, and evaluating thousands of applications as to whether they meet minimum job requirements. An early business case for adding an ATS also included automatic triggers for internal process (e.g., developing an offer, filling out I-9 forms) and responding to or communicating with high volumes of applicants.

Sample Case Study: When a Small Business Needs an ATS

Let's consider the needs of a hypothetical manufacturing business in Texas. When you have 200 people and 12% attrition with flat growth, your workforce plans call for about 24 hires per year (replacements only), which in a non-seasonal business works out to about two per month. To get two hires per month, someone has to do the following work: define the open roles, decide on qualifications needed, decide where to post the job, get any approvals required, post it, pay for posting, read incoming résumés, decide whom to call for an interview, schedule interviews, conduct interviews, decide on whom to hire, make the offer, onboard, and complete paperwork to ensure compliance. To get two hires you may have to post the opening in four places, review 60 résumés, do 12 screening calls, and interview six candidates. An ATS can automate many of these tasks for you. The ATS can take out filtering steps, review résumés, apply screening questions to improve the odds of a viable candidate (e.g., in terms of hours/schedule, location, certifications), and automatically file paperwork for any available government funds (e.g., tax credits for hiring veterans). The hiring manager will still need to conduct the interview and decide when to make an offer (and for how much), but a number of manual steps can be reduced or eliminated.

Small firms usually lack resources for TA dashboards or deep analysis of hiring metrics, but if their accounting or finance team can track their cost of hiring and time spent to fill a typical opening, it will pay dividends and enable more efficient candidate targeting. Managers may spend 6 to 30 hours of their time and take 30 to 90 days to fill a job depending on skill scarcity, company reputation, location, and compensation. If a firm hires two people per month and can save 40% of that time, it works out to a median of 14.4 hours per month in savings. An ATS will also automate a career page connection, automatically email candidates, track them through the hiring process, and allow compliance and ROI reporting. Depending on the system, it can cost from $50,000 to $150,000 to put in. The managers' time needs to be highly valuable (e.g., $250 per hour) to make this a break-even move for a small business unless they really need those compliance reports, are in a tightly regulated industry, had government contracts, etc. For most small businesses, an ATS makes good financial sense once hiring reaches 100 full-time or 300 part-time employees per year, or if the company is so understaffed that managers simply cannot absorb this time and therefore contract recruiters are doing a lot of manual tracking in Excel.

For companies that hire at scale (10,000-plus per year), other modules that are normally optional add-ons to the ATS start to make sense. For each 10,000 hires at a company with a strong brand there might be 1 million applicants, so an AI screening tool to automate résumé review can save hundreds of hours of recruiter or contractor time (some companies hire contractors to source and screen initial candidate slates). At larger organizations a small change to usage of manager time scales quickly, so standardized employment testing that improves the ratio of interviews to hires becomes valuable, and a TA team can justify a new hire survey to generate performance criteria around quality of hire without waiting for an annual review or relying on a criterion of retention alone. Larger companies can also take advantage of smaller effect sizes from hiring a social media recruitment specialist to post jobs and do search engine optimization to drive traffic. At large-scale companies that hire 500,000 per year or more (e.g., Walmart, Amazon), even smaller improvements to the recruiting process are cost-justifiable (e.g., automating laptop procurement for new hires, onboarding plans, security clearances).

When considering a new ATS component, a TA team can check ROI by looking for:

1. *Adoption rates*—anticipated degree of cultural acceptance (e.g., how it will be received, how I will sell it, learning curve)
2. *Cost*—time and money involved for set-up and maintenance
3. *Metric impact*—impact on recruiter/requisition productivity, time to fill, candidate experience, EVP, application rates, quality of applicants, Service Level Agreements, response times, downtimes, etc.
4. *Systems integration*—implications for payroll, benefits enrollment, new hire training, compliance filing, GDPR, etc.

Deep Dive: AI

AI is at the cutting edge of recruiting technology today and offers an interesting path forward, with standard tools and practices just beginning to emerge and compete. Josh Bersin (2023) compared the likely impact of AI to the cloud and mobile in terms of level of technological disruption. While a detailed review of AI standards and use in selection is beyond the scope of this book, I will briefly discuss use cases, evaluation principles, tips for DEI, and fundamental AI concepts and will offer several examples of how to apply AI in the recruitment process. Due to the current pace of innovation in the AI space, the user should expect significant change after publication of this chapter.

Here are some potential use cases for AI in recruiting:

1. Develop profiles of a candidate for whom a role would be attractive prior to sourcing
2. Create personas for EVPs
3. Analyze pay versus benchmarks when selecting a job title (and offer alternative titles)
4. Auto-populate onboarding plans
5. Build competency guides

AI offers significant benefits to the ATS. In the past, the ATS tool could only do keyword searches, but integrated AI allows automation of far more sophisticated algorithms for selecting a candidate from internal and external applicants, and even predicting when a position may become available. The volume of online applications and access to passive candidates in social media creates incentives for the automation trend to continue in recruiting, as an automated AI surfacing tool makes it easier for recruiters to find candidates and for AI tools to surface potentially suitable jobs to candidates to encourage applications. AI has the potential here to increase talent pools for hiring organizations, broadening and deepening sources of talent while simultaneously providing cost-free visibility to candidates about jobs and companies they might never have considered. For example, uploading a résumé in Word or Acrobat or even just the URL to a LinkedIn page allows some ATS tools to auto-upload all the work experience, dates, and education information, allowing the candidate to simply review it for accuracy and then click submit, making it a low-effort way to apply for many jobs. This can result in high volumes of applications to manage, but it also appeals to more passive candidates who are not motivated to spend 30 minutes on completing a job application. The challenge then becomes managing the ratio of qualified candidates to total applicants. If the AI is sending a lot of spam to either candidates (unsuitable job postings) or hiring organizations (unqualified applicants to sift through), then it is likely to be tweaked or dropped from the hiring process.

When you couple the competing demands of increased hiring volume and decreased recruiter headcount, AI and other automation tools will continue to see development, especially as organizations get better at addressing their weaknesses, such as what data they use to train the algorithms (see Chapter 6 for more on this issue). Previously, AI algorithms showed the same bias against diverse candidates that was reflected in many organizations in terms of lower representation of diverse talent at higher levels and with lower performance ratings. If clean, accurate criteria for selection can be developed and workflow metrics are available so that recruiting leaders can check each step of the pipeline for impact on the diversity of the candidate pool, this could open up the promise of AI's power in this domain.

For example, recruiters could track data on the diversity of an initial candidate pool, then see if diverse talent was proportionally moving on to the screening calls, then to the assessment phase, then to the onsite or hiring manager virtual interviews, then to the offer, then to offer acceptance. Seeing where in this pipeline diverse populations are disproportionately not moving on will tell you where to inspect. If you have a lack of diverse populations in the pipeline in the first place, check the labor pool and your sourcing strategies (see Chapter 3 for more). Because AI data now uses emails, texts, chats, assessments, résumé content, and even social media to determine candidate attractiveness, it is important to build bias detection into the technology itself. In terms of pure predictive power, AI for selection has been found to be at least as accurate as multiple regression models for predicting outcomes. Landers, Auer, Dunk, Langer, and Tran (2023) ran simulations on actual scores from 1.2 billion validation-study participants and examined thousands of different selection systems and scoring approaches. Modern machine learning (MML) techniques used by AI offered similar predictive power to multiple regression in most scenarios but were able to do so in many cases by dropping predictors, which simplified the model. One practical suggestion emerging from their work is to stick with MML to predict performance instead of psychometric scale composites in smaller sample sizes or when you have many scales. Their rule of thumb is to choose MML over regression when the ratio of sample size to scale count is less than 3.

Generative AI is experiencing high growth at the time of this writing, with ChatGPT becoming the fastest-growing app ever as of summer 2023 (Chui et al., 2023): over 100 million users in only two months. "Generative AI" refers to a class of AI models and algorithms that can create new content, including text, images, or videos, using rules and summations from a training dataset. As always, the key is to feed the AI good, representative data with sufficient variance and sample size. Google's Gemini (or Med-PaLM specifically for medical domain), Microsoft's GPT-4 which can write emails and generate code, and Kosmos-1, which can respond to image and audio prompts), Meta (LLaMA is small but efficient), and Amazon's Bedrock which lets you customize models and build agents all collect and sell data as foundational data models. These models are based on deep learning techniques, particularly generative models, which aim to mimic the creative and pattern-recognition abilities of the human brain. These models allow generative AI chatbots to perform a wide range of tasks and can be used by users who do not have a deep background in ML. Risks include the fact that the AI model sometimes generates fictitious sources when asked to do a literature review, or imaginary information for a biography. The training data includes only open-source information, so research published behind a paywall is not included. Transformers are key components of foundation models—GPT stands for generative pretrained transformer. A transformer is a type of artificial neural network that is trained using deep learning, a term that alludes to the many (deep) layers within neural networks. Deep learning has powered many of the recent advances in AI. A type of foundation model called a large language model can be trained on vast amounts of text that is publicly available on the internet and covers many different topics. While other deep learning models can operate on sizable amounts of unstructured data, they are usually trained on a more specific dataset. For example, a model might be trained on a specific set of images to enable it to recognize certain objects in photographs.

Evaluating the fairness of AI models is a concern in this rapidly growing field. Landers and Behrend (2023) offer an evaluation framework for HR teams planning to develop or apply AI tools. See their article for more specifics on the 12 components underlying these three broad lenses:

1. *Individual attitudes*—assess the procedural, distributive, and interactional justice perceptions toward the AI model and its recommendations
2. *Legality, ethicality, and morality*—applies the American Psychological Association (APA) ethical principles and current federal law, such as Title VII of the Civil Rights Act, to assess fairness in AI decisions
3. *Technical domain embedded meanings*—describe psychometric errors, such as error of estimates and differential prediction

Fundamental AI Concepts

When people say "use AI," what is it and how does it work? While a comprehensive treatment is beyond the scope of this chapter, I will introduce some key concepts. First, we will review how a commonly used generative AI model (generative adversarial network [GAN]) works.

- **Training data:** The first step in building a generative AI model is to gather a large dataset of the type of content the model will generate. This is commonly purchased (e.g., from Amazon, Google, or Microsoft) and can be part of an Amazon Web Services (AWS) offering when buying cloud services. Purchase a training set that will equip your AI to answer the questions and develop the capabilities you need.
- **Model architecture:** The model's architecture is designed to capture patterns and representations present in the training data. For GANs, the two primary components are the generator and the discriminator.

- *Generator*: The generator creates new content that mimics the patterns and characteristics found in the training data. During training, the generator gradually improves its ability to produce more realistic content.
- *Discriminator*: The discriminator is a separate neural network that is trained to distinguish between real data from the training set and fake data generated by the generator. Its goal is to become better at differentiating between real and generated content.
- **Adversarial training:** This phase involves a competition between the generator and the discriminator where the generator attempts to produce content realistic enough to fool the discriminator into thinking it is real data. At the same time, the discriminator attempts to more accurately separate real cases/data from fake cases/data. This competition continues, with both improving, until convergence is achieved.
- **Convergence:** This is reached when the generator becomes so proficient at creating realistic content that it is nearly indistinguishable from real data, and the discriminator struggles to spot the difference. This is the point at which a generative AI model is considered ready for use in production.
- **Generating new content:** Once the GAN model is trained, the generator can take random noise as input and generate new content. For example, if the model was trained on text, the generator could generate new sentences that resemble the writing style and patterns found in the training data.

Generative AI models can be further fine-tuned and controlled to generate content with specific attributes or follow certain constraints, making them incredibly versatile for creative applications, content generation, and data augmentation in various fields. One limitation of generative AI models is that they are very resource-intensive, requiring substantial computational power, skilled staff, and training data to produce high-quality results.

Example Usage—ChatGPT

ChatGPT (from OpenAI) is an example of generative AI that offers many potential game-changing applications for recruiting. For example, for the prompt "Provide a short job description for a software engineer that will appeal to candidates who might want to work at Amazon," the AI response is shown in Table 5.1.

Table 5.1 AI Job Description

Job Title: Software Engineer—Innovative Solutions at Amazon

Are you passionate about pushing the boundaries of technology to create groundbreaking solutions that impact millions of customers worldwide? If you thrive in a fast-paced, dynamic environment and want to be part of an innovative team that drives global change, then Amazon's Software Engineer position might be the perfect fit for you!

About Us: Amazon is the world's leading e-commerce and cloud computing company, revolutionizing the way people shop and interact online. Our commitment to customer obsession drives us to constantly challenge the status quo and invent new ways to enhance the customer experience.

Job Overview: As a Software Engineer on the Innovative Solutions team at Amazon, you will play a pivotal role in developing cutting-edge technologies that redefine customer interactions and propel our business to new heights. You will work alongside some of the brightest minds in the industry and collaborate on projects that span various domains, from supply chain optimization to personalized recommendations.

Key Responsibilities:
- Design and implement scalable and high-performance software solutions that solve complex technical challenges.
- Collaborate with cross-functional teams to identify business requirements and translate them into practical, robust software solutions.
- Participate in the complete software development lifecycle, from ideation and design to deployment and maintenance.
- Innovate and explore emerging technologies to improve system efficiency and performance continuously.
- Conduct thorough testing and debugging to ensure the quality, reliability, and security of our software products.
- Contribute to code reviews and provide constructive feedback to fellow team members.

Required Qualifications:
- Bachelor's or Master's degree in Computer Science, Software Engineering, or a related technical field.
- Proficiency in one or more programming languages (e.g., Java, C++, Python) and experience with object-oriented design principles.
- Strong understanding of data structures, algorithms, and software design patterns.
- Proven track record of delivering scalable and reliable software applications.
- Ability to work in a collaborative and agile environment, adapting quickly to changing priorities.
- Excellent problem-solving and communication skills.

Preferred Qualifications:
- Experience with cloud computing platforms, such as Amazon Web Services (AWS).
- Familiarity with distributed systems and large-scale data processing.
- Knowledge of machine learning concepts and their practical applications.
- Previous experience in e-commerce or retail-related technology.

Join Us: At Amazon, we value diversity and foster a culture of innovation, where every idea counts and everyone's voice is heard. Join our dynamic team, and together, let's shape the future of commerce and revolutionize the way the world shops!

ChatGPT can also be used for just-in-time onboarding. For example, a generative AI tool might suggest upselling opportunities to the newly hired salesperson in real time based on the actual content of the conversation, drawing from internal customer data, external market trends, and social media influencer data (Chui et al., 2023). This could greatly accelerate the time to productivity and improve performance.

A risk of ChatGPT's training set, which is a large language model (LLM), is that it can be prone to "hallucination," or answering questions with plausible but untrue assertions. Generative AI is also currently unsuited for directly analyzing large amounts of tabular data, or solving advanced numerical-optimization problems. Other risks cited by Chui and colleagues (2023) and Kim-Schmid and Raveendhran (2022) include privacy, fairness, intellectual property, and security, and there could even be liability for a company if its AI exhibits bias in material decisions. As a user, I am sometimes frustrated that ChatGPT refuses to form a judgment or opinion as to the best option even if it is given weighted decision criteria, and, of course, if the training data does not include proprietary content behind a paywall, that will be reflected in ChatGPT's product.

ChatGPT is already very helpful for other applications. For instance, automated job postings take only seconds to generate and can be edited and customized, resulting in much higher productivity in creating job postings. Companies with the necessary data architecture, technical skill base, and risk management processes will be able to embed AI functionality in many aspects of HR, significantly enhancing productivity.

ATS and AI in Gamification and Selection

An important area within hiring involves selection assessment/employment testing. Selection assessment is well covered by other volumes in the Professional Practice series (e.g., Tippins & Adler, 2011), so a detailed discussion is beyond the scope of this book. However, a key part of recruiting technology includes screening questions built into the ATS or even the job posting vendor. Naturally these must pass all the usual APA and SIOP guidelines for job-relevant, validated selection procedures, just as interviews do. The trend appears to be further integration of assessment with TA (e.g., testing platforms like Quintela compatible with Success Factors, Workday, Oracle, etc.). Some recruiting technology could be considered to include gamified assessment tools (e.g., HireVue), and some of the technology gains are about integrating automation into scoring and interviewing processes, as in HackerRank. Video games are a $138 billion industry and are popular among younger candidate demographics, especially in high-demand technology jobs. Gamified hiring elements contribute to perceptions of an organization's brand, adding a "cool factor" that can be important in attracting in-demand candidates; however, games can be expensive and time-consuming to develop. In the early 2010s hiring games offered limited plotlines and were sometimes only graphical or video versions of multiple-choice tests. In 2022 games are combining situational judgment with simulated scenarios to immerse candidates in the stories and allow a variety of responses. The feel of new hiring games is closer to interactive "edutainment" training approaches that can be found from Skillsoft or in immersive experiences. "Edutainment," a blend of entertainment and traditional learning/education, can include gaming, films, or even physical toys designed to integrate fun into training. Gamified hiring can be applied to selection in sample use cases such as competitive gaming using variations of Tetris (for hiring packers in logistics centers), virtual combat (Army), or store management (mall retail). Games may tap constructs like risk tolerance, decision-making under time pressure, resource allocation, or short-term memory, all of which can map to job-related constructs. Like any selection device, games must be carefully developed and validated for the roles they seek to fill, checked for adverse impact, and reviewed regularly. Games can be less efficient than other AI-driven mass scanning approaches. Games can also create a "fun" impression, so if your employment brand or industry requires a more serious orientation, then they may not be the best choice.

In the TA space, technology developers are leveraging the competitiveness of recruiters to apply gamification to performance. One example of the SaaS options for this includes niche products like Spinify or Engagedly that use points systems, badges, and recognition to provide incentives for internal recruiter competition. Earning badges for completing training, hitting a number of referrals, meeting an SLA, or getting good candidate feedback can motivate and even retain recruiters as well as create proxy performance measures. Recruiter productivity is a key focus for fast-growing teams, and gamified approaches such as earning a cool icon next to your name in the online phone directory or in your training transcript can both motivate and contribute to a fun work environment while simultaneously allowing leaders to manage performance.

Other ATS Add-ons

Chatbots

Chatbot software allows automated responses based on an AI parsing text, which can include a simple keyword search. The chatbot may go beyond responses to performing simple tasks (such as scheduling an interview or collecting basic information) and can offer a step toward mass personalization. A recruitment chatbot may respond to potential hires during off hours, answer common questions, or even ask screening questions tied to a specific requisition while saving labor costs. At this time, savvy users are often able to spot a chatbot, and the goal of creating a positive candidate experience is at risk if the chatbot usage is not judicious. AI Chatbot tools can be included in your ATS or added separately. Microsoft's ChatGPT, IBM's Watson chatbot, or GoHire can be customized to your business. AI chat tools are developing rapidly and use cases change daily. TA leaders should consider where they fit in the portfolio of candidate touch, and where direct human contact offers added value.

Social Media and DEI

Below are two basic approaches for recruiters to consider when sourcing on social media. The first approach involves marketing the requisition you're posting and can include a tool like CareerArc, which will amplify and automatically market your post on X (formerly Twitter) and other sites, getting it front of many more candidates than your career site on the web. These recruitment marketing tools can be used to advertise job openings, engage with candidates, and nurture interest. These systems have social recruiting and CRM capabilities and are typically used to help build talent pipelines as companies grow. See Chapter 2 on building on your employment brand first, as you'll want to select recruitment marketing tools that drive your branding on career sites and job portals and integrate with your ATS.

AI has made important strides in evolving from a powerful tool with a risk of prediction bias to a weapon that can actively reduce bias in job descriptions and ad postings. AI tools like Textio, ChatGPT, or Pymetrics can check job postings for potentially biased language prior to posting. The AI can then suggest rewording alternatives before the post is seen by potential candidates. After the tragic deaths of Breonna Taylor, Ahmaud Arbery, and George Floyd in the summer of 2020, many organizations are more sensitive to the implicit bias in job postings. The cues you could be inadvertently including in a job ad may reduce applications from qualified diverse candidates. How to efficiently check for potential bias? The AI tools mentioned above can be used for ads, text on career sites, and other augmented writing so you can foresee likely responses and even set up alerts for risky wording. Augmented writing searches language patterns in job postings that have good results and suggests them to you. If you want to get started in this space, run your job ad through an online gender decoder, like the free one by Kat Matfield (https://gender-decoder.katmatfield.com/), to do a quick check for potential bias. This tool includes many adjectives and adverbs in its list, so if you paste a job ad into Kat Matfield's gender decoder, apply your good judgment to the list of masculine-coded words identified before editing your ad.

Crowdsourced Video

Companies like Amazon use tools like Seenit to manage video content produced by a user community. A company can use their studio to set up a story concept and invite any users (fans, customers, employees, etc.) with a smartphone to contribute. Once all the contributions are uploaded, the recruiting team can edit them together and make it available on a YouTube channel. Since non-corporate videos about companies can have good credibility with potential candidates and tend to get high engagement with sought-after talent, this can be a useful tool to add to your recruiting technology team. While the recruiting team still must be able to cobble together a story, come up with general guidelines for content creators, and then do the editing, it does save time to have content created for free.

Automating Onboarding

While some companies use their own proprietary onboarding tools (e.g., Amazon's Embark), your organization may want to add a third-party tool to enhance the basics offered in your ATS. Onboarding should be carefully managed to meet the cultural needs of your organization and represent you in the best light to retain new hires and avoid new hire attrition. Tools offer turnkey Application Program Interfacs (APIs) that can often be dropped right into your current process, creating notifications, nudges and checklists for required training, paperwork, people to meet, etc. Electronically triggered based on user-configurable criteria, nudges are a potential new area for automating support and can be particularly useful for new hires or new managers if they are not so frequent as to be tuned out due to overuse. Nudges are like email reminders but specific to a program or product. These preprogrammed nudges include notifications, messages, in-product dialog boxes, or emails to managers to remind them to set up a career discussion, or to begin requests for technical assessment prior to promotions, update successor development plans, etc.

Overall, I anticipate the future of TA to be strongly linked with the adoption of new technology that allows a faster, simpler candidate and hiring manager experience with quicker applications, easier-to-check status, data visualization of hiring metrics, and integration with workforce plans and external tools such as AI and social media. Be intentional in choosing technology tools that will create an experience that is consistent with your employment brand and integrates well with your existing technical architecture and process infrastructure. Different industries and newer or smaller companies may be at different stages of maturity and hence have different candidate expectations, and this should be reflected in the technology choices that offer the candidate a window into your organization's culture. Companies with limited resources in and knowledge of AI should carefully identify where to include it in the hiring processes and consider retaining expert assistance if using it for prediction or other material employment decisions.

References

Axon, S. (2021). Big tech companies are at war with workers over return to work. Ars Technica. https://arstechnica.com/gadgets/2021/08/vaccines-reopenings-and-wor ker-revolts-big-techs-contentious-return-to-the-office/.

Bersin, J. (2023). The role of generative AI and large language models in HR. https://jos hbersin.com/2023/03/the-role-of-generative-ai-and-large-language-models-in-hr/.

Bersin, J., & Enderes, K. (2021). Rise of the talent intelligence platform. https://eightfold. ai/wp-content/uploads/Rise_of_Intelligence_Platform_Bersin.pdf.

Bloom, N., Barrero, J. M., Davis, S., Meyer, B., & Mihaylov, E. (2023). Survey: Remote work isn't going away and executives know it. https://www.shrm.org/executive-netw ork/insights/survey-remote-work-isnt-going-away-executives-know

Cerrato, J., & Freyermuth, J. (2020). Gartner market guide for talent acquisition applications. https://www.gartner.com/doc/reprints?id=124DSFP22&ct=201016&st=sb.

Chui, M., Roberts, R., Rodchenko, T., Singla, A., Sukharevsky, A., Yee, L., & Zurkiya, D. (2023). What every CEO should know about generative AI. https://www.mckinsey. com/capabilities/mckinsey-digital/our-insights/what-every-ceo-should-know-about-generative-ai.

Cocca, N. (2019). Ten trends in AR recruitment technology for 2019. https://recruitingda ily.com/10-trends-in-ai-recruitment-technology-for-2019/

Heger, B. (2024). Return to Office Updates. Gartner (2020) survey of 130 HR leaders found that 90% intended to allow at least partial work-from-home options for remote workers.

HireVue. (2022, February). Global trends report: The state of talent experience 2022. https://www.hirevue.com/resources/report/report-hirevue-2022-global-trends-report.

Kim-Schmid, J., & Raveendhran, R. (2022). Where AI can and can't help talent management. *Harvard Business Review*. https://hbr.org/2022/10/where-ai-can-and-cant-help-talent-management.

Landers, R. N., & Behrend, T. S. (2023). Auditing the AI auditors: A framework for evaluating fairness and bias in high stakes AI predictive models. *American Psychologist, 78*(1), 36–49. https://doi.org/10.1037/amp0000972.

Landers, R. N., Auer, E. M., Dunk, L., Langer, M., & Tran, K. N. (2023). A simulation of the impacts of machine learning to combine psychometric employee selection system predictors on performance prediction, adverse impact, and number of dropped predictors. *Personnel Psychology, 76*(4), 1037–1060.

Mondal, S. (2021). The top 25 recruiting software tools of 2021. https://ideal.com/top-recruiting-software/.

Ongig (2020). Top Applicant Tracking Systems. https://blog.ongig.com/applicant-tracking-system/top-applicant-tracking-systems-ats-software-2020/

Popovic, J. (2020). Survey: More than half of companies hired new staff remotely during the pandemic. https://rh-us.mediaroom.com/2020-09-30-Survey-More-Than-Half-Of-Companies-Hired-New-Staff-Remotely-During-The-Pandemic.

Sethi, B. (2020). 23rd Annual Global CEO Panel Survey. https://www.pwc.com/gx/en/ceo-survey/2020/reports/pwc-23rd-global-ceo-survey.pdf

Shufran, L. (2021). Reflections, initiatives, predictions.https://lp.gem.com/2021-recruiting-reflections-initiatives-predictions-ws.html.

Tippins, N. T., & Adler, S. (2011) (Eds.). *Technology-enhanced assessment of talent*. San Francisco: Jossey-Bass.

Zhao, D. (2019). The rise of mobile devices in job search. https://www.glassdoor.com/research/app/uploads/sites/2/2019/06/Mobile-Job-Search-1.pdf.

6

Talent Metrics and Analytics in a Sea of Data

Alexis A. Fink
Meta
Tanya Delany
Philip Morris International
Jay Steffensmeier
Amazon

As seen in the previous chapter, advances in technology have spurred tremendous evolution across the landscape of talent practices but particularly in the area of talent acquisition (TA). Technology has profoundly changed how candidates and jobs find and evaluate one another, altering every stage of the recruitment and selection process. In this chapter, we will consider TA measurement and analytics, exploring how selected advances in technology have substantially changed what is possible in terms of both the effectiveness and efficiency of TA. We will describe new data sources made possible by advances in technology, as well as exploring the fundamentals of staffing process measurement and selection analytics.

The Evolving World of TA

The past decade has seen a dramatic explosion in analytics and technology applied to talent opportunities in organizations. Perhaps the most obvious change to TA measurement and analytics with the advent of technology is the explosion of variables to consider (the "sea of data"). Some of these have changed the process of recruitment, selection, and job consideration for both candidates and employees, and some more directly inform one party or the other.

Alexis A. Fink, Tanya Delany, and Jay Steffensmeier, *Talent Metrics and Analytics in a Sea of Data* In: *Becoming a Talent Magnet*. Edited by: Mark A. Morris, Oxford University Press. © Oxford University Press 2024.
DOI: 10.1093/oso/9780190938512.003.0006

Technologies that enhance the information available on the employer side include text analytics such as natural language processing (NLP), artificial intelligence (AI), pre-employment tests, simulations, video evaluations, and "digital exhaust." Text analytics and AI can be used to automatically and efficiently evaluate candidates' capabilities, based on their résumé, work sample, formal application, or other available and relevant information, and may act as a complement or supplement to the traditional résumé or application form. These technologies can also ingest and categorize the information present in a job posting, as well as the characteristics of successful incumbents or recent successful hires into the role. These techniques can evaluate large bodies of work-related documents to build engines that can infer adjacent skills that might not be mentioned but are likely present, moving far beyond a standard keyword search in the ability to source quality talent and reduce false negatives in the sourcing process. They can then match candidates to available roles where they are likely to succeed.

As new data sources and analytic techniques become available, it is critical for TA professionals to remain vigilant about protecting ethics and privacy. Candidate information must be gathered, analyzed, and stored thoughtfully, ensuring that only relevant and actionable data for which appropriate consent has been given is used. Further, it is worth noting that many of the techniques and advances discussed in this chapter are only relevant at scale, where an organization may need to evaluate and hire many hundreds or thousands of employees into a job or family of jobs. In those cases, appropriate validity evidence and proof of fairness (e.g., absence of adverse impact) for the specific jobs under examination can be demonstrated and monitored over time. Techniques that simply render an assessment of an individual without solid evidence of job relatedness and fairness for the job under consideration should not be used.

New Approaches to Data and Evaluation

Advances in technology and sophistication have combined in recent years to significantly enhance recruitment and selection work. Simulations have moved far beyond the inbox exercises of past decades. Videos can now remove scheduling barriers by making interviews asynchronous, as well as more efficient through the use of technology to transcribe and analyze the content of the interview. Digital processes mean that organizations have additional data about the ways candidates are engaging with their organization and the recruitment process. Examination of social patterns through organization network analysis (ONA) can help identify new types of talent-relevant patterns, and candidates can learn a great deal about what it's like to work at various organizations. Organizations can make their recruitment and assessment processes more engaging through gamification. Together, these innovations have substantially improved selection and recruiting for organizations and candidates.

Simulations

Simulations continue to evolve to meet candidates where they are (i.e., mobile delivery), providing realistic previews of the jobs to which they are applying while measuring skills and abilities shown to be predictive of on-the-job performance. Virtual and augmented reality hold the potential to create simulations with very high fidelity to real job tasks, particularly those that are risky, as well as providing some immediacy in response without revealing potentially sensitive demographic information such as race, ethnicity, gender, or disability to the interviewer. However, in many cases augmented and virtual reality still require special equipment that can be cumbersome and that may not be available to all individuals, particularly those who may be economically disadvantaged or who may lack access to the high-speed internet typically required for such platforms to function effectively.

In particular, simulations and augmented or virtual reality have significant potential to mitigate for disability. However, if poorly designed, these same systems may exclude some persons with disabilities. Careful consideration of accessibility is important when designing and potentially choosing simulations or augmented reality experiences as part of a selection process.

Video Assessment

Video assessments are providing new sources of job-related data through richer information, and the ability of machine learning models to more thoroughly assess a larger number of candidates that a human recruiter could through screening calls. When paired with technology to translate text to speech and analyze the resulting text, it is possible to create summaries or assessments of the responses given, which can yield efficiency for the recruiter, and potentially limit bias as the recruiter may not have demographic information attached to the candidate record. However, virtual interviews also create risk in that AI can detect variables that are not appropriate to consider as part of most selection processes, such as some speech patterns or facial symmetry. Virtual interviewing, or indeed any assessment, that uses a "black box" to evaluate candidates creates risk that inappropriate variables are being incorporated into candidate scores; we still have an obligation to ensure that only relevant and nondiscriminatory criteria are used in evaluating candidates even when these techniques are used.

Candidate Behavior

Candidate digital exhaust, the record of behavior on the job search site, such as time spent, number of jobs applied to, number of visits, and so on, can also provide information related to job success. Indeed, with enough cases, even very small effects can become statistically significant, and tempting to include in an effort to gain as much precision in prediction as possible. However, this remains an area of potential concern. Where many may approach the problem of predicting job success from a purely quantitative lens, requirements such as the Uniform Guidelines for Selection Procedures (Uniform Guidelines) require a higher standard than simple prediction. The burden of proof, then, rests on the employer to ensure that the candidate behavior captured and assessed is indeed job-related and fair as well as predictive of success on the job.

Organization Networks and Social Media

Deloitte's *Global Human Capital Trends* (Deloitte, 2019) survey reported that 48% of companies were experimenting with the use of ONA for a range of purposes. One key use case of ONA is to identify highly connected people who essentially represent untapped expertise and underutilized resources within an organization. When applied to an entire labor market or talent pool (e.g., when applied outside of an organization), ONA may be a way to identify high-potentials or "influencers" earlier in their careers, giving companies a head start in acquiring them as talent. Solutions like these are sometimes proposed as a means to surface passive candidates who may be interesting to organizations or well suited to particular roles.

As organizations consider technologies such as ONA, it is critical to be mindful of appropriate use of data. The European Union's General Data Protection Regulation (GDPR) requires explicit user consent to develop ONA insights. While ONA insights can be calculated with a proportion of employees not opting in, there is a needed critical mass of employees who give user consent in order to enable acceptable and reliable ONA insights. Thus, while it may be technically possible to produce useful ONA insights for selection purposes, given the nature of ONA, the use cases are likely stronger for other talent management applications, such as discovering high potentials, assigning mentors, or diagnosing organization-level collaboration patterns, rather than for TA.

Social media activity and digital footprints are often suggested as data sources to assess skills and capabilities or risks associated with candidates, although this area of inquiry also raises significant questions around both privacy and efficacy. Social media has been explored as a data source for selection purposes (e.g., Roth, Bobko, Van Iddekinge, & Thatcher, 2016), and, in many cases, those studies are relying on some form of NLP (discussed later in this chapter) as they create indices for the attributes being assessed, such as personality variables. Other attributes have been inferred from metadata, such as the number of connections one has on a given social media platform and the frequency, complexity, variability, or amount of interaction generated by public social media posting behavior. As these tools have become more ubiquitous and embedded in everyday life, additional scrutiny and changing utilization patterns have resulted in mixed findings about their efficacy. As individuals increasingly move toward more digital privacy by using controls to restrict what information is available on the public web, it becomes harder to mine this data source. Additionally, not all social media platforms are similarly situated.

Beyond concerns around veracity, the use of social media data poses several other challenges, specifically around privacy and ethics. Indeed, entire popular social media platforms (e.g., Snapchat) have been built on their very lack of permanence, where posts disappear as soon as they are viewed, leaving no searchable record behind. Candidate perceptions from using their publicly available data to make inferences of measurable attributes will likely differ based on the source. Where the content is professional in nature (e.g., LinkedIn, WeChat), social media data may be seen as fair game by candidates, but there is less candidate acceptance for screening use of social media data that is more personal in nature (e.g., Facebook, Instagram, etc.). These factors combine to limit the effectiveness of these data sources in most situations. Of course, unscrupulous employers (and admissions officers) have been accused of demanding social media passwords for purposes of reviewing private data; we view this practice as intrusive, inappropriate, and to be avoided. Overall, while it may be tempting for recruiters and hiring managers to use social media information as part of a selection process, evidence suggests that it is simply inappropriate for these purposes (e.g., Vosen, 2021).

Candidate Value Proposition

Candidates also enjoy new tools with which to evaluate the attractiveness of a potential employer. Until recently, candidates might have been restricted to asking friends, family, or school alumni "what it's like" at a particular employer, or, for larger or more prominent employers, significant details are available in the many "Best Employers for . . ." lists published by various magazines and organizations, such as Fortune's "Best Companies to Work For." Today, several anonymous websites exist where current and former employees can provide their perspective on a huge range of employers (e.g., Glassdoor, Comparably, Blind). Non-anonymous networking tools like LinkedIn can help job seekers gain realistic job previews from a much larger universe of potential connections. In some industries and geographies, in-person networking and professional development opportunities provide a rich trove of information on employers. Employers, feeling a crunch to recruit high-quality talent, may produce recruiting assets that include video tours, employee profiles, and extensive information about the company's working culture, values, and benefits. Increasingly, savvy candidates may take advantage of all of these opportunities to come to the table with a solid sense of "what it's like to work here," which implies that traditional realistic job previews may decline in value as part of a selection process for tech-savvy candidates. This process offers an opportunity to enhance selection as well, through helping candidates "opt out" proactively if concerns about fit arise during this period of exploration. As a result, candidate experience is a key focus for many recruiters, especially in competitive industries (e.g., technology).

Gamification

Pre-employment tests in some domains can now take the form of highly engaging puzzles and games. Gamification has the benefit of immediate personalized feedback and, depending on the design, can be used to assess the candidate's ability to make effective decisions and consider complex information. It thus can yield insights about a variety of candidate skills and abilities that might be harder to detect and assess through traditional approaches. The use of gamification may increase signal quality on core job-relevant skills that may be hard to determine from a résumé or traditional interview.

The scenarios and answers with game elements might make the expected behaviors less obvious to candidates and, as a result, more difficult to distort or fake than traditional assessment approaches (Nikolaou, Georgiou, & Kotsasarlidou, 2019). However, simply adding game-type elements to an assessment experience is not likely to provide these potential advantages (Landers, 2019). Organizations that are considering using such gamified elements or products must also understand the underlying psychological constructs being measured and require assessment vendors to provide adequate validity evidence when choosing whether and how to use these products. In essence, gamification offers advantages of an engaging candidate experience, process efficiency, and potentially good validity; thoughtfully designed and implemented in a relevant context, it can offer substantial benefits to an organization.

Summary

Advances in technology have created new opportunities to add efficiency and nuance to the process of evaluating candidates, as well as leveling the information inequality between candidate and organization during the selection process. Yet, despite the new and exciting opportunities, TA professionals must remain diligent in ensuring ethical use of data and appropriate variables in selection processes.

Metric and Analytic Foundations

Both metrics and analytics have important roles to play in designing and delivering a powerful, data-driven TA function. Metrics are generally regarded as evaluative in nature, assessing the efficiency, effectiveness, or impact of a product or process (e.g., Boudreau & Ramstad, 2007; Dulebohn & Johnson, 2013). Analytics, on the other hand, are often designed to help inform design decisions. Most organizations have evolved their data-driven talent function over time, moving along a path of increasing sophistication. Several models of this evolution are available, but in general they share a framework moving from simple descriptive and operational reporting to advanced analytic work. A typical progression among these models will include several steps:

1. **Basic reporting**: The first challenge for organizations is to be able to accurately and consistently describe the organization. The focus may be on collecting and ensuring clean data. Typical metrics at this stage in a staffing framework might include pass-through rates at different points in the recruiting funnel, offer conversions and acceptance rates, the number of open requisitions at any given time, time to hire, channel mix, hiring yield, attrition of new hires, and quality of hire. In their simplest form, these reports may be tabular; with increasing sophistication in data management and display, organizations may use elegant data visualizations to convey basic reporting efficiently and effectively.

2. **Advanced reporting**: As organizations gain sophistication, they often look not only to report what is happening but also to evaluate those results. At this stage of sophistication, we begin to see effectiveness and efficiency metrics aligned, such as goal percentage achieved, heat maps, and benchmarking comparisons. The clean data may now be cut or filtered in many ways to answer business questions. Here again, data visualization, such as comparisons to a prior period or to a goal, may be employed to efficiently convey large volumes of information to stakeholders. With the additional context provided in advanced reporting, organizations are better able to make decisions and adjustments to their recruiting strategies.

3. **Analysis**: The next analytic challenge for most organizations is to determine not only what is happening, but also why it is happening. Here, we see organizations beginning to look for meaning in their data, and

organizations at this stage might begin to deploy more sophisticated analytic methods. For example, teams may look for patterns common to their best hires, sourcing effectiveness, or patterns among reasons for declining an offer.

4. **Prediction:** Increasingly, organizations are looking to statistical methods to help them make more informed choices, and prediction is a key maturity stage. At this stage, organizations may engage in analysis to determine how a change in sourcing channels could increase candidate volume, which would be difficult to manage without rightsizing the support staff, or how a change in benefits could negatively impact candidate attraction. Research questions can include sourcing effectiveness, linkage between early engagement and attrition behavior, or connecting the success of new hire onboarding to elements of the hiring process.

5. **Prescription:** As organizations continue to gain sophistication they deploy "sustainable analytic loops." These loops leverage algorithms for ongoing system evaluation, using its data to predict future issues (e.g., future data integrity issues, rise in skill requirements in specific locations) and recommend solutions before the data integrity breaches occur. As the title suggests, this enables the organization to prescribe paths and make effective decisions. Some of these systems may even be fully automated and run in the background, suggesting specific adjustments to humans as situations warrant.

For many large organizations, attrition rates are important to understand and serve as an example of this progression, with the objective being to understand how often and which factors might be contributing to the observed rates. For example, accurate basic reporting at the site, region, and overall organization levels will be useful as an initial step to understanding the employee experience and is necessary to build a foundational dataset that can be used for later modeling. From this, organizational researchers can begin to provide more advanced reporting such as rates and seasonality of attrition in order to better understand how those rates may fluctuate and further benchmark against this data. Merging candidate data with employee retention records will enable the organization to better predict the candidate and situational characteristics leading to attrition, but here again, care must be taken to ensure that appropriate consent is given and data is used and stored ethically. Tracking those interventions will lead to more sustainable analytic loops that will allow decision-makers to make meaningful changes to the recruiting process and/or the employee experience to interrupt those factors and increase the probability of retaining successful employees for longer periods.

Key Analytical Methods and Concepts

A full exploration of statistical methods and concepts is beyond the scope of this chapter, although many useful texts exist (e.g., Cascio, Boudreau & Fink, 2019). However, there are a few methods and concepts that are particularly relevant for staffing and selection work. Additionally, research into selection has additional constraints, beyond those of many other types of projects. While many areas of research can take advantage of any predictor that yields a contribution to accuracy, employment law, notably the Uniform Guideline for Selection Procedures, requires that organizations use only predictors that are relevant to the job.

Increasingly, we are seeing data scientists using a data-first approach to identifying predictors, rather than starting with a job analysis. Traditionally, a theory of what may contribute to job success was proven by laboriously gathering specific structured data to prove a theory. Today, we have the ability to gather and analyze unstructured and structured data, allowing us access to new insights into relationships between predictors and job success.

The risk here is ensuring that researchers remain mindful of the legal and ethical implications around job relatedness and avoidance of bias when developing these models. It is incumbent upon researchers to use methods that allow them to have clarity regarding the items and attributes in predictive models. To use a classic example, zip code/postal code may indeed emerge as a significant predictor of the likelihood that a candidate is offered a job, or of promotion velocity within an organization. However, zip code may also simply encode socioeconomic or other demographic traits status into these models. Similarly, including seemingly innocuous résumé variables, such as a break in employment, might be discriminating illegally against those, typically women, who are more likely to have gaps in employment related to care work, such as caring for a child or older relative. It is critically important to ensure that the variables being included are appropriate, and that the outcomes considered are not only the increased efficiency of prediction, but also the absence of illegal and unethical discrimination against protected groups. Additionally, in an environment where the availability of talent is constrained, organizations cannot afford to decline capable candidates for non–job-related reasons. False negatives can significantly slow hiring.

When well executed, these advanced models can serve to overcome human biases and bring visibility to and exposure by auto-surfacing additional candidates who might not have been considered (e.g., "diamonds in the rough"). This opportunity to overcome human biases holds tremendous promise; however, to do so requires very thoughtful construction of training databases and transparent analyses.

The zip code example does not render all geographic information inappropriate or useless. For example, organizations may wish to consider the locations of key talent pools when deciding where to open a new office or facility, or when building sourcing strategies. This is a talent-relevant decision that uses zip code data but does not discriminate against specific individuals in hiring decisions.

Much of the predictive work described above relies on scaled extraction of data from some form of text, commonly including interviews and résumés or experience profiles. Advances in computing power have enabled a transformation in the accuracy and availability of text analytics over the past decade. Machines can now greatly expedite the assessment of candidates' skills and experiences, leading to more efficient matching of candidates to jobs. Additionally, advanced NLP can support staffing function process improvements, such as chatbots to manage candidate scheduling.

NLP is a general term for a family of methods that deconstruct unstructured written content and extract meaning from the component parts (e.g., Dutta & O'Rourke, 2020). Deploying NLP not only massively increases speed but also, with well-constructed training sets, can remove bias and increase accuracy. By grouping families of related skills and capabilities, NLP can match candidates to roles in a way that traditional keyword searches cannot, thus reducing the number of false negatives, and expanding the pool of candidates for consideration. That is, NLP can "understand" that, for example, candidates who list regression on their résumé are also likely to be able to perform machine learning, a related skill, where a traditional keyword search would likely miss that candidate. As long as the training sets and methodologies have been carefully constructed and checked to avoid building in biases, the addition of NLP can dramatically increase organizations' ability to find additional qualified candidates from within their existing candidate pools.

Ultimately, the purpose of analysis is to inform decision-making. In most cases, that will require not only an assessment of whether a given assessment or business process is efficient and effective, but also whether it is more efficient or more effective than other alternatives. This leads us to consider concepts such as utility and return on investment (ROI; e.g., Cascio, 1996).

Managing the TA Function

In addition to the data and analytics available to evaluate candidates, there are a host of variables and analytic considerations around the process of operating a recruiting function. At a minimum, most organizations will monitor metrics such as time to fill, offer accept rate, cost per hire, and the average recruiting load carried by individual recruiters. Determining the optimal number of recruiters, sourcers, recruiting coordinators, and interviewers, for example, is an important function for a growing organization and often ties directly to workforce planning initiatives. Recruiting organizations may be asked to estimate the anticipated attrition in the coming year to plan appropriately for replacement hiring. A strong recruiting function will do each of the following in this context:

- Identifying which content areas to address at which stage of the recruiting funnel for a specific role or family of roles
- Establishing best practices and resources like interview questions and skills assessments for interviewers
- Monitoring candidate value proposition information such as decline reasons

High volumes of data are creating exciting new opportunities but also new challenges. Specifically, new data streams require architecting data storage in a way that is accessible and efficient and protects candidate data privacy appropriately. The 2016 passage of the GDPR in Europe and similar regulations emerging in different jurisdictions are creating new standards for protecting and in some cases removing data.

One critical implication for staffing organizations is the deletion of candidate data rather than maintaining it indefinitely. Further, any organizations that wish to use candidate data to improve their own processes (e.g., using it as training data for model development) must be thoughtful in their disclosures. Finally, specific to diversity data, organizations must tread carefully regarding what data to collect and store regarding which candidates in which geographies. It is critical to consult with your legal representatives as local requirements vary widely.

Most treatment of selection from the perspective of industrial/organizational (I/O) psychology begins and ends with the technical aspects of prediction. For organizations, however, the ability to effectively manage the staffing function overall is at least as important. Fortunately, as technology has genuinely revolutionized the practice of staffing, it has created enormous opportunity to extract insight and carefully manage the function for efficiency and effectiveness.

The nature of identifying, evaluating, selecting, and dispositioning candidates offers a host of data along a process with several discrete steps. Large organizations may hire tens of thousands of individuals each year, and their applicant databases might contain millions of records. Making sense of all that data and moving the best-qualified individuals efficiently through that system, while ensuring fairness and a positive candidate experience, is a tremendous task.

Most staffing functions will consider metrics across major categories—cost, time, volume or yield, diversity and EEO compliance, customer or constituent reactions, quality of hire, and value impact of talent (Cascio, Boudreau & Fink, 2019). For example, cost metrics might include advertising costs, event costs, assessment costs, any travel costs to participate in the interview, and the time value of any sourcers, recruiters, or schedulers involved in the recruitment process (Table 6.1). An obvious and traditional time metric is time to hire or time to fill (TTF), which is the time that elapses from the time a requisition is opened to the start date of the new employee. Some companies have adopted a time to accept (TTA) metric in place of TTF, especially in highly competitive labor markets where organizations often are recruiting passive candidates who may need to relocate or require more time before starting. TTA therefore better describes the attraction elements of the hiring company without the masking effects of a hard-to-fill role and enables more standardized recruiter productivity scorecards. For normal roles at a high-performing company, one expect typical recruiters to handle 20 open requisitions at any one time (in different stages) and hire two people per month. For executive roles and hard-to-fill roles, this can drop to below one hire per month.

Table 6.1 Common Staffing Metrics

Metric	Definition	Purpose
Time to fill	Number of days from job opening to new employee start	Time
Time to accept	Number of days from job requisition being posted to signed offer letter	Time
Time to first day	Number of days from offer to new hire start date	Time
Cost per hire	Ratio of dollars spent per job filled	Cost
Interviewer hours per candidate	Ratio of total number of hours spent by interviewers divided by total number of candidates. Useful for tracking opportunity cost for the business/recruiting and projecting future interviewer demand.	Cost
Exception rates	Percentage of offers that must have compensation outside the normal range to get an accept	Cost
Time to productivity	Number of days from new hire start to reaching typical productivity	Quality
Quality of hire	Can include defect rates (percentage with lowest performance rating, percentage who leave within six months) or preliminary performance rating or "would rehire" from hiring manager	Quality
Diversity, equity, and inclusion (DEI)	Percentage of slates with a diverse candidate interviewed onsite	Quality
Interview to offer conversion ratio/ Offer acceptance rates	Most commonly used to identify average number of candidates receiving offers divided by total number of candidates interviewed. This can also be created for any step in the hiring process where candidate decisions are made. Can also be intern conversion rates. Trends can show attractiveness of brand.	Yield
Recruiter productivity	Rolling 12-month average number of new hires starting per month from this recruiter's "owned" requisitions	Yield
Sourcing productivity	Percentage of acceptances from initial sourcing pool of candidates personally contacted	Yield
Fill mix	Percentage of internal fills by job level and job family	Yield
Candidate experience	Survey items such as "likely to recommend company to other candidates"; offer accept rates; percentage of candidates who were informed of hiring decision within five days, etc.	Branding

Quality metrics might include both quality of hire and the impact to product or outcome quality based on the skills and capabilities of new hires. Quality of hire has a myriad of definitions and no common understanding in the literature for what is being measured within organizations, nor is there a common prescription of what *to* measure.

When operationalizing the quality of hiring decisions it is important to separate the organization's appetite for quality of new hire performance versus quality of the hiring system itself. Quality of the hiring system is seen through process efficiency in reaching the right hires as well as indexes of candidate engagement. Quality of the hiring decision can be measured by success in performing the tasks of the job, lowered attrition rates, and proxies of performance available via organizational metrics (e.g., sales quota attainment, manager performance ratings).

Common metrics across candidate populations (e.g., hourly vs. salaried, technical vs. non-technical, university vs. experienced hires, internal transfers vs. external hires) are only as good as they are comparable. A challenge faced by practitioners is the ability to understand the underlying source of the data and the confidence that is collected accurately and systematically. Within-role variation in the recruiting cycle must also be known in order to accurately make decisions. University recruiting functions will likely have an annual cadence of pre-employment recruiting activities and new employee start dates. These new hires will be most effectively treated as cohorts. Where these same job roles are filled by both university and non-university hiring sources, care must be taken to understand how the cohorts interact with organizational phenomena (e.g., formal performance reviews). These within-role hiring channels will not be accurately comparable without some treatment of the confounds that cohort hiring brings.

Candidate attitudes and reactions to an organization's hiring process are also a key input to managing the TA function, particularly in markets where talent is scarce or in high demand. The ability to attract candidates with the necessary skills for an organization is critical to ensuring that an organization can deliver on its goals. Candidates' first direct experience with an organization is often through the recruiting function; thus, a well-organized, efficient, effective, and engaging hiring process is important to an organization's ability to hire high-quality candidates and fulfill its mission.

As with most metrics, an over-reliance on any single metric can create unintended consequences in another area. For example, a firm can dramatically reduce time to hire by removing hiring criteria but in the process might create significant challenges with candidate quality. Effective organizations must thoughtfully consider their entire universe of measurement and make intentional tradeoffs to manage these tensions.

In addition to these common overall metrics, many organizations find value in examining individual steps in their recruiting funnels. In particular, candidates who decline to move forward with an organization can be a valuable source of feedback regarding features such as external sentiment, competitiveness of compensation, benefits, career potential, work environment, or other key elements of the employee value proposition or working conditions. The ability to extract narrower and narrower proxies of the candidate experience can be used by recruiting teams to inform tactical decisions and will be critical to inform system-level decisions. Outcomes at a later stage can be a source of information for modifying prior stages. For example, conversion of onsite interviews to full-time offers and acceptance rates of those offers can be compared and used as a set of criteria to evaluate prior efficacy of recruiting activities or changes in compensation. Developing systems by which recruiters can easily record factors that contribute to a candidate's decision to decline can help inform an organization's talent and recruiting strategies proactively.

Practitioners in employee selection will often look to traditional utility analyses to quantify changes in validity for new selection methods (e.g., Boudreau & Ramstad, 2003; Cascio, Boudreau, & Fink, 2019). While important for practitioners, their usefulness in influencing organizational decision-makers is questionable (Drasgow, Nye, & Tay, 2010). These analyses tend to isolate the estimated opportunity cost or monetary savings of one selection component compared to using a selection component with lesser validity in the same stage. While useful, it ignores the broader systemic effects on the recruiting system itself (Cascio & Boudreau, 2011). Concrete savings such as interviewer time or recruiter time when more valid *and* more efficient recruiting methods are being proposed can be more attractive to organizational stakeholders. Simply supplying efficiencies to the business can free recruiters and interviewers to engage in potentially more valuable activities for the organization (Cascio & Boudreau, 2011). Repetitive elements of a hiring process that can be automated should generally be automated if there is no cost in terms of effectiveness, legal risks, diversity, or other valued outcomes. However, not all changes to a selection system will be more efficient. Showing the value in increased performance, longer tenure, or similar outcomes can help to bridge this gap. The Uniform Guidelines recognizes reduction of attrition as a valid criterion to consider in validation studies.

Bringing Metrics and Analytics to Life

Once the data is collected, it needs to be understood and presented to the end users and stakeholders who will then move from data-driven insights to actions. Historically, creating these reports was time- and resource-intensive. The emergence of real-time cloud-based business intelligence reporting tools has changed the data reporting game, making insights available instantly and visually easier for decision-makers to grasp difficult concepts or identify new patterns. A well-designed dashboard should not only show the summaries, trends, and analysis of the data but should also let the users take action on that data. Based on our experience and frequent benchmarking with global Fortune 500 companies, the current state of maturity is usually a mass of web-based reporting tools with many filters and cuts, usually exported to a spreadsheet. Investing in visualization represents a key opportunity for recruiting organizations. When developing a dashboard, consider the following in deciding what to present:

1. **Know your key metrics.** Before you build the dashboard, know what metrics are important for your audience and how they tie to critical business performance metrics like sales, profits, productivity, etc. In many cases, organizations have different metrics updated on different cadences (e.g., hourly, daily, weekly, monthly, or quarterly). It is important to ensure that your dashboard's update schedule is coordinated with the cadence of the underlying data. Additionally, a top-line label might be calculated in many different ways. For example, organizations may use cost centers to define hiring pipelines in some cases, or use job codes in other cases. Precision and transparency in definitions is critical. Clarity regarding the formula, source, operational definitions, and any unique quirks for your organization will help data professionals build credibility and do good quality control to ensure the data for these metrics are clean and accurate.

2. **Know your audience.** The universe of available metrics is vast. A good deal of effective data and metrics work is in ensuring that the data presented is relevant and compelling for the specific audience being addressed. The data that is relevant for the operational owners of a process will likely need to be more granular than that for executive stakeholders. Good design will be visually appealing, intuitive, and

clearly focused on the information that is meaningful or required to make decisions. Further, audiences differ in their technical sophistication and in the nature of metrics used in operational areas of the business. Professionals can increase their impact by thoughtfully incorporating the organization's data habits into their own data-sharing strategies. In many cases, this will be simple, such as counts, ratios, or percentages.

In working with dashboards, deciding how to present data is nearly as important as identifying what data to include in the first place. Several excellent primers on data visualization exist (e.g., Sinar, 2015). Below are some key considerations for designing compelling and informative dashboards:

1. **Leverage high-impact visual real estate for high-impact findings.** Most Western cultures read left to right, top to bottom. Therefore, top left is considered the starting point for most users. Be thoughtful regarding what information is displayed in this premium visual real estate.

2. **Avoid visual overload.** Color, used correctly, enhances analysis and understanding. However, too many colors, or incompatible colors, can create visual overload for your audience, slowing cognitive processing and sometimes preventing it. Be mindful of accessibility issues, including color blindness. Several color-blindness color palettes are available and should be used whenever possible (e.g., WCAG 2.0 Level AA, Guideline 1.4[1]). Unfortunately, typical "traffic light"–style color palettes—red, yellow, and green—are not color-blindness friendly and should be avoided where possible. A palette of reds, grays, and blues can be a useful alternative.

3. **Create balance.** Ensure key visuals are distributed across the frame, and use white space effectively to create separation and meaning.

4. **Emphasize key findings.** Draw the user's attention to key messages. Highlight the important and impactful data by using color, font size, shapes, highlighting, etc.

5. **Create patterns to reduce cognitive load.** Display similar sets of information the same way, decreasing the cognitive load for the user. Lead

[1] Web Content Accessibility Guidelines (WCAG) were established by the World Wide Web Consortium under its Web Accessibility Initiative.

the viewer from one to the next based on a logical flow. For example, if turnover slowed, it might be important to review the total headcount of hires, average compensation/job family mix, and top talent exit ratios to see what may have been traded off.

6. **Give context for the numbers.** Provide guidance via color, trends, etc. if numbers are good or bad, making it easier for the user to interpret the results accurately and decipher the story of the data. This can be done through annotation with text and symbols.

It is important to build a plan for protecting, anonymizing, and purging the data to stay aligned with changing legislation as you are designing your dashboard and constructing the data that will flow into it. Data owners need to be conscious of what data will be needed in the future and how long that data will need to be retained. As data has become a critical resource for companies, evolving legislation (e.g., GDPR, as mentioned earlier) is focused on protecting an individual's (e.g., candidate, employee) personal information. Thus, organizations that process personal information or control its processing must consider and protect the personal data of candidates, current employees, and former employees. No longer can researchers collect and retain data for the potential of future analysis without fair disclosure and a legitimate justification for retaining it. Today, legislation worldwide is being enforced requiring knowledge of how data will be used and retention periods.

As a data-oriented function, human resource departments should align with their legal and privacy departments to ensure proper handling of candidate and employee data. The purpose of data retention policies is to systematically retain only data that is needed in the future, to retain the data in a manner in which it can be searched and accessed at a later date, and to systematically purge data when it is no longer needed. Unfortunately, the retention periods for different records can vary dramatically. These requirements and guidelines are subject to change, and data retention practices and policies should be reviewed frequently.

Although records retention is important, much of the focus today is on data privacy. A large and growing number of countries have adopted some form of data privacy legislation. In most cases, the legislation requires clarity as to the purpose of the collected data, how the data will be used once collected, where it will reside, and for how long it will be stored. Additionally, data managers must specify what measures will be taken to ensure the data, once collected, is protected. Individuals have the right to make inquiries to see any of their data.

Although many of these data privacy laws have been in place for decades (e.g., Data Protection Act 1998, Freedom of Information Act, Swiss Federal Data Protection [1992], and Canadian Personal Information Protection and Electronic Documents Act), it was the introduction of the GDPR that has triggered companies to rethink their approach to data privacy, as it is seeks to harmonize the legislation regarding data in general. Equally, individuals are becoming savvier and are taking a more active role in protecting their data. Eighty-one percent of consumers say they've become more concerned about how companies use their data, while 87% think companies should be more heavily regulated on personal data management. Three-quarters of the people felt like they were less likely to trust companies with data and 89% said companies should be clearer about how their products use data, according to the 20th edition of IBM's global C-suite study (IBM Institute for Business Value, 2019).

Bringing It Together

Human resources is becoming even more of a data-driven function. We rely on our data to execute and evolve our offerings across the employee lifecycle. To retain the privilege of using candidate and employee data in our offerings, we need to be diligent in aligning our needs across our function. Human resources organizations that understand their data map and can articulate it will be positioned for success in navigating the increasing number of regulations being adopted globally. Equally important, they will build the trust of the data owners, including potential candidates, their workforce, and their customers.

Managed effectively, the staffing and selection processes will yield an enormous treasure trove of data at both the individual and aggregate level. Most of the time, this data is not put to any other talent management purpose, which is a significant missed opportunity. At a philosophical level, it makes sense to align the priorities and criteria used on the selection process to other essential talent management functions such as learning and performance evaluation. Organizations that center their talent management processes on competencies will thread the same concepts throughout their system, which is a good step for now, but both roles and competencies continue to become more fluid and new paradigms of job and person measurement are needed that can be built much faster to keep pace with the speed of business (e.g., Jesuthasan & Boudreau, 2022). Utilizing some of the advanced techniques noted above (e.g., NLP) to monitor evolving skills and capabilities can offer one mechanism for ensuring that talent management systems stay current and effective.

Organizations generally miss the opportunity to use information regarding an individual candidate's strengths and weaknesses relative to a new role beyond the hiring decision. Organizations can use that data to build custom onboarding or learning plans, including perhaps to identify particularly relevant onboarding buddies or learning content that should be prioritized to support the candidate in achieving full performance as quickly as possible.

Similarly, though few organizations do this, it is possible to look at broad patterns within the candidate pool and identify, for example, skills that are not in sufficient supply in the external market and explicitly build or adapt learning programs to intentionally and dynamically fill those gaps. While this may include formal learning, organizations can also experiment with strategies to support employees in learning on the job, through activities such as being paired with a deep expert. This opportunity for insight equips organizations with multiple channels to meet their business needs and can reduce business risks.

Organizations that gather good data on candidate preferences throughout the recruiting funnel up to and including decline reasons are missing a powerful influencing opportunity if they do not connect candidate data to exits. Structuring those programs to make it easier to match up decline and exit reasons will make it much simpler to tell a clear and compelling story about, for example, an organization that is losing a strong competitive position with regards to pay or career opportunities and needs to adjust its overall talent management strategies. In the same vein, organizations can look at exit rates and offer decline rates together by job type or location for clues as to where their pay may be out of line, their value proposition needs modification, or their community reputation might be poor.

Generally, this exit data will reveal that career opportunities are a key exit reason, especially for top talent. As human resources data systems are increasingly integrated, and data systems improve, it is increasingly feasible to consider selection and career development not as entirely separate silos but as part of an overall employee lifecycle. Organizations that invest in career development and especially in technology-enabled career development platforms can treat the recruitment and selection phase as the first step in an overall career plan. Here again, however, it is important to mention the obligation to ensure appropriate consent and data use, particularly being mindful that data is not being stored for excessive periods of time or being used beyond the original purpose for which it was gathered.

Conclusion

Talent acquisition has experienced hypergrowth during the past decade, fueled by the use of technology. The technology is enabling new, data-driven approaches for gathering insights regarding candidates, employees, and leavers, promoting TA's role as a key business partner and influencer. With this enhanced credibility, there is also a responsibility to balance the speed and quality of the inferences being made with fair and ethical practices. We have only just begun to harness this data to gain insights that will improve the TA offerings.

References

Boudreau, J. W., & Ramstad, P. M. (2003). Strategic industrial and organizational psychology and the role of utility analysis models. In W. C. Borman, D. R. Ilgen, & R. J. Klimoski (Volume Eds.), *Handbook of psychology: Volume 12, Industrial and organizational psychology* (pp. 193–221). Hoboken, NJ: Wiley.

Boudreau, J. W., & Ramstad, P. M. (2007). *Beyond HR: The new science of human capital.* Boston: Harvard Business School Press.

Cascio, W. F. (1996). The role of utility analysis in the strategic management of organizations. *Journal of Human Resource Costing & Accounting, 1*(2), 85–95. https://doi.org/10.1108/eb029032.

Cascio, W. F., & Boudreau, J. B. (2011). Utility of selection systems: Supply-chain analysis applied to staffing decisions. In S. Zedek (Ed.), *APA handbook of industrial and organizational psychology, Volume 2* (pp. 421–444). Washington, DC: American Psychological Association.

Cascio, W. F., Boudreau, J. B., & Fink, A. A. (2019). *Investing in people: Financial impact of human resource initiatives* (3rd ed). Alexandria, VA: Society for Human Resources Management.

Deloitte. (2019). *Leading the social enterprise: Reinvent with a human focus.* 2019 Deloitte Human Capital Trends. https://www2.deloitte.com/content/dam/insights/us/articles/5136_HC-Trends-2019/DI_HC-Trends-2019.pdf.

Drasgow, F., Nye, C. D., & Tay, L. (2010). Indicators of quality assessment. In J. C. Scott & D. H. Reynolds (Eds.), *Handbook of workplace assessment: Evidence-based practices for selecting and developing organizational talent* (pp. 27–59). San Francisco: Jossey Bass.

Dulebohn, J. H., & Johnson, R. D. (2013). Human resource metrics and decision support: A classification framework. *Human Resource Management Review, 23*, 71–83.

Dutta, S., & O'Rourke, E. (2020). Open-ended questions: The role of natural language processing and text analytics. In W. H. Macey & A. A. Fink (Eds.), *Employee surveys and sensing: Driving organizational culture and performance* (pp. 202–218). New York: Oxford University Press.

IBM Institute for Business Value. (2019). *Build your trust advantage: Leadership in the era of data and AI everywhere.* https://www.ibm.com/downloads/cas/K1OGEMA9.

Jesuthasan, R., & Boudreau, J. W. (2022). *Work without jobs: How to reboot your organization's work operating system.* Cambridge, MA: MIT Press.

Landers, R. N. (2019). Gamification misunderstood: How badly executed and rhetorical gamification obscures its transformative potential. *Journal of Management Inquiry, 28*(2), 137–140.

Nikolaou, I., Georgiou, K., & Kotsasarlidou, V. (2019). Exploring the relationship of a gamified assessment with performance. *Spanish Journal of Psychology, 22*, 1–10.

Roth, P. L., Bobko, P., Van Iddekinge, C. H., & Thatcher, J. B. (2016). Social media in employee selection: Research needs and reasons for caution in uncharted territory. *Journal of Management, 42*, 269–298.

Sinar, E. F. (2015). Data visualization. In S. Tonidandel, E. King, & J. Cortina (Eds.), *Big data at work: The data science revolution and organizational psychology* (pp. 115–157). New York: Taylor & Francis.

Vosen, E. (2021). Social media screening and procedural justice: Towards fairer use of social media in selection. *Employee Responsibilities & Rights Journal, 33*(4), 281–309.

7

Onboarding During Transformational Times

Responding to Business Trends with Technology and Best Practices

Deborah K. Ford

Actium Health

Talya N. Bauer

Portland State University

In today's competitive climate where industry leaders must battle for top talent, onboarding emerges as a critical differentiator for reinforcing the employer value proposition (EVP), instilling commitment, and accelerating time to productivity. A rigorous and intimate onboarding program that reinforces interpersonal connection has become critical during COVID-19 isolation. Speed and ease are enabled and accelerated given the technological transformation. Employee-centric design methodology seeks to create thoughtful experiences for those "moments that matter" in the employee journey.

Sharp competition for talent creates even more pressure for practitioners to place greater importance on attracting, onboarding, and accelerating the productivity of top talent, while instilling along the way a greater sense of commitment to drive retention. Indeed, the contribution of onboarding efforts to meaningful bottom-line results is being well documented. For example, standardized onboarding processes were associated with 54% greater new hire productivity and 52% greater retention (Aberdeen, 2016; Cleary, 2018). Yet most organizations do not believe they do it well (Brandon Hall Group, 2014). Consequently, transformational initiatives within an organization's onboarding practices can influence organizational outcomes in nontrivial ways. In this chapter, we overview extensive endeavors and relatively easy ways to drive meaningful impact for your hiring managers, human resources (HR) talent operational staff, and new joiners.

Deborah K. Ford and Talya N. Bauer, *Onboarding During Transformational Times* In: *Becoming a Talent Magnet.*
Edited by: Mark A. Morris, Oxford University Press. © Oxford University Press 2024.
DOI: 10.1093/oso/9780190938512.003.0007

During a time of intense disruption with increasing pressure on industry leaders to meet challenging goals, onboarding practices have evolved exponentially. The evolution of onboarding is also partially a result of the rise in consumer-like expectations of employers to deliver simplicity, delight, and distinction. Digital and artificial intelligence (AI) technology has also notably allowed for substantial opportunities to up-level services to employees without increasing operational expenses. For example, at Twitter, "managers start thinking about onboarding well before a new hire's first day by streamlining the many steps and interactions that must occur to make a new hire's first days at the company welcoming and successful" (Ellis, Nifadkar, Bauer, & Erdogan, 2017a). Traditionally thought of as a process starting on Day 1 that largely involved the completion of paperwork and an overview of one's job, onboarding efforts have evolved into a comprehensive set of operational and psychological processes that emphasize a new employee's socialization and understanding of an organization's purpose, values, and competitive advantages (Bauer, Erdogan, Caughlin, Ellis, & Kurkoski, 2021). Thus, successful onboarding today is multifaceted: It must support and amplify the EVP, simplify the processes for recruiters and hiring managers, delight candidates, accelerate the productivity of new joiners, and provide a competitive edge.

The 5 Cs of Onboarding

Research suggests that more than 80% of new employees decide whether to stay with their new organization within the first few months, yet only 76% of HR leaders believe they are effectively onboarding their new employees (Maurer, 2018; SAP, 2018). Never before has the pace of change been faster or the level of job mobility (both within and across organizations) been so high. The median job tenure by age now ranges from 1.42 years for those 25 to 35 years old to a high of 2.53 for those 55 to 65 years old (Wilkie, 2017). Effective onboarding not only has been shown to get new employees off to a fast and productive start (Wynhurst, 2014) but also is associated with longer tenure (Bauer, Bodner, Erdogan, Truxillo, & Tucker, 2007).

Individuals have increasingly come to expect the same seamlessness, personalization, and automation that they experience as consumers to exist in their work environments. Employers are leveraging technology and customer-centric unique design solutions to effectively combat the very real challenges associated with the high pace of mobility within the workforce. The "5 Cs of onboarding" have emerged in recent history to provide a framework for onboarding drivers: compliance, clarification, confidence, connection, and culture (Bauer, 2010). Organizations that focus on the 5 Cs demonstrate more successful onboarding and business outcomes than those that do not (Laurano, 2013), and research has found that new employees who experienced connection as part of their onboarding process had higher perceptions of onboarding usefulness, organizational commitment, perceived organizational support, and job satisfaction (Meyer & Bartels, 2017). We will go through and define each of the 5 Cs in detail while highlighting empirical support for creating positive employee experiences throughout.

Compliance

Compliance refers to things that must be done, like getting paperwork completed, the badging process, and provisioning tasks like equipping new employees with computers and phones, as well as a workspace. Although you might think of this task as something to get through and move on from, organizations are working tirelessly to put an end to the frustration that employees feel by elevating this experience and improving organizational efficiency. New joiners can complete required paperwork online prior to their start; this allows for an optimized first-day experience that is focused more on role alignment and networking rather than bureaucratic activities. By eliminating the paper trail and embracing e-sign functionality, organizations are able to increase time to proficiency and optimize process performance for scale.

Given how busy everyone is doing their own day-to-day work, it can be challenging to connect and engage with stakeholders in the planning for onboarding of new employees. Using technology so that no one has to start all over again every time is helpful. It also makes engaging with stakeholders less tedious as planning can be done across individuals and then applied to cases as needed.

Recruitment should lead seamlessly into onboarding with a smooth handoff. Industry leaders "aspire to provide a consumer-grade experience to their workforce that treats employees as customers of HR" (Lougee, Chandra, & Burden, 2017). Using a pre-entry onboarding portal is a great way to align new employees with other newcomers, share information about the company, and get them set up with pre-hire paperwork. The time between them signing the offer letter and starting their new job is a golden opportunity to start building a connection. Employees want the capability to work anytime, anywhere, on any device, including laptops, tablets, and smartphones. Digital HR applications like Adobe Acrobat DC and "sign and scan" apps are being widely applied to offer employees light, mobile, and efficient self-service capabilities. These types of digital applications are being used to allow applicants and employees to conveniently complete, sign, and return documents securely, which drastically reduces the drain experienced during a highly administratively tedious process.

Similarly, virtual support agents for enterprise service management are being applied to deliver a personalized user experience with instant responses to common inquiries that decrease support call volume. Some traditional HR questions are "How much available personal time off do I have?" or "What is our sick leave policy?" The application of digital technology continues to evolve, and we can expect that creative solutions will be adding significantly to the onboarding experience. These are similar to the chatbots described in Chapter 5 (see that chapter for more on onboarding technology).

Remember that new employees are excited to join the organization. Streamlining administrative processes rather than burying them under a mountain of paperwork will allow organizations to capitalize on that initial rush of enthusiasm. Utilizing technology to allow new joiners to complete paperwork before the first day on the job or anytime anywhere is increasingly becoming commonplace. In fact, *gamification* techniques are being applied creatively to excite employees and solidify learning. Elements of progress and achievement are built-in characteristics that can turn around traditionally mundane tasks like enrolling in benefit programs, completing tax paperwork, and creating processes to set up badge IDs. From the outset, new joiners can be rewarded for small achievements to minimize the pains associated with overly laborious moments in the onboarding processes.

The global COVID-19 pandemic highlighted the need for well-thought-out remote onboarding programs. Newcomers at Microsoft were surveyed and reported that making social connections within their teams was challenging without ever meeting in person (Rodeghero, Zimmerman, Houck, & Ford, 2021). Remote onboarding and training of new program coordinators into medical education offices led to insights regarding best practices, such as being specific during communication, thinking a step ahead, and reassuring employees (Goodermote, 2020). In addition, eight actionable items were identified to remotely onboard and train newcomers:

1. Creating a virtual workday
2. Planning for purposeful learning
3. Developing spreadsheets for process flow
4. Engaging other staff in mini-tutorials
5. Scheduling remote meet-and-greets
6. Assigning supplemental self-learning modules
7. Establishing standard virtual meeting formats
8. Conducting regular one-on-one check-ins.

Onboarding designers can enhance engagement by creating "leveling up" tasks that must be completed before additional steps can be taken within the new hire orientation and training. For example, you may ask sales staff to complete a number of pipeline management activities in order to "level up" to support a client sales meeting. Often incremental goals can build self-efficacy, reinforce desired behaviors, and motivate new joiners to greater productivity goals.

Gamification "quests" can also be applied to a wide range of training subjects to offer active learning methods. Rather than requiring a new sales-person to attend a lengthy training session, new joiners could be asked to interview veteran employees about their top sales pipeline tactics and present their findings to a group of fellow new joiners. A facilitator could drive discussions about how the new joiner's previous experiences and tactics fit with some of the themes that were uncovered from veterans. While you may think that having your new employees watch videos or read through manuals will help them understand the information, having them seek out the information is a much more active process that will help to solidify their learning. It is also a more enjoyable way to learn.

Clarification

Clarification refers to how well new employees understand the organization, their roles, and performance expectations. Fundamental to clarification are basics like showing new joiners what it is they need to function daily (e.g., booking and locating meeting spaces, enrolling in employee wellness benefits, and understanding policies and regulations). Often organizations take extra steps to support new joiners in learning the workplace "language," acronyms, and history. Simple reference guides can be powerful in removing those feelings of being lost or overwhelmed.

Critical to performance success and feelings of early accomplishment are role clarity activities that provide direction for executing the major functions of the job. As such, proper alignment and coaching sessions are strategically timed throughout the first year. Because of the demanding business climate, it is easy to lose track of time, progress, and focus. Using a framework with timed milestones, such as 30, 60, 90, and 120 days on the job, up through the one-year post-organizational entry, to check in on employee progress provides a valuable mechanism for ensuring role clarity due diligence (Bauer, 2010). That is especially true with new joiners who are eager to shed their newness status and demonstrate immediate value.

Developing an understanding of objectives, timelines, roles, and responsibilities can be intimidating and overwhelming, so organizations often build out structured integration plans and assign team members to support. Integration team members might include the manager, a buddy, and other assistants. Managers work with new joiners to ensure they understand the bigger picture of what they need to know to be successful on the team and with key stakeholders. Managers help set goals/objectives, meet regularly with new joiners, and share guidance on their work. A buddy is often asked to be that "lifeline" into both how the team works and where to find things in the organization. A buddy may also serve as an independent resource to give new joiners additional perspective and counsel as needed.

An integration plan helps to accelerate a new joiner's business impact and provide valuable insights into the who, what, when, where, and why of successful integration. An integration plan may include an overview of expectations, goals, and objectives; network/stakeholder analysis; and a review of key meetings and resources. The integration plan may provide a high-level 30/60/90 plan that can be fleshed out further by the new joiner.

With that said, providing support and clarification is even more important for those entering leadership roles. Often new business leaders complete an onboarding analysis, which can begin in the first 30 days and continue over the course of their first 90 days. Conducting this onboarding analysis ensures that leaders are not making changes simply for the sake of making changes. Instead, they conduct a comprehensive assessment of six key areas to identify priorities at the end of their first 90 days: strategy, programs, processes, culture, organizational structure and talent, and stakeholder network. An onboarding analysis can help leaders examine what is working well to help achieve that strategy and what additional needs exist. Critical to early success is the ability to determine any immediate issues and assess if the programs are appropriately resourced. Leaders can begin understanding the current culture and evaluate challenges, strengths, and weaknesses. Through this analysis, leaders determine what should remain the same, what should be modified, and what should be discontinued.

Some key questions within the onboarding analysis may include:

- Is there a clear vision of what success looks like for the team?
- Do goals and priorities cascade down?
- Do all team members understand the role they contribute to the strategy?
- How efficient and effective are your operational processes? What are any apparent bottlenecks?
- In what areas are you likely to face stiff challenges in the coming year? What can be done to prepare for those challenges?
- What are the most promising opportunities for growth?

Let's not forget the monumental role of leaders in onboarding, assimilating, and supporting new joiners. It is easy for managers to be swept away in the day-to-day demands of quarterly reviews, demanding clients, and intense stakeholder meetings. All leaders want to support their teams, but the overwhelming resources needed to tackle the day-to-day grind may distract managers from executing onboarding activities fully and effectively. This is especially true given the current talent market, with many organizations experiencing high volatility and frequent team onboarding.

As a result, savvy organizations are providing manager "nudges" that essentially spoon-feed managers content to support onboarding efforts. This might include templates, talking points, worksheets, and job aids at the exact moment they are needed. These bite-sized just-in-time managerial support materials are friendly nudges that reinforce positive managerial behaviors. The impacts can be nontrivial. For example, when Google sent a short email reminder to hiring managers containing tips in the form of a new hire checklist the day before orientation, they were able to jump-start new employee productivity by a month (Bock, 2015; Sullivan, 2015).

Confidence

Confidence refers to how much new employees feel like they can do the job well and tackle new challenges. The importance of establishing early moments of adjustment (also referred to as accommodation) for new joiners has been well established. Early research supports that self-efficacy (learning the tasks of the new job and gaining confidence in the role), role clarity (understanding job tasks to understanding task priorities and time allocation), and social acceptance (coming to feel liked and accepted by peers) were not only integral to successful onboarding but were also formed early in the tenure and were long-lasting (Feldman, 1981).

Managers will frequently provide new joiners with initial priorities and goals they are confident the new joiner can achieve. Establishing quick wins helps to build self-efficacy and momentum for more challenging endeavors. This is also true for transfers within the organization. While individuals moving from one role to the next may have established connections and have completed the compliance aspects of their employment previously, their confidence and understanding of the culture throughout the organization should be augmented with new information and a well-thought-out process rather than leaving things to chance.

Progressively increasing the complexity of goals will allow employees to expand their initial contributions and show more meaningful value to the business. Through this process, it is critical that managers openly discuss gaps in their skill set and work to close them. Striving to go beyond priorities and goals, inspiring employees, and instilling a sense of meaningfulness associated with their work can have profound impacts.

As noted earlier, some organizations are seeing the power of technological "nudges" to target employee actions toward larger goals. Nudges are simple Twitter-like short messages that allow recipients to act immediately. Machine learning is being used to craft the ideal content and time for messages to employees. As pointed out by Laszlo Bock, "We want to be the person we hope we can be. But we need to be reminded. A nudge can have a powerful impact if correctly deployed on how people behave and on human performance" (Wakabayashi, 2019).

Connection

Connection refers to how accepted and valued new employees feel. Make the first day on the job special to leverage connection. Plato once rightfully posited that "you can discover more about a person in an hour of play than in a year of conversation." Although making connections is critical for new joiners, tenured employees also benefit from activities that build in the "stickiness" that promotes organizational commitment, energizes people to come to work, creates a fun environment of high achievement, and reinforces those social bonds that keep the inner workings of the organization moving smoothly. Clearly the first day on the job is critical. To the degree that you can help new employees feel valued and special, they will be relieved and happy that they made the right choice to join your organization. But treat them like just another number and they probably won't stay long.

Research has consistently shown that new employees' peers and managers are crucial for maximizing onboarding success (Ellis, Nifadkar, Bauer, & Erdogan, 2017b; Nifadkar & Bauer, 2016; Wanberg, 2012). The more support that is offered to new employees, the better the chances are they will integrate successfully into the team structure. Thus, onboarding should not be thought of as just one department's or person's job; rather, it should be something that everyone invests in over time. When more people are involved, newcomers are less likely to fall through the cracks of the system. Research has established that a large factor in team success is members' sense of psychological safety. When teams feel safe, they experience better outcomes because team members are more likely to speak up and participate. This is especially pronounced early in a team member's life (Edmondson & Polzer, 2016). For new employees this may mean not feeling afraid to ask a "silly" question or seeking help for the information they need to do their job well. Managers play a critical role in creating a safe space; further, they assign buddies and peers to help new employees adjust and feel like they belong and are accepted. Research shows that this is critical for igniting new employee confidence and motivation to fully engage in onboarding activities (Bauer et al., 2007). Thus, taking an "it takes a village" approach to onboarding should be considered when designing and implementing onboarding programs to help new employees with connection and confidence.

Culture

Culture refers to how well new employees understand the norms, values, stories, and symbols of their new organization. Because employees are changing employers and jobs more frequently, organizations must employ targeted and impactful tactics that build excitement and enthusiasm, contributing to greater levels of commitment and retention. According to Tim Campos, former chief information officer of Facebook, "If a company does not manage to arouse a level of interest among employees about the company culture and work and make them more productive in the very first 45 minutes, then something is certainly not done right. Such companies need to seriously rethink their employee onboarding strategies" (Bhaswati, 2016).

The development of corporate pride and the internalization of values can provide that stickiness that makes newcomers feel that they are part of a community and identify with the organization. It is important to alert new employees to the social nuances or unwritten rules throughout the organization (Stein & Christiansen, 2010). To accelerate this often gradual process, organizations are using storytelling approaches during onboarding, including vignettes, scenario-based learning that highlights norms and values, and high-level messaging from organizational leaders. Using such tactics will often help new joiners quickly accelerate out of that uncomfortable phase of feeling like "such an outsider."

Additionally, research is reinforcing the importance of reframing socialization toward individual self-expression. This suggests that including messages that emphasize new joiners' authentic best selves during the onboarding process reinforces personal identities, which drives some nontrivial results. Cable, Gino, and Staats (2013) found quite astounding evidence for the power of reframing messaging during onboarding. Their research showed that focusing messaging on the value a new joiner brings to the organization led to greater performance and levels of retention.

With that said, it is important to note that many organizations miss the opportunity to learn from new hires. This is a shame, as a key reason that organizations hire is to get "new blood" into the organization. If you don't ask what works for them or how you're doing, that learning gets stymied. Rather than reinforcing the existing "way we do things here," seek to optimize the ways in which your organization works by gaining insights and learnings from a new joiner's previous work experience and educational background. Not only does this reinforce a growth mindset within your organizational culture, but it also signals to new joiners that your organization appreciates their self-expression and individual contributions.

One phenomenon that is pervasive across organizations to drive connection, culture, and employee bonding is the utilization of employee resource groups (ERGs). These can be grassroots efforts tied to global diversity and inclusion strategies that serve to provide a sense of belonging and create relationships with people of similar backgrounds (Brown, 2019). ERG members engage in numerous prosocial and advocacy activities such as information sharing, mentoring, and initiatives improving their communities (Welbourne, Rolf, & Schlachter, 2017).

Despite their wide popularity, ERGs are largely unexplored and lacking in empirical examination. Welbourne and colleagues (2017) make a strong theoretical linkage from ERGs to social identity theory (SIT) and offer a series of propositions for future research into ERG effects on individual, group, and organizational outcomes. With that said, we propose that during those early onboarding stages noted by heightened levels of insecurity, ERGs may be far more impactful. ERGs can provide reaffirmation for individual identity and expression, while also offering social support for understanding the intricate organizational dynamics. All of this can drastically reduce anxiety, uncertainty, and feelings of being an "outsider." Additionally, it is possible that new joiners will find their performance enhanced by a greater sense of self and social identity.

Onboarding Trends That Address Challenges

In the next half of this chapter, we focus on challenges and onboarding trends that have borrowed at times from marketing and customer-focused practices and methodology. We explore technology solutions to common challenges and revisit the role of the recruiter in the future, as well as the role of the new employee. We highlight advancements in the field and identify opportunities for further exploration. Table 7.1 includes some examples of opportunities and associated approaches.

Table 7.1 Examples of Potential Onboarding Opportunities and Associated Recommendations

Onboarding Opportunity	Recommendation
Automation	Consider where automation can help make onboarding more efficient and effective.
Technology	Leverage technology with nudges and reminders.
Social onboarding	Connect new employees to other new employees and/or organizational insiders even before they join the organization.
Buddy assignments	Connect new employees to organizational insiders by assigning a specific buddy who can help answer questions as they come up.
Time	Time can be leveraged to help organizations maximize onboarding success by remembering that onboarding takes place across months and years, not just during orientation.
Initial onboarding contact (first day on the job)	Remember that new employees are excited to join the organization. Energize them instead of burying them under paperwork. Use technology to allow them to complete paperwork before the first day on the job or away from in-person time.

Marketing and Design Methodologies

During the pandemic, the job market has altered: In some industries, there is a surplus of talent, while in highly valued and scarce jobs, the market continues to be hypercompetitive. Regardless of job, the macro trend continues to shift toward the candidate experience, where employees' perceptions are more important than in previous hiring eras. This is exemplified by the increased level of transparency in the job market provided by online websites (e.g., glassdoor.com) and widely available insider salary information for some jobs (e.g., levels.fyi for technology jobs). In fact, anonymous crowdsourced salary data was widely distributed via social media applications in 2021. As a result, progressive organizations are focusing extensively on being "brand forward" in their social media strategy, in their workspace, and in the experiences reinforced throughout the employee journey, which starts during the attraction stage of the hiring process and solidifies during those onboarding moments that span much of their first year. EVPs and a corporate brand analysis are two methods useful for informing talent sourcing, attraction, hiring, and onboarding processes. Additionally, employee journey mapping is a user-experience design methodology that combines a comprehensive listening strategy with process redesign that is aimed to delight employees with intelligent processes customized to their unique needs. We next look more closely at each of these three methods and how they can be used to methodologically redefine an organization's onboarding strategy.

Employer Value Proposition

Strong employer brand messaging attracts quality candidates that will thrive in your organization (Brandon Hall Group, 2015). An EVP would highlight such topics as culture, career growth opportunities, and workplace amenities (see Chapter 2 for a thorough discussion and guidelines for building your EVP). The most competitive organizations are rigorous in their efforts to cultivate a corporate brand within their onboarding activities that reinforces their EVP. The central premise of the EVP is in creating and promoting an employment brand that assimilates, inspires, and motivates new joiners. You might think of an organization's EVP as a market-driven campaign that clearly expresses the organizational culture with the employer benefits.

In developing an EVP, practitioners conduct traditional active listening strategies that might include analyzing metrics related to recruitment, retention, employee engagement, and exit interviews. Increasingly, however, organizations are being required to stand up and take notice of passive feedback mechanisms. The digital employer marketplace is largely enabled by online websites designed to share information online; this has introduced greater levels of transparency that can either bolster your cultural image or create considerable brand damage. Applicants and employees can post reviews on social media and digital platforms that will not only directly impact the employment brand, but also indirectly impact the corporate brand. Consider the devastating effects on employment brands that resulted from employee public statements. For example, Susan Fowler publicly wrote about Uber's toxic misogynist corporate culture (Dowd, 2017). In another example, Fawzi Kamel released a video of then Uber CEO Travis Kalanick's outburst over questions related to the recent changes to the ride-hailing pay structure (Isaac, 2017). And, finally, Loretta Lee, a Google engineer, blogged about the poor state of gender inclusion within the technology industry (Ghosh, 2018). Each of these messages had an impactful negative influence on the organization's employment image, damaging recruitment and onboarding but also bleeding into the consumer image.

Industry leaders are proactively promoting their EVP throughout the onboarding journey, while actively monitoring their corporate employment brand using passive listening analysis such as third-party public surveys and sentiment analysis (i.e., content analysis of open text responses) of employment social media platforms like LinkedIn, Blind, and Fairygodboss, which focuses on an organization's support for women in the workplace. Machine learning is often used to accelerate sentiment analysis across social media platforms to understand the corporate image. Some organizations are also comparing their own public sentiments with those of their primary talent competitors.

During information-gathering efforts associated with building an EVP, organizations will inevitably be confronted with less desirable information, but this can be used to help inform cultural interventions. Taking a strategic approach to monitoring and addressing the passive messages that shape your employment brand is important to ensure you attract top talent and are proactive in reinforcing your EVP. With that said, EVPs traditionally take on a positive light and are crafted using an employee-design approach to ensure that the messaging does not ring false and actually portrays the genuine strengths of the organization.

Employment Brand Analysis

During the recruitment and selection process, a mutual assessment exists whereby candidates draw conclusions about the organization on a multitude of criteria, such as career growth opportunities, values, and fun. Building an employment brand to attract top key talent can directly impact productivity, innovation, customer satisfaction, and operational spend. In fact, Fortune 500 companies who ranked in the top 10 for employment brand showed combined revenues *four times greater* than organizations ranked in the bottom 10 (Wilson, 2017). However, what is cutting edge today can become commonplace tomorrow. Therefore, great value is derived by rigorously examining the trends within the employment market, with a special focus on the organizations with which you compete for talent. Integrating those elements that differentiate your employment brand from those of your competitors throughout the onboarding program in thoughtful ways is essential for not only reinforcing your organization's culture but also demonstrating and living corporate values within onboarding moments.

Because candidates and current employees compare their own experiences with the meaningful experiences of others within their own organization and other leading employers across all industries, it is important to gather specific information on the practices of competitive employers. Unlike the product market competition, the employer competition may require organizations like Boeing to compete on a global scale for engineering and cyber security talent with very different product competitors like Tesla, Amazon, and Meta/Facebook. Benchmarking an organization's EVP and onboarding efforts against those of other competitor employers is often referred to as an *employment brand analysis*.

To drive a rigorous analysis, organizational psychology methods combined with market analysis techniques can ensure that organizations gather actionable insights that yield the greatest return on investment. First, identify a group of direct top competitors for talent to benchmark your organization against by identifying (1) those organizations that are winning the candidates who declined your offer of employment and (2) those organizations that are winning the talent leaving your organization.

Next, identify criteria to compare these organizations systematically. We suggest conducting a rigorous content analysis using publicly available information tied to organizational design features and EVP elements. Gather insights for each competitor related to key focus areas such as:

1. Type of work climate (e.g., quality and innovation, mission and purpose)
2. Organizational structure (e.g., future career opportunities, compensation)
3. Organizational culture (e.g., diversity and inclusion, corporate responsibility, fun)
4. Quality of people (e.g., quality of talent, senior leader reputation).

In evaluating the competitiveness of your onboarding design, you might assess how your organization compares to others in terms of the length of the in-person sessions, type of welcome gifts provided, level of worker getting a job offer e.g., executives, university, interns), social engagements, and networking opportunities.

Finally, it is beneficial to sample existing employees to evaluate the "value" they place on each organizational design feature (e.g., quality and innovation, diversity and inclusion) gathered in the content analysis. Such an analysis of individual differences related to these values not only helps support recruiting strategies but also ensures business dollars are invested in those areas that would yield the greatest value to your customers, your employees. All in all, it is wise for organizations to shape and form their own unique brand that is genuine to the mission and values of the organization, while still maintaining a distinct competitive edge by scanning the practices of employment market competitors.

Employee-Centric Design Thinking

Design thinking puts the focus on your target audience, which allows you to create experiences uniquely matched to their needs. Taking insights from your EVP and employer brand analysis and systematically redesigning your onboarding program in a thoughtful manner can be accomplished in many ways. Employee journey mapping is gaining in popularity with leading companies. For example, Adobe applied the employee-centric design methodology, just as they would for consumers. When journey mapping the onboarding process, you might interpret the customer as the new joiner, but it is advantageous to evaluate the employee experiences for all of those involved in the onboarding experience (i.e., employee personas). A process that is completely delightful for new joiners might be extraordinarily painful for hiring managers or unscalable for the talent team. It is essential to optimize the experiences for each of the employees involved in the process, including those delivering the services and those receiving services. As depicted in Figure 7.1, the stages of customer-centric design efforts might include discovery, definition, ideation, test/prototype, and implementation. We will highlight each of these stages with related activities.

Stage 1: Discovery
The discovery phase often includes the development of current-state process maps, review of survey data, and development of the employee personas. *Employee personas* are another example of marketing methodology that can be applied well within strategic HR. They are frequently used in journey-mapping efforts to ensure that individual differences across generations, genders, roles, cultures, and geographies are proactively captured. A persona is a fictional representation for various segments of employees, with comparable demographics, behavior patterns, motivations, and goals (Haak, 2017).

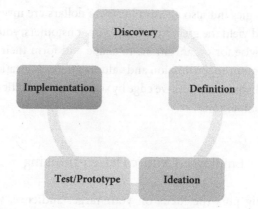

Figure 7.1 Stages of customer-centric design efforts

Capturing diverse employee drivers supports the design of experiences with broad employee appeal. Adobe's onboarding journey-mapping sessions utilized personas that included different types of candidate characteristics (e.g., university graduates, interns, executives, gender and ethnic diversity, and different roles, like creative vs. engineering), hiring manager characteristics (e.g., high-volume vs. low-volume hiring, remote office hiring), and delivery team characteristics (e.g., recruiters, information technology [IT] support, onboarding administrators). Including the delivery team as an employee persona was a progressive approach. If the onboarding process is overly laborious for recruiters or IT support, it cannot be optimized for the ultimate customer, the candidate/new joiner.

Stage 2: Definition

Building from the previous stage, practitioners often conduct open conversational interviews with employees to uncover rich stories that bring their current experiences to light. Although probing questions are prepared, the interviews allow employees to share their interests. The definition stage often involves techniques for completing an *affinity analysis*, which applies a high-level process map to uncover the pains and gains experienced by each employee persona. First, practitioners identify the *moments that matter* (MTMs) in the employee onboarding journey derived from process maps, interviews, and insights from surveys. MTMs represent the key events in the employee lifecycle that are most important and distinctive for each persona. For example, MTMs for onboarding include several major moments and micro-moments like accepting the job offer (example micro-moments include pre-employment documentations, offer email), introductions to employees (example micro-moments include social clubs, networking activities), and arrival activities (example micro-moment includes clean desk, proper equipment, badge functionality).

Focus groups are conducted with persona representatives (e.g., new joiners, hiring managers, delivery team members) to identify the pains and gains for each MTM. Personas are used in these sessions to ensure a representative focus is placed on each of the key stakeholders with distinct motives and preferences. Diversity of representation is absolutely critical for an optimized design.

Stage 3: Innovation/Ideation
In the innovation/ideation phase, focus is placed on North Star sessions to solicit ideas on valuable design experiences for the MTMs for the different employee personas, while also reflecting the corporate EVP. Bringing the corporate EVP to life and enhancing key moments in a way that is meaningful to employees without being disingenuous or too self-aggrandizing is important. Actionable insights are documented and placed into logical groupings to support the prioritization effort.

In this phase efforts are conducted to identify the *minimum viable employee experience* to drive design features that are seamless and simple and deliver the greatest value. Examples of ways to operationalize Adobe's EVP within their onboarding experience include escorting candidates through the workplace in a strategic way during their interviews to highlight the workspace features favored by employees (e.g., rooftop basketball court, Instagrammable creative installations) or conducting an informal interview in a café booth rather than in a conference room. Operationalizing and living your EVP throughout the major MTMs will start that enculturation process before the employee accepts the position. Other ways organizations look to transform their onboarding is by educating new joiners about their organization's market distinction and brand by means of the company swag gifted to new joiners and activities that reinforce the values of the organization. Rather than passively gifting swag with little or no in-person meeting, employers can look to drive understanding in the corporate offerings, while instilling pride. Networking events can be centered around a volunteer activity that has societal impact.

Phase 4: Test/Prototype
The stage largely involves piloting and learning from your design efforts. Often research studies are conducted and feedback is gathered to allow for course corrections and design refinement. During this phase, often an end-of-life plan is created for a successful transition to the new ways of running the business.

Phase 5: Implementation
The final phase focuses on deploying new capabilities and adoption plans with corresponding change-management strategies. This includes an evaluation and analysis component that requires the tracking of key performance indicators, performing health checks, and supporting mechanisms for continuous improvement.

Digital Technology

The impact of technology to address many of the challenges faced by organizations and talent management is undeniable. Digital capabilities permeate every aspect of the onboarding process and present new possibilities. Organizations that leverage technology to help with efficiency, especially when it comes to onboarding, stand to reap major advantages. Rather than relying on manual processes, organizations would be well served to focus on specific technologies designed not only to enhance operational ease but also to enhance the experiences of the new joiner.

Technology can also aid in the monitoring of programs over time. Are new employees using the system? Are they accessing information? Are they being assigned buddies? Are team members welcoming them to the organization using the system? All of these aspects, among others, are important for new employees, so onboarding dashboards can be a great tool for keeping up with utilization.

Onboarding best practices are enhanced when using the right technology. Below are examples of potential ways to leverage each of the onboarding 5 Cs for onboarding success using technology.

- *Implement the basics prior to the first day on the job to leverage compliance.* Using a pre-entry onboarding portal is a great way to align new employees with other newcomers, share information about the company, and get them set up with pre-hire paperwork. The time between them signing the offer letter and starting their new job is a golden opportunity to start building a connection. And recruitment should lead seamlessly into onboarding with a smooth handoff.

- *Make the first day on the job special to leverage connection.* Research is clear that the first day on the job is critical. To the degree that you can help a new employee feel valued and special, they will be relieved and happy that they made the right choice to join your organization. Treat them like just another number and they probably won't last long.

- *Use formal orientation programs to leverage all five of the onboarding Cs.* Research is also clear that formal onboarding is more effective than informal onboarding, so seek to create a formal orientation program to help new employees understand the Cs of onboarding.

- *Develop a written onboarding plan to leverage clarity and connection.* It is tough to formalize an onboarding plan without documenting it. Once you determine what works in terms of onboarding within your organization, formalize it in writing.

- *Make onboarding participatory to leverage clarity and connection.* Many organizations miss the opportunity to learn from new hires. That is a shame, as a key reason that organizations hire new employees is to get "new blood" into the organization. If you don't ask what works for them or how you're doing, that learning gets stymied.

- *Be sure your program is consistently implemented to leverage all five of the onboarding Cs.* The more consistent you can become with your onboarding process, the more effective you will be. Technology is critical in allowing for both consistency and customization, as both can be needed at different times for different employees. However, the goal of consistency is a good one.

- *Ensure that the program is monitored over time to leverage all five of the onboarding Cs.* Track usage for new employees and buddy assignments. If you track productivity of new hires this is a good place for it, such as when they get laptops, submitted first code commits, etc.Onboarding metrics should be part of talent dashboards used by recruiters and HR leaders.

- *Use technology to facilitate the process to leverage all five of the onboarding Cs.* Again, sending welcome messages, having managers assign mentors and buddies to new employees, and making introductions can all be facilitated seamlessly using the right technology.

- *Use milestones, such as 30, 60, 90, and 120 days on the job and up to one year post-organizational entry, to check in on employee progress to leverage all five of the onboarding Cs.* It is easy to lose track of time. That is especially true with new employees, who are eager to be seen as "regular" employees rather than new ones. However, research shows that key milestones are important for new employees, and setting up check-ins at these key points using technology can be effective at heading off little issues before they become big problems that result in great employees leaving.
- *Engage stakeholders in planning to leverage connection.* Given how busy everyone is doing their own day-to-day work, it can be challenging to connect and engage with stakeholders in the planning for onboarding of new employees. Using technology so that no one has to start all over again every time is helpful. It also makes engaging with stakeholders less tedious as planning can be done across individuals and then applied to cases as needed.
- *Include key stakeholder meetings as part of the onboarding program to drive clarity, connection, and confidence in your new hires.* Assigning key stakeholder meetings to new employees with specific time guidelines (e.g., "Meet with Barbara in the finance department within your first 30 days on the job") can be facilitated and tracked over time using technology.
- *Be crystal clear with new employees in terms of objectives, timelines, roles, and responsibilities to leverage clarity.* Information can be efficiently and conveniently stored and accessed for new employees. A personalized onboarding access portal with information, forms, activities, to-do lists, maps, and photos of team members goes a long way toward helping with onboarding success.

Role of the Recruiter

Given these recent AI and machine learning advancements, the role of the recruiter is likely to be redefined. We might look at technological impacts on similar jobs in the past for inspiration on how to transform the role of the recruiter in a way that provides greater value to the organization and support for new joiners. For example, bank tellers were once the sole dispensers of money within a bank. When ATM machines were introduced, bank teller positions did not go away or diminish; they simply optimized and became more service-oriented around the bank's product offerings. Similarly, as recruitment tasks are automated with machine learning and AI capabilities, we see great opportunities to evolve the role of the recruiter to enhance the level of service for employee onboarding and counseling. Because of the relationships built during the application attraction and screening stages, recruiters often have an intimate rapport with new joiners that can be leveraged to reduce new joiners' anxiety and accelerate their success.

Starting the onboarding process early, even before the first day on the job, is gaining more attention, as pointed out by the role of marketing methods. Onboarding has become part of a fluid talent strategy that no longer is thought to begin on the new joiner's first day; rather, it begins with the very first impressions formed of the company. Multiple interactions with hiring managers, recruiters, talent scouts, and interviewers provide a plethora of opportunities for candidates to derive meaningful and lasting impressions of the organization. An emerging practice is to be far more thoughtful in the messages put forth to candidates during the hiring process. Consistency of messaging, from the job announcement to the recruiter to the interviewers, needs to be reinforced throughout and must be genuine. Authenticity is critical to ensure that messages ring clear not only for the candidate but also for those delivering the message.

Emerging opportunities may exist in the role definition of recruiters. One of the earliest relationships a candidate forms is with the recruiter. A pervasive challenge for new joiners is that their bonds with a recruiter quickly dissipate. Many new joiners are dismayed when the contact with a recruiter often drops abruptly once the offer is signed. Within the recruitment and selection process a multitude of technological advancements are in play or quickly emerging, including the use of machine learning to scan for candidates through résumés and job boards, technology-enabled interview scheduling, and even more progressive simulated interviews. We anticipate great opportunities to reinvent the role of the recruiter to drive greater value in the strategic support to new joiners.

The Role of the New Employee

In addition, research has consistently found that new employee proactivity plays a critical role in onboarding success. New hires may help or hinder their own success by asking questions, observing others, searching for information, experimenting with different ways of doing things (Ashford & Black, 1996; Bauer et al., 2007; Bauer & Erdogan, 2011; Wanberg & Kammeyer-Mueller, 2000), and being curious (Harrison, Sluss, & Ashforth, 2011). Anything that organizations can do to help new employees feel less stressed (Ellis et al., 2015) and more comfortable and confident can help them become successfully onboarded. As noted earlier, in a unique and compelling study of new employee onboarding, researchers found that initial onboarding processes that encouraged new employees to express their own identities led to several key onboarding success outcomes (Cable et al., 2013).

Progressive organizations are setting some standards for talent acquisition processes. According to Bortz (2017), Facebook has a "45-minute rule," which means all new employees can begin to work within 45 minutes of arriving because all of their systems and devices have been set up before they report for their first day. To drive candidate experience, Amazon has a "2&5 promise" for which the recruiting team is accountable. The promise is that a candidate will hear about the decision within two days of the phone screen and within five days of the interview loop.

Providing a culturally honest flavor is key to setting expectations for the work environment. Before their first day at the Motley Fool, new hires complete questionnaires about their favorite color, snacks, music, sports team, and other interests. The company then uses that information to "deck out" each employee's desk with items they love (Bortz, 2017) along with a "first-day survival kit" with Uno cards, Silly Putty, and a Nerf gun. The first day starts with culture and a tour and ends with $100 per person to celebrate their new job over the weekend. On the following Monday, new hires take part in a scavenger hunt ("Fool's Errand") that pushes them outside their comfort zones. Many companies, especially those with "strong culture," assign a buddy, a more experienced employee who helps the new hire navigate the culture.

Conclusion

As the new normal is continuous change, particularly in how work gets done, what work gets done, and who does it, onboarding technology and employee experience design methods can help organizations stay on top of things during these times of transition. The fast pace of change and mobility mean that onboarding is even more important than ever before. Onboarding technology can help with the 5 Cs: supporting compliance issues such as paperwork and procurement, providing clarification to help new employees understand their roles, enhancing confidence as new employees get accustomed to knowing who to ask and what to do, building connection and becoming "part of the organization" (even before organizational entry), and teaching culture, which is communicated by videos, stories, and symbols throughout the organization. Onboarding success can be maximized by applying an employee-centric design strategy, while leveraging the use of technology to respond to the opportunities and challenges of today, as well as those that will be encountered tomorrow. Organizations only get one chance to make a great first impression with new employees, and those positive first impressions can set the organization up for a positive relationship with new employees or lead to the best candidates expressing buyer's remorse in their job choice. Strategic onboarding takes planning, coordination, and consistency. Technology and intelligent design features can aid in every aspect of onboarding, freeing up managers and organizational veterans to connect to new employees in meaningful ways that can differentiate employers in today's uniquely competitive climate.

References

Aberdeen. (2016). Perfecting the onboarding funnel. https://www.aberdeen.com/hcm-essentials/perfecting-onboarding-funnel/.

Ashford, S. J., & Black, J. S. (1996). Proactivity during organizational entry: The role of desire for control. *Journal of Applied Psychology, 81*, 199–214.

Bauer, T. N. (2010). Onboarding new employees: Maximizing success. SHRM Foundation's Effective Practice Guidelines Series. https://www.shrm.org/foundation/ourwork/initiatives/resources-from-past-initiatives/Documents/Onboarding%20New%20Employees.pdf.

Bauer, T. N., Bodner, T., Erdogan, B., Truxillo, D. M., & Tucker, J. S. (2007). Newcomer adjustment during organizational socialization: A meta-analytic review of antecedents, outcomes, and methods. *Journal of Applied Psychology, 92*, 707–721.

Bauer, T. N., & Erdogan, B. (2011). Organizational socialization: The effective onboarding of new employees. In S. Zedeck (Ed.), *APA handbook of industrial and organizational psychology, Vol. 3. Maintaining, expanding, and contracting the organization* (pp. 51–64). American Psychological Association. https://doi.org/10.1037/12171-002.

Bauer, T. N., Erdogan, B., Caughlin, D., Ellis, A. M., & Kurkoski, J. (2021). Jump-starting the socialization experience: The longitudinal role of Day 1 newcomer resources on adjustment. *Journal of Management, 47*, 2226–2261.

Bhaswati, B. (2016). Employee onboarding at Facebook, Google and Apple. Capabiliti. https://blog.capabiliti.co/employee-onboarding-facebook-google-apple/.

Bock, L. (2015). *Work rules!: Insights from inside Google that will transform how you live and lead*. New York: Twelve.

Bortz, D. (2017). Original onboarding options from 4 HR leaders. https://www.shrm.org/topics-tools/news/hr-magazine/original-onboarding-options-4-hr-leaders

Brandon Hall Group. (2014). High-performance onboarding as a driver of employee engagement. https://static1.squarespace.com/static/567c3751d8af10f889926467/t/56f9a48540261d5bd4e9bcae/1459201167374/BHG_HighPerformanceOnboarding_Final.pdf.

Brandon Hall Group. (2015). Talent shortage and hiring practices study. https://membership.brandonhall.com/posts/2403003-research-summary-talent-shortage-hiring-practices.

Brown, E. I. (2019). Why employee resource groups still matter. Bloomberg. https://www.bloomberg.com/diversity-inclusion/blog/employee-resource-groups-still-matter/.

Cable, D. M., Gino, F., & Staats, B. (2013) Breaking them in or eliciting their best? Reframing socialization around newcomers' authentic self-expression. *Administrative Science Quarterly, 58*, 1–36.

Cleary, B. (2018). Strategic onboarding. Helping new hires succeed. Deloitte: Human Resources Today. http://www.humanresourcestoday.com/onboarding/retention-and-turnover/study/?open-article-id=9033920&article-title=strategic-onboarding&blog-domain=hrtimesblog.com&blog-title=hr-times.

Dowd, M. (2017). She's 26, and brought down Uber's C.E.O. What's next? *New York Times*. https://www.nytimes.com/2017/10/21/style/susan-fowler-uber.html.

Edmondson, A., & Polzer, J. (2016). Why psychological safety matters and what to do about it. Re:Work. https://rework.withgoogle.com/blog/how-to-foster-psychological-safety/.

Ellis, A. M., Bauer, T. N., Mansfield, L. R., Erdogan, B., Truxillo, D. M., & Simon, L. S. (2015). Navigating uncharted waters: Newcomer socialization through the lens of stress theory. *Journal of Management, 41*, 203–235.

Ellis, A. M., Nifadkar, S. S., Bauer, T. N., & Erdogan, B. (2017a). Your new hires won't succeed unless you onboard them properly. *Harvard Business Review*. https://hbr.org/2017/06/your-new-hires-wont-succeed-unless-you-onboard-them-properly.

Ellis, A. M., Nifadkar, S. S., Bauer, T. N., & Erdogan, B. (2017b). Newcomer adjustment: Examining the role of managers' perception of newcomer proactive behavior during organizational socialization. *Journal of Applied Psychology, 102*, 993–1001.

Feldman, D. (1981). The multiple socialization of organization members. *Academy of Management Review, 6*, 309–318.

Ghosh, S. (2018). An ex-Google engineer's sexual-harassment lawsuit claims she found a male coworker hiding under her desk. Business Insider. https://www.businessinsider.com/google-loretta-lee-lawsuit-alleges-harassment-2018-3.

Goodermote, C. (2020). Remote onboarding and training of new program coordinators into the medical education office during Covid-19 social distance quarantine: Process and recommendations. *Journal of Community Hospital Internal Medicine Perspectives*, *10*, 399–401.

Haak, T. (2017). The use of personas. HR Trend Institute. https://hrtrendinstitute.com/2017/05/11/personas/.

Harrison, S. H., Sluss, D. M., & Ashforth, B. E. (2011). Curiosity adapted the cat: The role of trait curiosity in newcomer adaptation. *Journal of Applied Psychology*, *96*, 211–220.

Isaac, M. (2017, March 1). Travis Kalanick, Uber chief, apologizes after fight with driver. *New York Times*. https://www.nytimes.com/2017/03/01/technology/uber-chief-apologizes-after-video-shows-him-arguing-with-driver.html.

Laurano, M. (2013). Onboarding 2013: A new look at new hires. Aberdeen Group. https://deliberatepractice.com.au/wp-content/uploads/2013/04/Onboarding-2013.pdf

Lougee, M., Chandra, R., & Burden, M. (2017). Gartner market guide for integrated HR service delivery solutions. https://www.servicenow.com/lpayr/gartner-guide-for-integrated-hr-service-delivery-solutions.html.

Maurer, R. (2018). Employers risk driving new hires away with poor onboarding. SHRM. https://www.shrm.org/resourcesandtools/hr-topics/talent-acquisition/pages/employers-new-hires-poor-onboarding.aspx.

Meyer, A. M., & Bartels, L. K. (2017). The impact of onboarding levels on perceived utility, organizational commitment, organizational support, and job satisfaction. *Journal of Organizational Psychology*, *17*, 10–27.

Nifadkar, S. S., & Bauer, T. N. (2016). Breach of belongingness: Newcomer relationship conflict, information, and task-related outcomes during organizational socialization. *Journal of Applied Psychology*, *101*, 1–13.

Rodeghero, P., Zimmermann, T., Houck, B., & Ford, D. (2021, May). Please turn your cameras on: Remote onboarding of software developers during a pandemic. In *2021 IEEE/ACM 43rd International Conference on Software Engineering: Software Engineering in Practice (ICSE-SEIP)* (pp. 41–50). IEEE.

SAP. (2018). SAP SuccessFactors onboarding. https://assets.cdn.sap.com/agreements/product-policy/css/service-specifications/sap-successfactors-onboarding-english-v6-2021.pdf

Stein, M. A., & Christiansen, L. (2010). *Successful onboarding: A strategy to unlock hidden value within your organization*. New York: McGraw Hill.

Sullivan, J. (2015). WOW, Google's simple just-in-time checklist improves onboarding results by 25%. https://www.ere.net/wow-googles-simple-just-in-time-checklist-improves-onboarding-results-by-25/.

Wakabayashi, D. (2019, December 31). Firm led by Google veterans uses A.I. to "nudge" workers toward happiness. *New York Times*. https://www.nytimes.com/2018/12/31/technology/human-resources-artificial-intelligence-humu.html.

Wanberg, C. (2012). *The Oxford handbook of organizational socialization*. New York: Oxford University Press.

Wanberg, C. R., & Kammeyer-Mueller, J. D. (2000). Predictors and outcomes of proactivity in the socialization process. *Journal of Applied Psychology*, *85*, 373–385.

Welbourne, T. M., Rolf, S., & Schlachter, S. (2017). The case for employee resource groups: A review and social identity theory-based research agenda. *Personnel Review*, *46*, 1816–1834.

Wilkie, D. (2017, August). Who's job-hopping now? *HR Magazine*, p. 10.

Wilson, J. (2017) The future of work: In the digital age, employees can be your best recruiters or worst critics. GE Reports. https://www.ge.com/reports/digital-age-employees-can-best-recruiters-worst-critics/.

Wynhurst. (2014). Help new hires succeed: Beat the statistics. http://thewynhurstgroup.com/wp-content/uploads/2014/07/Help-New-Hires-Succeed.pdf.

Conclusion

Mark A. Morris

Amazon

In this concluding section I will briefly describe four key themes that touch on emerging trends in talent acquisition (TA), along with implications for practitioners for how best to address them. These themes dovetail nicely with the chapters in this book, the post-pandemic challenges of remote hiring, new ways of working, and the critical need to provide equity and inclusion in hiring practices to realize the full power of our diverse workforce.

Business Acumen

TA is never divorced from financial considerations such as budget for headcount, cash flow, and profit. Cash flow that could be spent on increased compensation or benefits to make a job or organization more attractive to external talent can also be spent on many other competing priorities, so the business case for any resource investments must be clarified and validated. Workforce planning is a disciplined, rigorous, and data-driven process that integrates well with financial planning. One reason for this is that human capital metrics such as time to fill and predictive attrition models and workforce (headcount or staffing) plans are usually easier to communicate to senior line executives. Recruiting technology can offer tremendous efficiencies at unearthing latent talent, spotting trends and opportunities, and handling vast volumes of work, but it can represent significant investments and so must clearly tie to strategy and have a plan for return on investment (such as recruiter productivity, reduced cost to hire, faster time to fill open roles, etc.).

Mark A. Morris, *Conclusion* In: *Becoming a Talent Magnet*. Edited by: Mark A. Morris, Oxford University Press.
© Oxford University Press 2024. DOI: 10.1093/oso/9780190938512.003.0008

Focus on the Experience

The counterpoint to the quantitative side to TA is the high-touch qualitative side. Recruiters and hiring managers sell the company, manage the employment brand, craft a compelling employee value proposition (EVP), and seek to keep its promises to maintain the psychological contract and earn the trust of candidates and employees alike. All hiring processes have multiple stakeholders that are affected when the process changes, such as recruiters, hiring managers, and candidates. Think through and role-play adjustments to the process from the perspective of an example candidate in each critical job family as they go through the process. How will they most likely react to each stage? Where is it unnecessarily burdensome on candidates? Where do they drop out? If you pilot a new approach, how will you know if it works? Can you track referrals, application and dropout rates, etc.? When testing your TA practices with this lens, it is important to ask how the hiring process is experienced by diverse candidates. I always like to sit back after designing onboarding and ask the team, "What will people say when they come home and family and friends ask how their first day went at the new job? What do we want them to say? To feel?" Then we can make design changes around the emotional goals.

Metrics Are Your Compass

Data will provide feedback on how well you are delivering to the business, to candidates, and to new hires, enabling your organization to nimbly adjust. Since you are using TA metrics to evaluate external talent pools, internal talent pools, leader accountability, etc., you will be able to set and communicate standards for performance at each stage of the hiring process. The key here (as seen in Chapter 6) is to select enough metrics to give you a full and representative picture of what's happening, figure out where to dive deep and what's working, and enable your team to connect some dots without being buried in endless tables, paralyzed by insignificant changes, and chasing wild geese or red herrings.

Balance

The key to balancing the other three themes lies in strategic deployment decisions. For example, don't automate a process with a chatbot that is a key differentiator of employee experience. Candidates want efficiency in applying to a job (vs. retyping all the information on their résumé into an applicant tracking system), but interactions with a live recruiter for screening can make them feel valued. For instance, State Farm uses a HireVue video screening interview tool for some jobs. Even with carefully selected questions and easy-to-use technology, this creates a notably different candidate experience than a human sourcer or screener who can read and respond to a candidate's confidence level, probe when needed, and offer clarifications to reduce anxiety. There may be diversity, equity, and inclusion implications in terms of reactions to these automated screening measures that should be investigated as artificial intelligence becomes more widespread. In State Farm's case this may be a realistic job preview from a data-driven actuarial company and may not alter candidate opinions (after all, they know they are applying to an insurance company), but it certainly should be intentionally aligned with State Farm's employer value proposition.

The findings from applicant reactions research could also be applied here when deciding where to leverage the efficiencies of technology in the TA value chain. Consider creating a process map and decide where the gains in time savings will offer return on investment. A matrix showing low candidate experience impact but high cost and time savings will help identify sweet spots, especially if the process is repeatable and data links are available.

It is my fervent hope that the reader of this book is able to spot and adapt at least one concept, tool, or technique that inspires them to take their own TA function to the next level, improving the experience for both candidates and employees and aiding their organization's success. Strike that balance and navigate your seas.

Index

For the benefit of digital users, indexed terms that span two pages (e.g., 52–53) may, on occasion, appear on only one of those pages.

Tables and figures are indicated by *t* and *f* following the page number

algorithm for flight risk, 8–9
advertisements. *See* job advertisements
affinity analysis, 178–79
affirmative action, 25. *See also* diversity,
    equity, and inclusion
aggregators, 98
AI. *See* artificial intelligence
analytics, leveraging for sourcing, 82–84.
    See also talent metrics and analytics
applicant tracking systems (ATS)
    add-ons for, 111
    alternatives to, 124–25
    benefits of, 10
    case study: small business, 125–27
    common tools, 124
    considerations for ATS components, 127
    current use of, 114–15
    future impact of, 115
    in gamification and selection, 133–34
    increasing velocity of hiring process
        with, 14–15
    integrating other tools with, 125
    interviewing process and, 18
    candidate experience effect, 16
    services included, 123–24
    widespread use of, 124
artificial intelligence (AI)
    advantages, 127–28
    balancing with human judgment, 23–24
    future use of, 128–29
    ethical use of, 140
    evaluating fairness of models, 130
    fundamental concepts, 130–31
    in gamification and selection, 133–34
    generative AI, 129–30, 131–33
    guarding against bias, 24–25

potential use cases for, 127
pre-hire assessments, 85
application by recruiters, 116–17, 140
ATS. *See* applicant tracking systems
Attrition. *See* turnover
automation
    balancing with bias reduction, 121
    benefits of, xiv, 127–28
    expectations of, 163–64
    integrating into scoring, 133–34
    of onboarding, 136–37, 173*t*
    when to use, 10, 119, 123

balance, 13–14, 23–24, 160, 190–91
bias
    evaluating and remedying in recruiting
        tools, 84
    guarding against in artificial
        intelligence, 24–25
    overcoming with advanced models, 149
    reducing in job advertisements, 135–36
big-data models. *See also* artificial
    intelligence
    balancing with human judgment, 23–24
    leveraging for sourcing, 82–84
brand, 33, 38, 39–40, 175–77
buddy assignments, 167, 173*t*

campus recruiting, 81
candidate experience
    balancing with valid and efficient
        selection, 13–14
    creating process maps, 191
    high-touch practices and, 190
    mapping out, xv
    role of EVP in, 9–10

candidate relationship management
    (CRM) software, 10, 86, 115, 117
candidate value proposition, 144–45
candidates
    appealing to, 101–2, 103f, 103t
    attracting attention, 100–1
    attracting diverse candidates, 103–4
    attracting high-quality, 12–13
    behavior on job search sites, 142
    candidate rediscovery, 86
    job advertisements and, 97–98
    lack of quality candidates, 1–2
    passive, 3–4, 11
    protecting privacy of, 140, 142
    use of organizational network
        analysis, 142–44
career sites, 117
chatbots, 86, 135
ChatGPT, 129–30, 131–33, 132t, 135–36
CIM tools, 115
company career websites, 77–78
competencies and skills, top 12 skills in
    demand, 11
compliance, 25, 164–66. See also diversity,
    equity, and inclusion
consumer brand, 38
continuous listening concept, 57
contrast, 101
core product, 37
cost metrics, 151
CRM. See customer relationship
    management software
crowdsourced video, 136
culture, role in onboarding, 171–72
customer-centric design, 178f

dashboards, 155–58
data retention policies, 157–58
data scraping, 107
digital exhaust, 142
digital footprints, 143
digital technology, 165, 180–82
diversity, equity, and inclusion
    effects of recruitment messages on, 108
    improving with recruiting
        technology, 122
    in job ads, 103–4
    in the workforce, 57

increased commitment to, 2–3
interventions for sourcing, 84
role in workforce planning, 25
social media and, 135–36

ECD. See employee-centric design
    thinking
employee mobility, increase in, 5–6
employee personas, 177–79
employee referrals, 76–77
employee resource groups (ERGs), 172
employee value proposition (EVP)
    central premise of, 174
    dealing with less desirable
        information, 175
    developing and deploying for sourcing,
        71–76, 78
    key elements of, 154
    promoting through onboarding, 175
    for remote versus physically present
        jobs, 9–10
    role in candidate experience, 190
    social media and, 79
employee-centric design thinking, 177–80
employees
    costs of turnover, 2
    high-performing as competitive
        advantage, 1–2
    internal talent marketplaces, 2–3
    role of new employees in
        onboarding, 183–84
employment brand, 33, 38, 39–40, 175–77
employment value proposition (EVP)
    budget restraints and, 33–34
    case study: EVP segment
        descriptions, 52t
    case study: financial services, 52–55
    case study: marketing write-ups for
        employee segments, 55t
    case study: more and less desirable EVP
        programs, 54t
    definition of term, 32–33
    differentiating yourself among
        employers, 32
    employment branding
        campaigns, 39–40
    future trends for, 56–59
    marketing strategy, 34–38

scope of, 56
structure of, 33
trends impacting employer-employee
    relationship, 55–56
environmental responsibility, 56
ERGs (employee resource groups), 172
ethics and privacy
    balancing speed of inferences with
        ethic, 160
    data retention policies, 157–58
    evaluating talent through social
        media, 143–44
    key analytical methods and
        concepts, 148–49
    protecting, 140, 142
    use of organizational network
        analysis, 142–43
EVP. See employee value proposition;
    employment value proposition
exit data, 159–60
external attrition, 2–3

5 Cs of onboarding
    benefits of effective
        onboarding, 163–64
    clarification, 166–69
    compliance, 164–66
    confidence, 169
    connection, 170
    culture, 171–72
    use of digital technology, 180–82
flight risk algorithm, 8–9
4 Ps/4Cs, 35–38, 36t

gamification, 133–34, 145, 165, 166
gap analysis, 70–71
General Data Protection Regulation (GDPR),
    2–3, 123–24, 127, 143, 150, 158
generative AI, 129–30
gig economy, 57–58, 67

hiring metrics, service-level agreements
    and, xiv
hiring process. See also candidate
        experience
    benefits of mapping out, xiv–xv
    improving velocity in, 14–16
    sample model of process, xvf

Hofstede cultural criteria, 64
HR. See human resources departments
human judgement, balancing with
    artificial intelligence, 23–24
human resources (HR) departments
    data retention policies, 157–58
    good practices for virtual
        interviews, 120
    tension with hiring managers, 8

integration plans for onboarding, 167
internal talent marketplaces, 2–3
interviewing process
    appropriate number of
        interviews, 17–18
    good design of, 19–20
    interviewing as recruiting event, 19
    purpose of multiple interviews, 18–19
    reducing cycle time for hiring, 17

job advertisements
    appealing to desired candidates, 101–2
    applying guidelines for, 105, 106f
    attracting candidate attention, 100–1
    current state of, 96–98
    demands versus needs in job
        descriptions, 103t
    drawing in diverse candidate
        pools, 103–4
    future of online advertisements, 106–7
    gendered versus neutral language, 105f
    guidelines for creating, 109–10
    new directions for research, 107–8
    organizing job ads around candidate
        concerns, 103f
    reducing bias in, 135–36
    trait versus behavioral statements
        in, 105t
job aggregators, 98
job boards, 80
job description optimization, 86
job market forecasting, 8–11, 86
job scraping, 107

knowledge, skills, abilities, and other
    characteristics (KSAOs), 4–5

large language models (LLM), 133

leadership roles, importance of support and clarification for, 167–69

marketing strategy (for EVPs)
  major components of, 34
  marketing mix, 35–38
  target marketing, 35
media richness, 101
metrics. *See also* talent metrics and analytics
  best use of, 190
  common staffing metrics, 152*t*
  cost metrics, 151
  hiring metrics and service level agreements, xiv
  leveraging for sourcing, 82–84
  quality metrics, 152–53
  quality-of-hire metric, 3–4
  time-to-fill vs. time-to-accept metrics, 3–4, 9–10, 151
  used in recruitment, 117–18
minimum viable employee experience, 179
mobile reference checking platforms, 118
moments that matter (MTMs), 178–79

natural language processing (NLP), 149
nudges, 168–69

ONA (organization network analysis), 140–41, 142–44
onboarding
  5 Cs of, 163–72
  automation of, 136–37
  digital technology for, 180–82
  employee-centric design thinking, 177–80
  employer value proposition, 174–75
  employment brand analysis, 175–77
  marketing and design methodologies for, 173–74
  opportunities and recommendations for, 173*t*
  role of new employees in, 183–84
  role of recruiters in, 182–83
  in transformational times, 162–63, 184–85
  virtual onboarding, 118
online databases, 117

organization network analysis (ONA), 140–41, 142–44
person–environment fit perceptions, 99–100
pre-entry onboarding portal, 180–81
privacy. *See* ethics and privacy
proof of fairness, 140
prospective employees. *See* candidates

quality metrics, 152–53
quality-of-hire metric, importance of, 3–4

realistic job previews (RJPs), 80–81
recruiter requisition loads, optimizing, 7, 11–12, 127
recruiting function. *See* talent acquisition (TA)
recruiting technology
  applicant tracking systems, 123–25
  artificial intelligence (AI), 127–30
  ATS add-ons, 111
  ATS and AI in gamification and selection, 133–34
  ATS components, 127
  case study: small business ATS, 125–27
  ChatGPT example usage, 131–33, 132*t*
  current state of practice, 114–18
  cutting-edge research on, 121–22
  improving diversity, equity, and inclusion, 122
  selecting, 122–23
  virtual interviews, 120
  virtual jobs/virtual hiring, 118–20
recruitment process. *See also* sourcing
  campus recruiting, 81
  developing models of effective recruiting, 26–27
  high-touch practices, 6, 123, 190
  job advertisements and, 96–97
  metrics, 154
recruitment process outsourcing (RPO) firms, 4
referrals, 76–77
remote onboarding, 165–66
RJPs (realistic job previews), 80–81

scenario planning, 9–10

service-level agreements, xiv
signal theory, 99–100
simulations, 141
SIPOC (Supplier, Input, Process, Output, Customer), 27
skills-based talent practices, 11
social identity theory, 99–100
social media
    candidate discovery software, 86
    diversity, equity, and inclusion and, 135–36
    evaluating talent through, 142–44
    impact on EVP, 58–59
    for recruitment, 78–79, 117
sourcing
    conducting a sourcing strategy, 65–67
    definition of term, 63–64
    EVP development and deployment, 71–76
    future trends in, 85–87
    impact of poor or distorted information, 64
    leveraging measurement and analytics, 82–84
    sourcing practitioner's checklist, 63t, 87
    tools for effective sourcing, 76–82
    workforce planning for, 67–71
staffing forecasts, 8–11
Supplier, Input, Process, Output, Customer (SIPOC), 27

talent acquisition (TA)
    challenges and rewards of, 3
    definition of term, 1–2
    list of toughest jobs to fill, 10–11
    managing the TA function, 150–54
    role in workforce planning, 2, 7–8
    role of diversity, equity, and inclusion in, 2–3
    role of metrics and analytics in, 146
    sample hiring process, xvf
    shift in metrics concerning, 3–4
    shortage of guidance concerning, 4
    technology used in (see recruiting technology)
    universal guidelines for, xiv–xv
talent hot spots, 5
Talent Intelligence Collective Battlecards, 64

talent metrics and analytics
    candidate behavior, 142
    common staffing metrics, 152t
    gamification, 145
    key methods and concepts, 148–50
    organization networks and social media, 142–44
    simulations, 141
    video assessment, 141–42
    visualizing results, 155–58
talent resources
    accurately forecasting talent demands, 8–11
    unique to strategy and culture, 3
target marketing, 35
technology. See digital technology; recruiting technology
text analytics, 140
time-to-fill vs. time-to-accept metrics, 3–4, 9–10, 151
TM. See talent management
total product offer, 37
turnover
    advanced flight risk algorithms, 8–9
    as a contagious process, 22–23
    costs of, 2
    estimating with HR business partners, 7
    EVPs and, 72, 73–74
    in hourly positions, 19
    of older workers, 86–87
    referral bonuses based on cost of, 13–14
    referred candidates and, 76–77
    risk of further, 18
    WFPs and, 70
2 & 5 Promise, xiv

unity, attracting candidate attention through, 100
utility analyses, 154

validity evidence, 140
value, creating, 29
video assessment, 141–42
virtual career fairs, 118
virtual interviews, 115–16, 120
virtual job tryouts (VJT), 80–81
virtual onboarding, 118
virtual referrals, 79

visualization, 155–58
VJT (virtual job tryouts), 80–81

workforce planning (WFP)
    accurately forecasting talent
        demands, 8–11
    attracting high-quality
        candidates, 12–13
    balancing candidate experience and
        efficient selection, 13–14
    diversity, equity, and inclusion in,
        2–3, 25

headcount/requisition approvals, 16–17
HR and hiring manager tension, 8
improving velocity in hiring
    process, 14–16
interviewing process, 17–20
optimizing recruiter requisition
    loads, 11–12
research necessary for, 20–27
role of talent acquisition in, 2, 7–8
sample workforce plan, 28f
for sourcing activities, 67–71
timing of, xiv